GRAMMAR

Level **2**

Grammar 공감 Level 2

지은이 넥서스영어교육연구소
펴낸이 임상진
펴낸곳 (주)넥서스

출판신고 1992년 4월 3일 제311-2002-2호 ⑰
10880 경기도 파주시 지목로 5
Tel (02)330-5500 Fax (02)330-5555

ISBN 978-89-6790-845-4 54740
        978-89-6790-843-0 (SET)

www.nexusEDU.kr

※ 집필에 도움을 주신 분
  : 김현진 선생님, 정혜영 선생님, 임현주 선생님, 임재원 선생님, 오선행 선생님

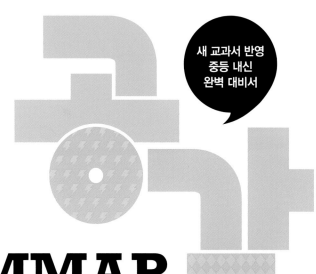

GRAMMAR

넥서스영어교육연구소 지음

Level 2

NEXUS Edu

새 교과서 반영
중등 내신
완벽 대비서

Grammar Gong Gam helps you...

Get high scores
2,500여 개의 전국 중학교 기출 문제를 분석하여 반영한 review test를 제공함으로써 내신 성적을 향상시켜 줍니다.

Obtain a wide vocabulary
풍부한 어휘 리스트를 제공, 기본적인 어휘 실력을 향상시켜 줍니다.

Nurture your English skills
최신 개정 교과서를 분석 반영한 문법 설명을 수록, 2,500여 개에 달하는 전국 중학교 최신 기출 문제를 분석하여 반영한 문제를 수록, 중등 과정에서 알아야 하는 풍부한 어휘를 제공함으로써 종합적인 영어 실력을 향상시켜 줍니다.

Get writing skills
서술형 평가 코너를 따로 수록해 새로운 교수 평가 방법에 대비할 수 있게 해 줍니다.

Get speaking skills
영어 회화로도 활용 가능한 예문을 제공하여 영어 말하기 능력을 향상시켜 줍니다.

Acquire good English sense
2,000여 개의 충분한 연습 문제를 풀어보게 해줌으로써 문법 감각을 습득시켜 줍니다.

Master the essentials of grammar
최신 교과서를 분석하여 반영한 문법 설명으로, 내신에 필수 불가결한 문법을 학습하게 해 줍니다.

Features

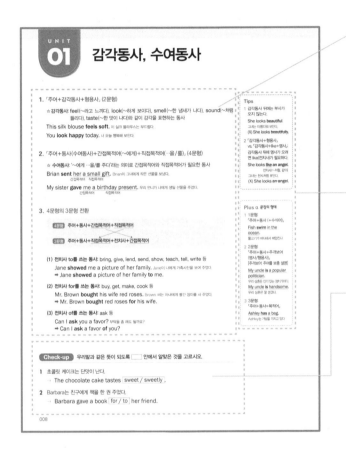

핵심 문법 정리

내신에 꼭 필요한 핵심 문법 사항들을 알기 쉽게 단계별로 설명하였습니다. 실용적인 예문과 간결하고 정확한 문법 설명을 제시하여 대표 예문만 봐도 문법의 개념을 이해할 수 있습니다. 시험에 꼭 나오는 문법 내용이 자연스럽게 반복되어 충분한 학습 효과를 볼 수 있습니다.

Plus α & Tips

핵심 문법 사항 이외에 추가로 심화 문법 사항과 학생들이 특히 주의해야 할 사항을 정리하였습니다.

Check-up

학습한 핵심 문법을 올바로 이해하였는지 바로 확인할 수 있는 문제로, 핵심 문법 사항만 숙지하였다면 누구나 쉽고 재미있게 풀 수 있는 기본 문제들로 구성하였습니다.

Exercises

해당 Unit에서 학습한 문법 사항을 다양한 유형의 주관식 문제를 통해 완벽하게 정리할 수 있도록 하였습니다. 단순 암기한 내용을 가지고 푸는 것이 아니라 직접 응용해서 써 보고 생각해 볼 수 있도록 구성하였습니다.

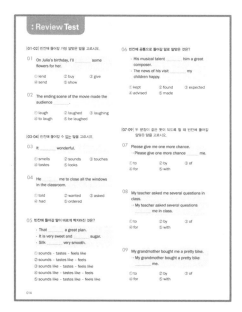

Review Test

해당 Chapter에서 학습한 내용을 통합형 문제 유형을 통해서 다시 한 번 정리할 수 있도록 하였습니다. 실제 학교 시험과 동일한 유형의 문제들로 구성하여 내신을 완벽하게 대비할 수 있습니다. 스스로 자신의 취약한 부분을 점검하며 문법에 대한 자신감을 기를 수 있습니다.

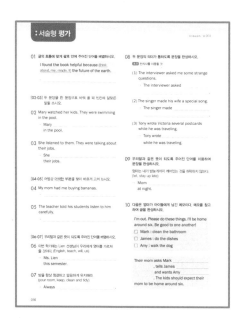

서술형 평가

최신 교수 평가 방법에 대비할 수 있도록 서술형 평가 코너를 따로 마련하였습니다. 학교 내신 시험에 자주 나오는 유형의 서술형 문제를 통해서 어떤 문제가 나와도 대비할 수 있도록 하였으며 학생들의 사고력과 창의력도 길러줍니다.

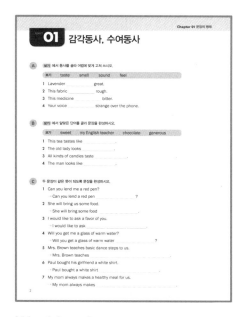

Workbook (서술형 대비)

본책에서 학습한 내용을 다양한 서술형 문제를 통해서 핵심 문법 사항을 충분히 연습할 수 있도록 하였습니다. 숙제나 자습을 통해 문법 사항을 최종 정리하며 복습할 수 있는 좋은 기회가 될 수 있습니다.

정답 및 해설

기존의 어렵고 복잡한 설명에서 벗어나 간결하고 정확한 설명을 통해서 해설집만 보고도 핵심 문법 정리를 한눈에 할 수 있도록 하였습니다.

Contents

Chapter 1

문장의 형태

감각동사, 수여동사

1. 「주어+감각동사+형용사」 (2문형)

☆ **감각동사**: feel(~라고 느끼다), look(~하게 보이다), smell(~한 냄새가 나다), sound(~처럼 들리다), taste(~한 맛이 나다)와 같이 감각을 표현하는 동사

This silk blouse **feels soft**. 이 실크 블라우스는 부드럽다.

You **look happy** today. 너 오늘 행복해 보인다.

2. 「주어+동사(수여동사)+간접목적어(~에게)+직접목적어(…을/를)」 (4문형)

☆ **수여동사**: '~에게 …을/를 주다'라는 의미로 간접목적어와 직접목적어가 필요한 동사

Brian **sent** <u>her</u> <u>a small gift</u>. Brian이 그녀에게 작은 선물을 보냈다.
　　　　　　간접목적어　직접목적어

My sister **gave** <u>me</u> <u>a birthday present</u>. 우리 언니가 나에게 생일 선물을 주었다.
　　　　　　　　간접목적어　　직접목적어

3. 4문형의 3문형 전환

　[4문형] 주어+동사+<u>간접목적어</u>+<u>직접목적어</u>

　[3문형] 주어+동사+<u>직접목적어</u>+<u>전치사</u>+<u>간접목적어</u>

(1) **전치사 to를 쓰는 동사**: bring, give, lend, send, show, teach, tell, write 등
　Jane **showed** me a picture of her family. Jane이 나에게 가족사진을 보여 주었다.
　➡ Jane **showed** a picture of her family **to** me.

(2) **전치사 for를 쓰는 동사**: buy, get, make, cook 등
　Mr. Brown **bought** his wife red roses. Brown 씨는 아내에게 빨간 장미를 사 주었다.
　➡ Mr. Brown **bought** red roses **for** his wife.

(3) **전치사 of를 쓰는 동사**: ask 등
　Can I **ask** you a favor? 부탁을 좀 해도 될까요?
　➡ Can I **ask** a favor **of** you?

Tips

1 감각동사 뒤에는 부사가 오지 않는다.

She looks **beautiful**.
그녀는 아름다워 보인다.
(X) She looks ~~beautifully~~.

2 「감각동사+형용사」 vs. 「감각동사+like+명사」: 감각동사 뒤에 명사가 오려면 like(전치사)가 필요하다.

She looks **like an angel**.
　　　　　전치사(~처럼, 같이)
그녀는 천사처럼 보인다.
(X) She looks ~~an angel~~.

Plus α 문장의 형태

1 1문형:
「주어+동사 (+수식어)」
<u>Fish</u> **swim** <u>in the ocean</u>.
물고기가 바다에서 헤엄친다.

2 2문형:
「주어+동사+주격보어 (명사/형용사)」
[주격보어: 주어를 보충 설명]
<u>My uncle</u> **is** <u>a popular politician</u>.
우리 삼촌은 인기 있는 정치가이다.
<u>My uncle</u> **is** <u>handsome</u>.
우리 삼촌은 잘 생겼다.

3 3문형:
「주어+동사+목적어」
<u>Ashley</u> **has** <u>a bag</u>.
Ashley는 가방을 가지고 있다.

Check-up 우리말과 같은 뜻이 되도록 □ 안에서 알맞은 것을 고르시오.

1 초콜릿 케이크는 단맛이 난다.
　→ The chocolate cake tastes [sweet / sweetly].

2 Barbara는 친구에게 책을 한 권 주었다.
　→ Barbara gave a book [for / to] her friend.

: EXERCISES

A [ ] 안에서 알맞은 것을 고르시오.

1 The coffee smells [strong / strongly].

2 The book [sounds / sounds like] a real story.

3 She gave good advice [for / to] me.

4 My mother bought [a new dress me / me a new dress].

strong
(형) (음식이) 향이 강한

real story 실화

advice (명) 조언, 충고

B 밑줄 친 부분을 어법에 맞게 고쳐 쓰시오.

1 Joseph really <u>looks</u> his mother.

2 The movie sounds <u>interestingly</u>.

3 The man asked a lot of questions <u>for</u> me.

4 She looks very <u>beautifully</u> in the red dress.

sound
(동) ～하게 들리다

a lot of 많은

C 두 문장이 같은 뜻이 되도록 문장을 완성하시오.

1 Cindy sent me a text message.

→ Cindy sent a text message _____ _____ .

2 Her fiancé bought her a beautiful ring.

→ Her fiancé bought a beautiful ring _____ _____ .

3 I brought some cookies to my sister.

→ I brought _____ _____ _____ _____ .

4 His grandmother made a nice sweater for him.

→ His grandmother made _____ _____ _____

_____ .

text message
(명) 문자 메시지

fiancé (명) 약혼자

D 우리말과 같은 뜻이 되도록 주어진 단어를 이용하여 문장을 완성하시오.

1 저기에 있는 소년은 외로워 보여요. (lonely)

→ The boy over there _____ _____ .

2 이 음식은 맵고 짜다. (spicy and salty)

→ The food _____ _____ _____ .

3 저에게 찬물을 한 잔 가져다주세요. (get)

→ Please _____ _____ a glass of cold water.

4 Jenny는 자신의 펜팔에게 편지를 썼다. (a letter)

→ Jenny _____ _____ _____ _____ her pen pal.

동사+목적어+명사/형용사/to부정사

☆ 5문형: 「주어+동사+목적어+목적격보어(명사/형용사/to부정사/동사원형/-ing)」
  목적격보어는 목적어와 동일한 사람[것]이거나 목적어의 상태나 동작을 보충 설명한다.

1. 「동사(make, call, elect 등)+목적어+명사」

☆ 목적격보어가 명사인 경우 목적어와 목적격보어는 동일한 사람[것]이다.

Shirley **made** <u>her daughter</u> **a great ballerina.** [her daughter = a great ballerina]
Shirley는 자신의 딸을 훌륭한 발레리나로 만들었다.

People **elected** <u>him</u> **President.** [him = President]
사람들이 그를 대통령으로 선출했다.

2. 「동사(make, keep, find, leave 등)+목적어+형용사」

☆ 목적격보어가 형용사인 경우 목적격보어는 목적어의 상태를 나타낸다.

I **found** <u>the man</u> **kind and funny.** [the man의 상태 = kind and funny]
나는 그 남자가 친절하고 재미있다는 것을 알았다.

Rules and laws **keep** <u>people</u> **safe.** [people의 상태 = safe]
규칙과 법률은 사람들을 안전하게 지켜준다.

3. 「동사(want, tell, ask, allow, advise, expect, order 등)+목적어+to부정사」

☆ 목적격보어가 to부정사인 경우 목적어와 목적격보어 간에 주어, 동사 관계가 성립한다.

My father **told** <u>me</u> **to go** to bed early. [me가 go to bed early하는 것]
아버지는 나에게 일찍 잠자리에 들라고 말씀하셨다.

I **want** <u>my children</u> **to be** honest. [my children이 be honest하는 것]
나는 내 아이들이 정직하기를 원한다.

Check-up 우리말과 같은 뜻이 되도록 ☐ 안에서 알맞은 것을 고르시오.

1 너는 그 책이 재미있다는 것을 알게 될 것이다.
  → You will find the book | interesting / interestingly |.

2 그 남자는 사람들이 자신의 거짓말을 믿기를 원했다.
  → The man wanted people | believe / to believe | his lies.

3 어떤 사람들은 Peter를 천재라고 부른다.
  → Some people call | Peter a genius / a genius Peter |.

4 우리 부모님이 내가 애완동물 기르는 것을 허락했다.
  → My parents allowed me | to keep / kept | a pet.

: EXERCISES

A [ ] 안에서 알맞은 것을 고르시오.

1 Please keep the classroom [clean / cleanly].

2 My father asked me [find / to find] his car key.

3 The band's performance made me [excited / excitedly].

4 She wanted me [wait / to wait] for her for thirty minutes.

keep 동 ~을 유지하다
cleanly 부 깨끗하게
performance 명 공연
excitedly
부 신이 나서, 흥분하여
wait for ~을 기다리다

B 보기 에서 알맞은 말을 골라 어법에 맞게 바꿔 문장을 완성하시오.

보기   take   stay   join   go

1 Brian asked Bell _____ to see a movie with him.

2 The soccer coach wanted Michael _____ his team.

3 She looks very tired, so I told her _____ a rest.

4 I like playing with my friends until late at night, but my parents don't allow me _____ up late.

join 동 함께 하다, 합류하다
rest 명 휴식
allow 동 허락하다

C 밑줄 친 부분을 어법에 맞게 고쳐 쓰시오.

1 Rainy days make me <u>sadness</u>.

2 I asked my mom <u>wake</u> me up early.

3 Listening to music makes me <u>happily</u>.

4 He wants me <u>arrive</u> by this afternoon.

rainy 형 비 오는
sadness 명 슬픔, 슬픈 일
wake A up A를 깨우다

D 우리말과 같은 뜻이 되도록 주어진 단어를 배열하시오.

1 나는 그 영화가 지루하다는 것을 알게 되었다. (found, boring, the movie)

→ I _____ .

2 나는 네가 나와 함께 그곳에 가기를 원해. (to, there, you, go, want)

→ I _____ with me.

3 학생들은 그 선생님을 '걸어 다니는 백과사전'이라고 부른다.
(call, a walking dictionary, the teacher)

→ The students _____ .

03 동사+목적어+동사원형/-ing

1. 「사역동사+목적어+동사원형」

☆ **사역동사**: make, have, let ～에게 …하도록 하다[시키다]

My mom **made** me **do** the dishes. 우리 엄마가 나에게 설거지를 시켰다.

His teacher **had** him **stay** after class. 그의 선생님이 그를 수업 후에 남게 했다.

> **Plus α**
> 1 get이 사역의 의미로 쓰인 경우, 목적격보어로 to부정사가 온다.
>   My father **got** me **to water** the plants. 우리 아버지가 나에게 꽃에 물을 주도록 시키셨다.
> 2 help의 목적격보어 자리에는 동사원형과 to부정사 모두 올 수 있다.
>   Will you **help** me **move[to move]** the table? 제가 테이블 옮기는 것을 도와주시겠어요?

2. 「지각동사+목적어+동사원형/-ing」

☆ **지각동사**: feel(느끼다), see(보다), hear(듣다), listen to(듣다), watch(보다), smell(～한 냄새가 나다) 등 사람이 감각 기관을 통해 사물을 인지하는 것을 표현하는 동사

I **heard** someone **sing[singing]** a song. 나는 누군가가 노래 부르는 것을 들었다.

We **felt** the ground **shake[shaking]**. 우리는 땅이 흔들리는 것을 느꼈다.

> **Tips**
> 지각동사의 목적격보어로 현재분사가 오면 동작이 진행되고 있다는 의미가 강조된다.
> I **heard** him **talking** on the phone.
> 나는 그가 통화하는 것을 들었다.

Check-up 우리말과 같은 뜻이 되도록 ☐ 안에서 알맞은 것을 고르시오.

1 나는 그에게 사실을 알게 해줄 것이다.
  → I will let him know / knowing the truth.

2 나는 누군가 우리 집에 들어가는 것을 보았다.
  → I saw someone enter / to enter my house.

3 그의 이야기는 많은 사람들을 울게 만들었다.
  → His story made a lot of people cry / to cry .

4 아이들은 바다에서 돌고래가 헤엄치는 것을 보았다.
  → The kids saw dolphins swimming / to swim in the sea.

: EXERCISES

A [   ] 안에서 알맞은 것을 고르시오.

1 He couldn't hear a car [coming / to come].

2 She made her son [carry / to carry] her bag.

3 I saw her [working / to work] hard in the garden.

4 This cartoon makes children [laugh / to laugh].

carry ⑧ 들고 있다, 나르다
cartoon ⑲ 만화, 만화 영화
laugh ⑧ (소리 내어) 웃다

B 보기 에서 알맞은 말을 골라 어법에 맞게 바꿔 문장을 완성하시오.

보기   touch   fix   do   call

1 Would you help me _____ my bicycle?

2 Can you hear someone _____ my name?

3 Ryan felt his father _____ his shoulder.

4 My teacher made me _____ my homework every day.

touch ⑧ 만지다
fix ⑧ 수리하다, 고치다

C 밑줄 친 부분을 어법에 맞게 고쳐 쓰시오.

1 Did you feel something to crawl on your hand?

2 His parents let him going to the summer camp.

3 My sister and I watched a sad movie, and it made her cried.

4 We watched our favorite singers to dance on the stage.

crawl ⑧ 기어가다
favorite ⑲ 가장 좋아하는

D 우리말과 같은 뜻이 되도록 주어진 단어를 배열하시오.

1 그는 아들에게 차를 운전하도록 시켰다. (his son, let, his car, drive)

 → He _____.

2 나는 두 명의 소녀가 벤치에서 얘기하는 것을 들었다. (two girls, listened to, talking)

 → I _____ on the bench.

3 그녀는 부엌에서 무엇인가 타는 냄새를 맡았다. (burning, smelled, something)

 → She _____ in the kitchen.

[01-02] 빈칸에 들어갈 가장 알맞은 말을 고르시오.

01
On Julia's birthday, I'll _____ some flowers for her.

① lend   ② buy   ③ give
④ send   ⑤ show

02
The ending scene of the movie made the audience _____.

① laugh   ② laughed   ③ laughing
④ to laugh   ⑤ be laughed

[03-04] 빈칸에 들어갈 수 <u>없는</u> 말을 고르시오.

03
It _____ wonderful.

① smells   ② sounds   ③ touches
④ tastes   ⑤ looks

04
He _____ me to close all the windows in the classroom.

① told   ② wanted   ③ asked
④ had   ⑤ ordered

05 빈칸에 들어갈 말이 바르게 짝지어진 것은?

· That _____ a great plan.
· It is very sweet and _____ sugar.
· Silk _____ very smooth.

① sounds – tastes – feels like
② sounds – tastes like – feels
③ sounds like – tastes – feels like
④ sounds like – tastes like – feels
⑤ sounds like – tastes like – feels like

06 빈칸에 공통으로 들어갈 말로 알맞은 것은?

· His musical talent _____ him a great composer.
· The news of his visit _____ my children happy.

① kept   ② found   ③ expected
④ advised   ⑤ made

[07-09] 두 문장이 같은 뜻이 되도록 할 때 빈칸에 들어갈 알맞은 말을 고르시오.

07
Please give me one more chance.
→ Please give one more chance _____ me.

① to   ② by   ③ of
④ for   ⑤ with

08
My teacher asked me several questions in class.
→ My teacher asked several questions _____ me in class.

① to   ② by   ③ of
④ for   ⑤ with

09
My grandmother bought me a pretty bike.
→ My grandmother bought a pretty bike _____ me.

① to   ② by   ③ of
④ for   ⑤ with

[10-11] 다음 중 어법상 <u>어색한</u> 문장을 고르시오.

10
① She let her brother to vacuum the house.
② Seat belts keep people safe while they are driving.
③ I didn't ask him to come and help me.
④ I want you to be quiet in the museum.
⑤ Ralph heard her playing the piano.

11
① I watched my dog running in the park.
② I felt very sleepy during the class.
③ My new neighbors look very friendly.
④ All of her songs sound beautifully to me.
⑤ I heard someone knocking on the door.

[12-13] 우리말을 영어로 바르게 옮긴 것을 <u>모두</u> 고르시오.

12 우리 엄마가 우리에게 초콜릿 케이크를 만들어 주셨다.

① My mom made us a chocolate cake.
② My mom made a chocolate cake us.
③ My mom made a chocolate cake of us.
④ My mom made a chocolate cake for us.
⑤ My mom made for us a chocolate cake.

13 나는 우리 할머니가 가방을 옮기는 것을 도와주었다.

① I helped my grandma of carrying her bag.
② I helped my grandma to carry her bag.
③ I helped my grandma carrying her bag.
④ I helped my grandma carries her bag.
⑤ I helped my grandma carry her bag.

[14-15] 글을 읽고, 물음에 답하시오.

What ❶ makes you happy? Everybody ❷ wants to be happy, and happiness comes in many different ways. (A) 어떤 사람들은 돈이 우리에게 행복을 가져다줄 거라고 믿는다. We need money to live, but it doesn't actually bring happiness. Other people feel happiness from small things. For example, they ❸ feel happy when they ❹ hear birds to sing a song or they ❺ see the sun shine brightly. Happiness is in our hands. Some experts say we can become happy with practice. One simple practice is smiling. So smile a lot, and be happy.

14 밑줄 친 ❶~❺ 중 어법상 어색한 것은?

15 밑줄 친 (A)를 바르게 영작한 것을 <u>모두</u> 고르시오.

① Some people believe that money brings happiness us.
② Some people believe that money brings happiness of us.
③ Some people believe that money brings us to happiness.
④ Some people believe that money brings us happiness.
⑤ Some people believe that money brings happiness to us.

01 글의 흐름에 맞게 괄호 안에 주어진 단어를 배열하시오.

I found the book helpful because (think about, me, made, it) the future of the earth.

→ _____

[02-03] 두 문장을 한 문장으로 바꿔 쓸 때 빈칸에 알맞은 말을 쓰시오.

02 Mary watched her kids. They were swimming in the pool.

→ Mary _____
in the pool.

03 She listened to them. They were talking about their jobs.

→ She _____
their jobs.

[04-05] 어법상 <u>어색한</u> 부분을 찾아 바르게 고쳐 쓰시오.

04 My mom had me buying bananas.

→ _____

05 The teacher told his students listen to him carefully.

→ _____

[06-07] 우리말과 같은 뜻이 되도록 주어진 단어를 배열하시오.

06 이번 학기에는 Lien 선생님이 우리에게 영어를 가르쳐 줄 것이다. (English, teach, will, us)

→ Ms. Lien _____
this semester.

07 방을 항상 청결하고 깔끔하게 유지해라.
(your room, keep, clean and tidy)

→ Always _____ .

08 두 문장의 의미가 통하도록 문장을 완성하시오.

조건 전치사를 이용할 것

(1) The interviewer asked me some strange questions.

→ The interviewer asked _____
_____ .

(2) The singer made his wife a special song.

→ The singer made _____
_____ .

(3) Tony wrote Victoria several postcards while he was traveling.

→ Tony wrote _____
while he was traveling.

09 우리말과 같은 뜻이 되도록 주어진 단어를 이용하여 문장을 완성하시오.

엄마는 내가 밤늦게까지 깨어있는 것을 허락하지 않는다. (let, stay up late)

→ Mom _____
at night.

10 다음은 엄마가 아이들에게 남긴 메모이다. 메모를 참고 하여 글을 완성하시오.

I'm out. Please do these things. I'll be home around six. Be good to one another!

☐ Mark : clean the bathroom

☐ James : do the dishes

☐ Amy : walk the dog

Their mom asks Mark _____
_____, tells James _____
_____, and wants Amy _____
_____. The kids should expect their
mom to be home around six.

Chapter 2

UNIT 01 명사적 쓰임

☆ to부정사의 명사적 쓰임: 「to+동사원형」의 형태로 문장에서 명사처럼 주어, 보어, 목적어 역할을 한다.

1. 주어 역할 ~하기는, ~하는 것은

To collect old coins is my hobby. 오래된 동전을 수집하는 것이 나의 취미이다.

To eat vegetables is good for your health. 채소를 먹는 것은 너의 건강에 좋다.

☆ to부정사가 주어로 오는 경우 그 자리에 It을 쓰고 to부정사를 문장 뒤로 보낸다. It을 '가주어', to부정사를 '진주어'라고 한다.

To study other cultures is interesting. 다른 문화를 배우는 것은 재미있다.

➡ **It** is interesting **to study other cultures**.
　　가주어　　　　　　　　　진주어

Plus α
to부정사가 주어로 쓰인 경우, 단수 취급한다.

To watch soccer games is exciting.
축구 경기를 보는 것은 흥미진진하다.

2. 보어 역할 ~하는 것(이다)

Her plan is **to learn** Spanish. 그녀의 계획은 스페인 어를 배우는 것이다.

My job is **to take** care of patients. 내 직업은 환자들을 돌보는 것이다.

Tips
to부정사의 부정:
「not[never]+to부정사」

He promised **not to be** late again.
그는 다시는 늦지 않겠다고 약속했다.

3. 목적어 역할 ~하기를, 하는 것을

☆ to부정사를 목적어로 취하는 동사: want, decide, plan, promise, hope, wish, expect, learn, refuse 등

They decided **to buy** a new house. 그들은 새집을 사기로 결정했다.

I hope **to make** many friends this year. 나는 올해 많은 친구를 사귀길 바란다.

4. 「의문사+to부정사」: 문장에서 명사처럼 주어, 보어, 목적어 역할을 한다.

　「what+to부정사」 무엇을 ~할지　　　　　「when+to부정사」 언제 ~할지
　「where+to부정사」 어디서[어디로] ~할지　　「how+to부정사」 어떻게 ~할지, ~하는 방법

Jonathan didn't know **what to do**. Jonathan은 무엇을 해야 할지 몰랐다.

Can you tell me **how to use** this camera? 이 카메라 사용법을 알려 줄래?

Plus α
「의문사+to부정사」= 「의문사+주어+should+동사원형」

I don't know **what to wear** tomorrow.
➡ I don't know **what I should wear** tomorrow.
나는 내일 무엇을 입어야 할지 모르겠다.

Check-up 우리말과 같은 뜻이 되도록 ☐ 안에서 알맞은 것을 고르시오.

1 내 목표는 한 달에 3킬로그램을 감량하는 것이다.
　→ My goal is ☐ lose / to lose ☐ 3 kg in a month.

2 그는 내 생일 파티에 오겠다고 약속했다.
　→ He promised ☐ come / to come ☐ to my birthday party.

3 나는 휴가에 어디를 갈지 결정할 수가 없었다.
　→ I couldn't decide ☐ where to go / where go ☐ on vacation.

: EXERCISES

A [ ] 안에서 알맞은 것을 고르시오.

1 [To watch / Watch] movies is my hobby.

2 [That / It] is difficult to learn foreign languages.

3 I plan [to stay / to staying] in Sydney for three days.

4 My dream is [to becoming / to become] a Nobel Prize winner.

foreign 형 외국어의 외국의

language 명 언어

Sydney 명 시드니(호주 동남부에 있는 항구 도시)

Nobel Prize 노벨상

B 두 문장이 같은 뜻이 되도록 문장을 완성하시오.

1 To change a habit is difficult.

→ _____ is difficult _____.

2 To ride a bike is a lot of fun.

→ _____ is a lot of fun _____.

3 Please tell me when to stop.

→ Please tell me _____.

4 She can't decide where to put the computer.

→ She can't decide _____.

habit 명 습관

put 동 놓다, 두다

C 보기 에서 알맞은 것을 골라 문장을 완성하시오.

보기   what to do   when to submit   where to find   how to read

1 I don't know _____ French.

2 I'll ask a waiter _____ the restroom.

3 Do you know _____ the science report?

4 I wanted to help her, but I didn't know _____.

submit 동 제출하다

restroom 명 화장실

D 우리말과 같은 뜻이 되도록 주어진 단어를 이용하여 문장을 완성하시오.

1 Kerry는 내 충고를 받아들이길 거부했다. (refuse, take)

→ Kerry _____ _____ _____ my advice.

2 불을 가지고 노는 것은 위험하다. (play with, fire)

→ _____ is dangerous _____ _____ _____ _____.

3 오후 5시까지 숙제를 끝내는 것이 그녀의 계획이다. (finish, one's homework)

→ _____ is her plan _____ _____ _____ _____ by
5 pm.

4 우체국에 어떻게 가는지 말씀해 주시겠어요? (get to)

→ Could you tell me _____ _____ _____ _____ the
post office?

UNIT 02 형용사적 쓰임

☆ **to부정사의 형용사적 쓰임**: 문장에서 형용사처럼 명사를 수식하거나 주어를 보충 설명한다.

1. 「명사+to부정사(+전치사)」

Amy has many <u>books</u> **to read** this week. Amy는 이번 주에 읽어야 할 책이 많다.

I'm looking for a <u>house</u> **to live in.** 나는 살 집을 찾고 있다.

2. 「be+to부정사」: 예정, 의무, 운명, 가능, 의도 등의 뜻을 나타낸다.

Miranda **is to leave** for Toronto tomorrow. [예정] Miranda는 내일 토론토로 떠날 예정이다.

We **are to respect** the elderly. [의무] 우리는 어른을 공경해야 한다.

He **was to become** a famous actor from birth. [운명]
그는 태어날 때부터 유명한 배우가 될 운명이었다.

Nobody **was to be seen** in the building. [가능] 건물에서는 아무도 볼 수 없었다.

If you **are to catch** the train, you have to hurry. [의도] 그 기차를 타려면 너는 서둘러야 한다.

> **Plus α**
>
> 「be+to부정사」는 다양한 의미를 가지므로 해석에 유의해야 한다.
>
> We **are to meet** at six. [We≠to meet at six, 형용사적 쓰임] 우리는 6시에 만날 예정이다.
>
> My hobby **is to read** books. [My hobby＝to read books, 명사적 쓰임] 내 취미는 책을 읽는 것이다.

> **Tips**
>
> 1 to부정사가 전치사를 필요로 하는지 아닌지는 to부정사 뒤에 목적어를 놓아 보면 알 수 있다.
>
> She needs <u>a pen</u> **to write with.**
> 그녀는 쓸 펜이 필요하다.
> (O) write with a pen
> (X) ~~write a pen~~
>
> 2 동사 뒤에 전치사가 오는 경우
> · <u>a pen</u> to **write with**
> (가지고) 쓸 펜
> · <u>a chair</u> to **sit on**
> (위에) 앉을 의자
> · <u>friends</u> to **play with**
> (같이) 놀 친구
> · <u>a knife</u> to **cut with**
> (가지고) 자를 칼

> **Plus α**
>
> 「-thing/-one/-body로 끝나는 대명사+형용사+to부정사」
>
> Would you like <u>something cold</u> **to drink**?
> 차가운 마실 것을 좀 원하세요?

Check-up 우리말과 같은 뜻이 되도록 ☐ 안에서 알맞은 것을 고르시오.

1 나는 함께 놀 친구를 원한다.

→ I want a friend │ to play / to play with │.

2 너는 도서관에서 조용히 해야 한다.

→ You are │ be to / to be │ quiet in the library.

3 John은 마실 물을 샀다.

→ John bought │ water to drink / to drink water │.

4 나는 해야 할 숙제가 많다.

→ I have │ a lot of homework to do / to do a lot of homework │.

5 성공하려면 열심히 일해야 한다.

→ If you │ are succeed / are to succeed │, you should work hard.

: EXERCISES

A [ ] 안에서 알맞은 것을 고르시오.

1 We are [follow / to follow] school rules.

2 We brought some chairs [to sit / to sit on].

3 It is a good [time to buy / to buy time] a house.

4 You'd better take [something warm / warm something] to wear.

follow
(동) 따르다, 따라 하다

bring (동) 가져오다

had better
~하는 편이 낫다

B 보기 에서 알맞은 말을 골라 to부정사로 바꿔 문장을 완성하시오.

보기   live in   visit   do   wear

1 I have a lot of work _____ this afternoon.

2 My husband and I want a cozy house _____.

3 There are lots of famous places _____ in New York.

4 You should bring sunglasses _____ in the strong sunlight.

cozy (형) 안락한

strong
(형) 강한; 힘센, 튼튼한

sunlight (명) 햇빛

C 밑줄 친 부분에 유의하여 해석을 완성하시오.

1 Nothing was to be found there.

→ 거기에서는 아무것도 _____.

2 Steve was to live alone for his whole life.

→ Steve는 평생 혼자 _____.

3 You are to finish the project by Friday.

→ 너는 금요일까지 그 프로젝트를 _____.

4 If you are to win the game, you should practice hard.

→ 경기에서 _____, 열심히 연습해야 한다.

D 우리말과 같은 뜻이 되도록 주어진 단어를 이용하여 문장을 완성하시오.

1 캘리포니아에 볼 만한 흥미로운 것이 있나요? (interesting, anything, see)

→ Is there _____ _____ _____ _____ in California?

2 그는 공항에 8시에 도착할 예정이다. (be, arrive at)

→ He _____ _____ _____ _____ the airport at eight.

3 나는 아프리카를 여행할 기회를 얻고 싶다. (a chance, travel)

→ I would like to have _____ _____ _____ _____ to Africa.

4 그는 같이 춤을 출 파트너를 찾고 있다. (a partner, dance with)

→ He is looking for _____ _____ _____ _____

_____.

부사적 쓰임

☆ **to부정사의 부사적 쓰임**: 문장에서 부사처럼 동사, 형용사, 다른 부사 등을 수식한다.

1. 목적(=in order to부정사, so as to부정사) ~하기 위해서, ~하러

He went to the market **to buy** some grapes. 그는 포도를 사러 시장에 갔다.
= in order to buy[so as to buy]

2. 감정의 원인 ~하니, ~해서

I'm sorry **to hurt** your feelings. 너의 기분을 상하게 해서 미안해.
She was very pleased **to see** him again. 그녀는 그를 다시 만나게 되어서 매우 기뻤다.

3. 결과 ~해서 …하다, 했지만 결국 ~하다

She grew up **to be** President. 그녀는 자라서 대통령이 되었다.
Sam studied hard, only **to fail** the test. Sam은 열심히 공부했지만 시험에 떨어졌다.

4. 판단의 근거 ~하다니, ~하는 것을 보니

He must be careless **to make** such a mistake. 그런 실수를 저지르다니 그는 부주의한 게 틀림없어.
They are very lucky **to win** the game. 대회에서 이기다니 그들은 운이 매우 좋다.

5. 형용사 수식 ~하기에, ~하는 데

His poems are easy **to understand**. 그의 시들은 이해하기 쉽다.
The weather is perfect **to go** for a walk. 날씨가 산책하기에 알맞다.

> **Plus α**
>
> to부정사의 부정은 to부정사 앞에 not을 붙이므로 in order to, so as to의 부정은 in order not to, so as not to로 쓴다.
>
> I got up early not to be late for school.
> ➡ I got up early **in order not to** be [**so as not to be**] late for school.
> 나는 학교에 늦지 않으려고 일찍 일어났다.

Check-up 우리말과 같은 뜻이 되도록 ☐ 안에서 알맞은 것을 고르시오.

1 나는 너에게 연락을 받아서 기뻤어.
→ I was happy ☐ hear / to hear ☐ from you.

2 우리 할머니는 90세까지 살았다.
→ My grandmother lived ☐ be / to be ☐ ninety.

3 그 문제는 해결하기 어렵다.
→ The problem is ☐ difficult to solve / to solve difficult ☐.

4 그는 책을 빌리기 위해 도서관에 갔다.
→ He went to the library ☐ borrowing / to borrow ☐ books.

: EXERCISES

A   [ ] 안에서 알맞은 것을 고르시오.

1 I'm so excited [go / to go] to the concert.

2 This new cell phone is [easy to use / to use easy].

3 Her paintings are very complicated [understand / to understand].

4 You should turn off your phone [not to make / to make not] noise in the library.

complicated 휑 복잡한
turn off ~을 끄다
make noise 소음을 내다

B   보기 에서 알맞은 말을 골라 to부정사로 바꿔 문장을 완성하시오.

보기	catch	celebrate	become	see

1 I work out hard _____ healthy.

2 She got up early _____ the first train.

3 My cousins will come to my house _____ me.

4 My family will get together _____ my grandfather's birthday.

celebrate 동 축하하다
work out 운동하다
get together
모이다, 모으다

C   밑줄 친 부분에 유의하여 해석을 완성하시오.

1 Sam was very excited to travel to Hawaii.

  → Sam은 하와이로 _____ 매우 신이 났다.

2 Clark was foolish to trust her again.

  → 그녀를 다시 _____ Clark은 어리석었어.

3 I'm going to Paris to learn French.

  → 나는 프랑스어를 _____ 파리로 갈 것이다.

4 The boy grew up to be a movie star.

  → 그 소년은 자라서 영화배우가 _____.

D   우리말과 같은 뜻이 되도록 주어진 단어를 이용하여 문장을 완성하시오.

1 그 물은 마시기에 적당하지 않다. (good, drink)

  → The water is not _____ _____ _____.

2 당신과 같이 일하게 되어 정말 행운이에요. (lucky, work with)

  → I'm so _____ _____ _____ you.

3 Kelly는 제 시간에 도착하기 위해서 학교로 달려가야 했다. (be, on time)

  → Kelly had to run to school _____ _____ _____

  _____.

UNIT 04 의미상의 주어, too ~to, enough to

1. 의미상의 주어: 문장의 주어와 to부정사의 행위자가 일치하지 않을 경우, to부정사 앞에 의미상의 주어를 쓴다.

(1) 「**for+목적격**」: 일반적인 형용사 뒤에서 to부정사의 주어를 나타낼 때 쓴다.

It is underlined{important} **for us** *to follow* the rules. 우리가 규칙을 지키는 것은 중요하다.

It was underlined{impossible} **for Jake** *to finish* his report. Jake가 보고서를 끝내는 것은 불가능했다.

(2) 「**of+목적격**」: 사람의 행동을 칭찬하거나 비판하는 형용사 뒤에서 to부정사의 주어를 나타낼 때 쓴다.
(nice, kind, clever, silly, careful, careless, wise 등)

It is very underlined{kind} **of Melanie** *to say* so. 그렇게 얘기하다니 Melanie는 정말 친절하구나.

It was underlined{silly} **of me** *to make* such a mistake. 그런 실수를 저지르다니 내가 어리석었어.

2. 「**too+형용사/부사+to+동사원형**」 너무 ~해서 …할 수 없다, …하기엔 너무 ~하다
= 「**so+형용사/부사+that+주어+can't /couldn't+동사원형**」

David was **too tired to drive** home. David는 너무 피곤해서 집까지 운전할 수 없었다.

➡ David was **so tired that he couldn't drive** home.

3. 「**형용사/부사+enough+to+동사원형**」 ~할 만큼 충분히 …하다
= 「**so+형용사/부사+that+주어+can/could+동사원형**」

She ran **fast enough to win** the race. 그녀는 경기에서 이길 만큼 충분히 빨리 달렸다.

➡ She ran **so fast that she could win** the race.

Plus α

1 「so+형용사/부사+that +주어+동사」[원인과 결과] 매우 ~하여 …하다

It was **so** hot **that** I opened the window. 날씨가 매우 더워서 나는 창문을 열었다.

2 so that [목적] ~하기위하여, ~하도록

She works out every day **so that** she can stay healthy. 그녀는 건강을 유지하기 위해 매일 운동을 한다.

Check-up 우리말과 같은 뜻이 되도록 ☐ 안에서 알맞은 것을 고르시오.

1 아이가 혼자 밖에 나가는 것은 위험하다.
→ It is dangerous ☐ for / of ☐ a child to go out alone.

2 나를 보러 오다니 그는 참 친절했다.
→ It was very kind ☐ for / of ☐ him to come and see me.

3 그 커피는 내가 마시기에는 너무 뜨겁다.
→ The coffee is ☐ hot too / too hot ☐ for me to drink.

4 그 강당은 천 명을 수용할 만큼 충분히 크다.
→ The hall is ☐ enough large / large enough ☐ to hold 1,000 people.

: EXERCISES

A [   ] 안에서 알맞은 것을 고르시오.

1 It was rude [for / of] him to keep us waiting.

2 It is necessary [for / of] you to do the work.

3 Tom studied hard [too / enough] to pass the exam.

4 They are [too / enough] young to watch the movie.

rude (형) 무례한, 버릇없는
keep (동) 계속~하게 하다
necessary (형) 필요한

B 빈칸에 of 또는 for를 넣어 문장을 완성하시오.

1 It was clever _____ him to solve the problem.

2 It is dangerous _____ her to go abroad alone.

3 It was brave _____ her to swim across the channel.

4 It was hard _____ me to answer all of the questions.

go abroad 외국에 가다
alone (부) 홀로, 혼자서
channel (명) 해협

C 두 문장이 같은 뜻이 되도록 문장을 완성하시오.

1 I was too busy to get enough sleep.

→ I was _____ enough sleep.

2 My sister is too young to ride a bike.

→ My sister is _____ a bike.

3 You are tall enough to reach the shelf.

→ You are _____ the shelf.

4 My brother was strong enough to move the desk alone.

→ My brother was _____ the desk alone.

ride (동) ~을 타다
reach (동) ~에 닿다; 도착하다
shelf (명) 선반

D 우리말과 같은 뜻이 되도록 주어진 단어를 이용하여 문장을 완성하시오.

1 그녀는 키가 너무 작아서 그 치마를 입을 수 없다. (short, wear)

→ She is _____ _____ _____ _____ the skirt.

2 그에게 돈을 빌려주다니 그녀는 어리석구나. (foolish, she, lend)

→ It is _____ _____ _____ _____ _____ him money.

3 그는 비밀을 지키기가 어려웠다. (hard, he, keep)

→ It was _____ _____ _____ _____ _____ a secret.

4 Brenda는 전문 수영 선수가 될 만큼 충분히 수영을 잘한다. (well, be)

→ Brenda swims _____ _____ _____ _____
   a professional swimmer.

: Review Test

[01-03] 빈칸에 들어갈 알맞은 말을 고르시오.

01

His dream is _____ to outer space.

① travel   ② traveled
③ to travel   ④ to travels
⑤ to traveling

02

_____ is impossible to remember everything.

① It   ② If   ③ That
④ When   ⑤ What

03

He told me _____ use the copy machine and I tried, but it didn't work.

① what to   ② when to
③ where to   ④ how to
⑤ who to

04 빈칸에 들어갈 수 없는 것은?

It is very _____ of her to do such a thing.

① kind   ② nice   ③ rude
④ stupid   ⑤ difficult

05 밑줄 친 우리말을 영어로 바르게 옮긴 것은?

A Would you like something to drink?
B Yes, please. Give me 시원한 마실 것.

① to drink cold something
② to drink something cold
③ cold to drink something
④ cold something to drink
⑤ something cold to drink

[06-07] 빈칸에 들어갈 말이 바르게 짝지어진 것을 고르시오.

06

· The boy is _____ weak to lift the box.
· He is strong _____ to lift four kids.

① too – enough   ② enough – enough
③ enough – too   ④ too – so
⑤ so – too

07

· It was important _____ me to pass the exam.
· It is wise _____ her to ask for his help.

① of – for   ② to – for   ③ for – of
④ for – to   ⑤ to – of

08 보기 의 밑줄 친 부분과 쓰임이 다른 것은?

보기   It is good for your health to take walks regularly.

① It is exciting to watch soccer games.
② The team expected to win the championship.
③ There are lots of interesting things to do in Seoul.
④ My plan was to stay in London for a month.
⑤ Do you want to go shopping today?

09 보기 의 밑줄 친 부분과 쓰임이 같은 것은?

보기   I had a chance to meet a famous singer.

① You should study hard to pass the test.
② Shelly went to the store to buy some milk.
③ The book is not easy for children to read.
④ I was surprised to see him at the police station.
⑤ The child has many friends to play with.

[10-11] 밑줄 친 부분이 어법상 어색한 것을 고르시오.

10 ① Judy grew up to be a great professor.
② Susie is enough tired to go out for dinner.
③ I will be so glad to hear from you soon.
④ My parents are to visit Paris next month.
⑤ It is necessary for us to respect other people.

11 ① Do you have something to say to me?
② I have something interesting to show you.
③ Linda plans to study history at university.
④ Lauren is kind enough to help me carry my luggage.
⑤ It was careless for me to leave my cell phone on the subway.

12 짝지어진 문장의 뜻이 서로 다른 것은?

① Please tell me when to start.
→ Please tell me when I should start.
② She is rich enough to buy a villa.
→ She is so rich that she can buy a villa.
③ He goes jogging to lose weight.
→ He goes jogging in order to lose weight.
④ To learn how to cook is not easy for me.
→ It is not easy for me to learn how to cook.
⑤ Ryan is too busy to meet his friends.
→ Ryan is so busy that he can meet his friends.

13 다음 중 어법상 바른 문장은?

① I have nobody to talk.
② She wants to buy a coat to wear.
③ The old man needs a chair to sit.
④ We are looking for a house to live.
⑤ Could you lend me a pen to write?

[14-15] 글을 읽고, 물음에 답하시오.

Dear Ms. Wilson,

Ann and I were best friends. But because of my mistake, she doesn't want to see me. I told her secret to other students, and everyone in school knows it now. I was so silly ❶ to do such a thing. I tried to apologize to her, but she refused ❷ to talk to me. I know that ❸ it will be difficult ❹ of Ann to forgive me because she trusted me, but I broke her heart. Would it be a good idea to write a letter asking her ❺ to accept my apology? What should I do (A) to change her mind about me?

Gloomy Sandy

14 밑줄 친 ❶~❺ 중 어법상 어색한 것은?

15 밑줄 친 (A)와 쓰임이 같은 것은?

① His wish is to make many friends in his new school.
② Joan came to Korea to see her friend, Kelly.
③ Smith decided to become a politician.
④ There is nothing to worry about.
⑤ To play the cello is not easy.

[01-02] 주어진 단어를 사용하여 우리말과 같은 뜻이 되도록 문장을 완성하시오.

01 나는 미안하다고 말하는 것이 어렵다. (difficult, I, say)

→ It is _____ sorry.

02 그녀에게 꽃을 사 주다니 그는 참 예의가 바르구나.
(polite, he, buy)

→ It is _____
her flowers.

[03-05] 두 문장이 같은 뜻이 되도록 문장을 완성하시오.

03 Lilly is so wise that she can make the right decision.

→ Lilly is _____ the right decision.

04 Tony was so busy that he couldn't go grocery shopping today.

→ Tony was _____ grocery shopping today.

05 Do you know where I should find the nearest subway station?

→ Do you know _____ the nearest subway station?

[06-07] 글을 읽고, 물음에 답하시오.

I went to a bookstore to buy an interesting book. But I couldn't decide **06** 무엇을 살지 because there were a lot of interesting books. It was hard **07** (me, choose) which book to buy.

06 밑줄 친 우리말과 같은 뜻이 되도록 영작하시오.

→ _____

07 주어진 단어를 문맥에 맞게 바꿔 쓰시오.

→ _____

[08-09] Anna의 할 일을 읽고, 대화를 완성하시오.

Anna's Things to Do:
- to go hiking with Kelly on Saturday
- to buy a book for her mother at the bookstore

조건 to부정사를 사용할 것

08 A What does Anna want to do on Saturday?
B She wants _____ with Kelly.

09 A Why does Anna want to go to the bookstore?
B Because she wants _____ for her mother.

10 현장 학습 유인물을 읽고, 밑줄 친 우리말을 영작하시오.

Field Trip to the National Park

Students are to go to the National Park.

When to go: September 5th
(1) 가는 장소: The National Park
(2) 가는 방법: By school bus

Don't forget:
- To bring (3) 마실 것
- To wear a warm jacket and a hat

* Students should be careful (4) 늦지 않도록 for the school bus.

(1) _____

(2) _____

(3) _____

(4) _____

Chapter 3

동명사

UNIT 01 동명사의 쓰임

☆ **동명사:** 「동사원형+ing」 형태로 명사처럼 문장에서 주어, 보어, 목적어 역할을 한다.

1. 주어 역할 ~하기는, ~하는 것은
Staying up late will make you tired. 밤늦게까지 안 자는 것은 너를 피곤하게 할 것이다.
Seeing her smile makes me happy. 그녀의 미소를 보는 것은 나를 행복하게 만든다.

2. 보어 역할 ~하는 것(이다)
Her job is **writing** cookbooks. 그녀의 직업은 요리책을 쓰는 것이다.
My favorite activity is **running** along the riverside.
내가 가장 좋아하는 운동은 강변을 따라 뛰는 것이다.

3. 목적어 역할 ~하기를, 하는 것을
Would you <u>mind</u> **opening** the window? [동사의 목적어] 창문을 좀 열어 주실래요?
Amy <u>finished</u> **doing** her homework. [동사의 목적어] Amy는 숙제 하는 것을 끝냈다.
Thank you <u>for</u> **inviting** me to dinner. [전치사의 목적어] 저를 저녁 식사에 초대해 주셔서 감사합니다.
I'm interested <u>in</u> **learning** new things. [전치사의 목적어] 나는 새로운 것을 배우는 데에 관심이 있다.

4. 자주 쓰이는 동명사 표현

be busy -ing ~하느라 바쁘다	how[what] about -ing ~하는 게 어때?
feel like -ing ~하고 싶다	look forward to -ing ~을 기대하다
be worth -ing ~할 가치가 있다	It is no use -ing ~해도 소용없다
on -ing ~하자마자	cannot help -ing[cannot but 동사원형] ~하지 않을 수 없다
go -ing ~하러 가다	spend + 시간[돈]+ -ing ~하는 데 …을 소비하다
be used to -ing ~에 익숙하다	have difficulty[trouble / a hard time] -ing ~하는 데 어려움을 겪다

I <u>was busy</u> **searching** for some information about stars. 나는 별에 관한 자료를 찾느라 바빴다.
The movie <u>is worth</u> **watching** twice. 그 영화는 두 번 볼 가치가 있다.

Plus α
1 동명사 주어는 단수로 취급해 단수 동사를 쓴다.
<u>Growing flowers **is**</u> my new hobby.
꽃을 기르는 것이 내 새로운 취미이다.

2 주어나 보어로 쓰인 동명사는 to부정사로 바꿔 쓸 수도 있다.
Seeing is **believing**.
➡ **To see** is **to believe**.
보는 것이 믿는 것이다.
(백문이 불여일견)

Tips
동명사의 부정:
「not[never]+동명사」
She apologized for **not coming** to the party.
그녀는 파티에 오지 않은 것에 대해 사과했다.

Check-up 우리말과 같은 뜻이 되도록 ☐ 안에서 알맞은 것을 고르시오.

1 친구를 사귀는 것은 신나는 일이다.
→ Make / Making new friends is exciting.

2 Rachel은 매일 아침 커피 마시는 것을 즐긴다.
→ Rachel enjoys have / having coffee every morning.

3 Joseph은 여행 가방을 싸느라 바쁘다.
→ Joseph is busy to pack / packing his suitcase.

: EXERCISES

A   [   ] 안에서 알맞은 것을 고르시오.

1   Dan is famous for [work / working] hard.

2   My brother's hobby is [raise / raising] spiders.

3   [Sleep / Sleeping] late is one of my bad habits.

4   How about [going / to go] to a movie tonight?

5   We love [taking / to taking] a walk along the beach.

be famous for
~로 유명하다

raise (동) 키우다, 기르다

sleep late 늦잠을 자다

go to a movie
영화 보러 가다

take a walk 산책하다

along (전) ~을 따라

B   밑줄 친 부분을 어법에 맞게 고쳐 쓰시오.

1   Peter gave up <u>learn</u> the guitar.

2   I feel like <u>to have</u> some ice cream.

3   I'm so excited about <u>go</u> to New Zealand.

4   Eating lots of vegetables <u>are</u> good for your health.

give up 포기하다

guitar (명) 〈악기〉 기타

feel like ~하고 싶다

New Zealand 뉴질랜드

C   보기 에서 알맞은 동사를 골라 동명사로 바꿔 문장을 완성하시오.

보기	be	read	say	watch

1   Science fiction is worth _____.

2   My father likes _____ sports on TV.

3   Chris left the party without _____ goodbye.

4   My dream is _____ a great painter like Picasso.

science fiction
공상 과학 소설

worth (형) ~의 가치가 있는

without (전) ~없이

painter (명) 화가

D   우리말과 같은 뜻이 되도록 주어진 단어를 이용하여 문장을 완성하시오.

1   토요일 아침 일찍 낚시하러 가자. (go, fish)

   → Let's _____ _____ early Saturday morning.

2   좋은 사진을 찍는 것은 쉽지 않다. (take, good pictures)

   → _____ _____ _____ is not easy.

3   다시 전화해 주셔서 감사합니다. (call, again)

   → Thank you for _____ _____.

4   우리는 크리스마스트리 장식을 끝냈다. (decorate, the Christmas tree)

   → We finished _____ _____ _____ _____.

UNIT 02 동명사와 to부정사

Plus α

1 「stop+동명사」
~하는 것을 멈추다

She **stopped talking** on the phone.
그녀는 통화하는 것을 멈췄다.

2 「stop+to부정사」
~하기 위해 멈추다

She **stopped to make** a phone call.
그녀는 전화를 하기 위해 멈췄다.

1. **동명사를 목적어로 취하는 동사:** avoid, delay, deny, dislike, enjoy, finish, give up, keep, mind, practice, put off, quit, stop, suggest 등

   I finished **taking** a shower just now. 나는 막 샤워를 끝냈다.

   Jack kept **talking** about his new classmate. Jack은 전학생에 대해 계속해서 이야기했다.

2. **to부정사를 목적어로 취하는 동사:** agree, ask, choose, decide, expect, hope, learn, plan, promise, refuse, want, wish 등

   I hope **to see** you more often. 나는 너를 더 자주 만나고 싶어.

   My father promised **to buy** me a bike. 우리 아버지께서 나에게 자전거를 사 준다고 약속하셨다.

3. **동명사와 to부정사를 목적어로 취하는 동사**

   (1) 의미 차이가 거의 없는 경우: begin, start, like, love, hate 등

   I began **working[to work]** for the company in 2013.
   나는 2013년에 그 회사에서 일하기 시작했다.

   My brother loves **making[to make]** model airplanes.
   내 남동생은 모형 비행기 만드는 것을 좋아한다.

   (2) 의미 차이가 있는 경우: remember, forget, try 등

remember+to부정사 ~할 일을 기억하다(아직 하지 않음)	remember+동명사 ~한 일을 기억하다(이미 했음)
forget+to부정사 ~할 일을 잊다(아직 하지 않음)	forget+동명사 ~한 일을 잊다(이미 했음)
try+to부정사 ~하려고 노력하다[애쓰다]	try+동명사 시험 삼아 (한번) ~하다

   I remember **getting** a phone call from you. 나는 너에게서 전화가 왔던 것을 기억한다.

   Remember **to call** me when you arrive home. 집에 도착하면 나에게 전화해야 하는 거 기억해.

   He forgot **leaving** his wallet at home. 그는 지갑을 집에 놓고 온 것을 잊었다.

   Don't forget **to tell** her the news. 그녀에게 그 소식을 전하는 거 잊지 마.

   I tried **to fix** the photocopier, but I couldn't. 나는 그 복사기를 고치려고 노력했지만, 고칠 수 없었다.

   The girl tried **putting** on her mom's shoes. 소녀는 엄마의 신발을 한번 신어 보았다.

Check-up 우리말과 같은 뜻이 되도록 □ 안에서 알맞은 것을 고르시오.

1 나는 식당에서 혼자 식사하는 것을 꺼려하지 않는다.
   → I don't mind eating / to eat alone in restaurants.

2 Emily는 직업을 바꾸기로 결심했다.
   → Emily decided changing / to change her job.

3 나는 뉴욕에 갔던 것을 기억한다. 즐거운 여행이었다.
   → I remember going / to go to New York. It was a good trip.

: EXERCISES

A [ ] 안에서 알맞은 것을 모두 고르시오.

1 Damon hates [driving / to drive] in snow.

2 I never expected [seeing / to see] her again.

3 Steve plans [studying / to study] Chinese in Beijing.

4 My friend and I like [going / to go] to the art gallery.

expect
⑧ 기대하다, 예상하다
art gallery 미술관

B 주어진 단어를 동명사 또는 to부정사로 바꿔 문장을 완성하시오.

1 The baseball player practiced _____ baseballs. (throw)

2 He promised _____ back the money within a month. (pay)

3 The baby kept _____, and I didn't know what to do. (cry)

4 Harry kindly agreed _____ me find a good doctor. (help)

practice
⑧ 연습하다; ⑲ 연습; 실행
throw ⑧ 던지다
pay back 갚다, 돌려주다
within ⑳ 이내에, 안에

C 두 문장의 의미가 통하도록 빈칸에 알맞은 말을 쓰시오.

1 Don't act like a child anymore.

→ Stop _____ like a child.

2 We wanted to enjoy the scenery, so we stopped.

→ We stopped _____ the scenery.

3 I forgot that I put my keys in my pocket.

→ I forgot _____ my keys in my pocket.

4 Remember that you should bring an umbrella with you.

→ Remember _____ an umbrella with you.

act like ~처럼 행동하다
scenery ⑲ 경치, 풍경

D 우리말과 같은 뜻이 되도록 주어진 단어를 이용하여 문장을 완성하시오.

1 Carrie에게 메시지를 남기고 싶어요. (want, leave a message)

→ I _____ _____ _____ _____ for Carrie.

2 내 아들은 4세 때 피아노를 연주하기 시작했다. (start, play the piano)

→ My son _____ _____ _____ _____ when he was four.

3 나는 공부에 집중하려고 노력했지만, 그럴 수 없었다. (try, concentrate on)

→ I _____ _____ _____ _____ studying, but I couldn't.

4 안전띠를 매는 거 잊지 마. (forget, fasten your seat belt)

→ Don't _____ _____ _____ _____ _____

_____.

동명사 vs. 현재분사

동명사 vs. 현재분사

Tips

현재분사는 주로 진행되고 있는 동작을 나타낸다.

She is **watching** a **swimming** boy.
➡ She is watching +
   A boy is swimming.
   그녀는 수영을 하는 소년을 보고 있다.

	동명사	현재분사
-ing + 명사	'~하기 위한'이라는 의미로 뒤에 나오는 명사의 용도나 목적을 나타낸다. • a **sleeping** car 침대차 [잠자기 위한 차: a car for sleeping] • a **waiting** room 대기실 [기다리기 위한 방: a room for waiting]	'~을 하고 있는'이라는 의미로 명사를 수식하거나 명사의 상태나 동작을 나타낸다. • a **sleeping** baby 잠자는 아기 [baby 수식: a baby is sleeping] • **waiting** people 기다리는 사람들 [people 수식: people are waiting]
be -ing	주격보어 역할: Her job is **designing** women' shoes. [her job = designing women' shoes] 그녀의 직업은 숙녀화를 디자인하는 것이다.	현재진행형: Karen is **designing** a house. Karen은 집을 디자인하고 있는 중이다.
주어	**Listening** to music is his hobby. 음악을 듣는 것은 그의 취미이다.	—
목적어	I like **listening** to music. 나는 음악 듣는 것을 좋아한다.	—
전치사의 목적어	I'm interested in **drawing** pictures. 나는 그림 그리는 데 관심이 있다.	—
목적격보어	—	I saw a boy **dancing** in the street. 나는 거리에서 춤추는 한 소년을 보았다.

Plus α

1 분사가 단독으로 명사를 수식할 경우 앞에서 수식한다.

There is a **sleeping** baby in the cradle. 요람에 잠자는 아기가 있다.

2 분사가 구를 이루어 명사를 수식할 경우 뒤에서 수식한다.

Who is the boy **sleeping in the back seat**? 뒤 좌석에서 잠을 자고 있는 소년은 누구니?

Check-up 우리말과 같은 뜻이 되도록 ☐ 안에서 알맞은 것을 고르시오.

1 그 춤추는 소녀는 나의 가장 친한 친구 Linda이다.

→ The ☐dancing / to dance☐ girl is my best friend, Linda.

2 우리 할아버지는 지팡이를 사용하신다.

→ My grandfather uses a ☐walked / walking☐ stick.

: EXERCISES

A [ ] 안에서 알맞은 것을 고르시오.

fit (동) 적합하다, 어울리다
calm (동) 진정시키다

1 There is a [to fit / fitting] room over there.

2 She is trying to calm the [cry / crying] child.

3 Is there a [smoke / smoking] room in this building?

4 My grandmother is [made / making] a cheesecake for me.

B 보기 에서 알맞은 단어를 골라 어법에 맞게 바꿔 문장을 완성하시오.

park (동) 주차하다
stand (동) 서다, 서 있다

| 보기 | listen to | park | stand | surprise |

1 My car is in the _____ lot.

2 Look at the girls _____ in line.

3 I heard _____ news from Samantha.

4 The boys are _____ rock music.

C 밑줄 친 부분에 유의하여 해석을 완성하시오.

1 Her hobby is <u>singing</u> pop songs.

→ 그녀의 취미는 대중가요를 _____이다.

2 She is <u>sitting</u> in the <u>waiting</u> room.

→ 그녀는 _____에 _____ 있다.

3 Clare saw the <u>singing</u> birds at the zoo.

→ Clare는 동물원에서 _____ 새들을 보았다.

4 My parents are <u>talking</u> in the <u>living</u> room.

→ 나의 부모님은 _____에서 _____ 있다.

D 우리말과 같은 뜻이 되도록 주어진 단어를 배열하시오.

1 너 선글라스를 쓰고 있는 소녀를 아니? (wearing, the girl, sunglasses, know)

→ Do you _____?

2 우리 아빠는 종종 재미있는 이야기를 해준다. (interesting, me, stories, tells)

→ My dad often _____.

3 아이들 몇 명이 수영장에서 놀고 있다. (in, playing, the swimming pool, are)

→ Some kids _____.

4 그녀의 목표는 전국 대회에서 우승하는 것이다.
(the national championship, her goal, winning, is)

→ _____

: Review Test

[01-02] 빈칸에 들어갈 알맞은 것을 고르시오.

01 _____ regularly is a good habit.

① Exercise   ② Exercises
③ Exercised   ④ Exercising
⑤ Being exercised

02 Greg is very interested in _____ foreign languages.

① study   ② studies   ③ studied
④ to study   ⑤ studying

[03-04] 빈칸에 들어갈 말로 알맞지 <u>않은</u> 것을 고르시오.

03 She _____ to study cooking in Paris.

① expects   ② enjoys   ③ wishes
④ hopes   ⑤ wants

04 Peter _____ writing his fifth novel.

① decided   ② gave up   ③ began
④ finished   ⑤ kept

05 보기 의 밑줄 친 부분과 쓰임이 같은 것은?

> 보기   My favorite activity is <u>riding</u> horses.

① The man <u>standing</u> over there is my father.
② My uncle is <u>designing</u> his own house.
③ Ruth is <u>washing</u> her car in the garage.
④ His hobby is <u>watching</u> sports on TV.
⑤ Look at the girl <u>wearing</u> red shoes.

[06-07] 빈칸에 들어갈 말이 바르게 짝지어진 것을 고르시오.

06 · Do you mind _____ for a moment?
· He proposed to her, and she agreed _____ him.

① wait – to marry
② waiting – to marry
③ to wait – marrying
④ waiting – marrying
⑤ to wait – marry

07 · The movie is worth _____ more than twice.
· I felt like _____ when I heard the sad news.

① to watch – cry   ② watch – to cry
③ to watch – crying   ④ watching – to cry
⑤ watching – crying

[08-09] 우리말을 영어로 바르게 옮긴 것을 고르시오.

08 Samuel은 강의에 집중하려고 애썼다.

① Samuel tried concentrate on the lecture.
② Samuel tried concentrates on the lecture.
③ Samuel tried to concentrate on the lecture.
④ Samuel tried concentrating on the lecture.
⑤ Samuel tried to concentrating on the lecture.

09 점심을 챙겨 오는 것을 잊지 마.

① Don't forget to bringing your own lunch.
② Don't forget to bring your own lunch.
③ Don't forget bringing your own lunch.
④ Don't forget brings your own lunch.
⑤ Don't forget bring your own lunch.

10 보기 의 밑줄 친 부분과 쓰임이 <u>다른</u> 것은?

> 보기   There are many children in the <u>swimming</u> pool.

① <u>Staying</u> up late is difficult for me.
② He avoids <u>driving</u> in heavy traffic.
③ My cousin is good at <u>playing</u> the violin.
④ The <u>waiting</u> room of the hospital is crowded.
⑤ She looked at the <u>sleeping</u> baby with a smile.

[11-12] 다음 중 어법상 <u>어색한</u> 것을 고르시오.

11 ① The boy promised to follow the rules.
② Dave is practicing shooting a basketball.
③ He started to repair the broken computer.
④ On to arrive in London, I called my parents.
⑤ They love to get together and have fun.

12 ① Remember to keep the secret.
② Rick gave up being a movie star.
③ She hates watching action movies.
④ Mom is busy cooking dinner in the kitchen.
⑤ They stopped to fight when they saw their teacher.

13 다음 대화 중 의미가 자연스럽지 <u>않은</u> 것은?

① A Do you want to go camping this weekend?
   B I'd love to, but I plan to do something else.
② A Did you send me the invitation card?
   B Sorry, I forgot to send it.
③ A What is Gary doing in the garden?
   B He is busy trimming trees.
④ A I will call and tell him not to go.
   B That's a good idea. It is no use talking to him.
⑤ A I'll meet James tonight. What is he like?
   B He is such a nice guy, so you cannot help liking him.

[14-15] 글을 읽고, 물음에 답하시오.

On a clear night, I enjoyed ❶ <u>looking</u> up at the sky. I counted stars and started ❷ <u>wondering</u> about a lot of things. Is space endless? Are there any aliens? Does the black hole really swallow everything near it? When I was young, I remembered ❸ <u>seeing</u> two round ❹ <u>flying</u> objects in the sky. Since then, my dream is always (A) <u>(be)</u> an astronaut. I wish (B) <u>(travel)</u> to outer space and study the stars and planets. These days, I'm thinking about how I can become an astronaut. I know that I need to study hard and be healthy. Even though it is very difficult to become an astronaut, I'll never give up ❺ <u>trying</u> to achieve my dream.

* astronaut 우주비행사

14 밑줄 친 ❶~❺ 중 쓰임이 나머지와 <u>다른</u> 것은?

15 밑줄 친 (A), (B)를 바르게 고친 것을 <u>모두</u> 고르시오.

	(A)		(B)
①	to being	----	to traveling
②	to be	----	traveling
③	to be	----	to travel
④	being	----	traveling
⑤	being	----	to travel

[01-02] 우리말과 같은 뜻이 되도록 주어진 단어를 이용하여
문장을 완성하시오.

01 나무 밑에 앉아 있는 소년은 내 남동생이다.
→ The boy _____ _____ _____
_____ is my brother. (sit, under the tree)

02 나는 수영하러 갈까 생각 중이다.
→ I _____ _____ _____
_____ for a swim. (be, think about, go)

[03-04] 두 문장이 같은 뜻이 되도록 문장을 완성하시오.

03 My brother plays sports very well.
→ My brother is very good at _____
_____.

04 I'll never forget that I had a good time in Guam.
→ I'll never forget _____
_____ in Guam.

[05-06] 우리말과 같은 뜻이 되도록 주어진 단어를 이용하여
문장을 완성하시오.

05 그는 주위를 둘러보기 위해 멈췄다. (stop, look around)
→ He _____.

06 그는 신문을 읽던 것을 멈췄다. (stop, read, newspapers)
→ He _____.

[07-08] 어법상 어색한 부분을 찾아 어법에 맞게 고쳐 쓰시오.

07 Thank you for help me move the table.
→ _____

08 Tiffany will go shop with Ann this afternoon.
→ _____

09 Peter에 대한 메모를 읽고, 동명사를 이용하여 글을 완성
하시오.

Name: Peter
· **Job:** English teacher
· **Things to enjoy:** to play all kinds of sports
· **Things to hate:** to do the housework
· **Things to do well:** to speak foreign languages

⇩

Let me introduce my brother, Peter.
His job is teaching English to high school
students. He enjoys _____
_____.
He hates _____.
He is good at _____.

10 대화를 읽고, 밑줄 친 우리말과 같은 뜻이 되도록 문장을
완성하시오.

A (1) 방과 후에 수영하러 가자.
B That sounds great. What should I bring?
A I'll bring some food. (2) 수영복과 수영모
가져오는 걸 잊지 마.
B Okay.

조건 동명사나 to부정사를 활용할 것

(1) Let's _____ after school.

(2) Don't _____ a swimsuit
and a swimming cap.

Chapter 4

대명사

부정대명사 I

☆ **부정대명사**: 불특정한 사물이나 사람을 막연하게 지칭하는 대명사이다. one, some, any, each, every, all, both 등과 같은 일부 부정대명사는 형용사로 쓰여 명사를 수식하기도 한다.

1. one(단수), ones(복수): 앞에 언급된 것과 같은 종류의 불특정한 것을 지칭한다.

Aiden sold his old car and bought a new **one**. [one = car] Aiden은 타던 차를 팔고 새 차를 샀다.

I like cookies, especially chocolate **ones**. [ones = cookies]
나는 쿠키를 좋아하는데, 특히 초콜릿 쿠키를 좋아한다.

Plus α

앞에 언급된 것과 같은 대상을 가리킬 때는 it을 사용한다.

Mom bought <u>a new dress</u> and gave **it** to me.
[it = a new dress]
엄마가 새 드레스를 샀고, 그 드레스를 나에게 주었다.

2. some 약간(의), 몇몇(의), 어떤 사람들: 주로 긍정문이나 권유를 나타내는 의문문에 사용한다.

Some of her books are very touching. [긍정문] 그녀의 책들 중 몇몇은 아주 감동적이다.

Would you like **some** coffee? [권유문] 커피 좀 드시겠어요?

3. any 어떤, 얼마간(의), 조금(의): 주로 부정문, 의문문에 사용한다.

A Are there **any** messages for me? 제 앞으로 온 메시지 있습니까?

B No. There aren't **any**. 아니요. 아무 것도 없어요.

Tips

any는 조건문에도 사용된다.

If you need **any** help, let me know.
어떤 도움이라도 필요하면 알려주세요.

4. all 모든 사람, 모든 것, 모든 ~: all이 사람이면 복수, 사물이나 상황을 의미하면 단수 취급한다.
「all+명사」는 명사의 수에 동사의 수를 일치시킨다.

All <u>looks</u> good to me. 나에게 모든 것이 좋아 보인다.

All my work <u>is</u> done now. 이제 내 모든 일이 끝났다.

All birds <u>have</u> wings and feathers. 모든 새는 날개와 깃털을 가지고 있다.

5. both 양쪽(의), 둘 다: 복수 취급

Both my parents <u>are</u> generous. 우리 부모님은 두 분 다 관대하시다.

Both (of us) <u>take</u> after our father. (우리) 둘 다 아버지를 닮았다.

6. each 각각(의) every 모든: 단수 취급

Each <u>student</u> <u>has</u> to write three reports. 학생들은 각각 세 개의 보고서를 작성해야 한다.

Each of them <u>comes</u> from a different country. 그들 각각은 다른 나라 출신이다.

Every <u>room</u> in the hotel <u>has</u> a nice view. 그 호텔은 모든 객실이 전망이 좋다.

Plus α

every 다음에는 단수 명사가 오지만, '~마다'의 뜻으로 쓰인 경우, 복수 명사가 오기도 한다.

There is a bus for downtown **every** <u>ten minutes</u>.
시내로 가는 버스가 10분마다 있다.

Check-up 우리말과 같은 뜻이 되도록 ☐ 안에서 알맞은 것을 고르시오.

1 아이들 두 명은 모두 그 답을 안다. → ☐Both / Each☐ of the kids know the answer.

2 펜이 필요하면 내가 하나 빌려 줄게. → If you need a pen, I will lend you ☐it / one☐.

3 그는 남자 형제가 한 명도 없다. → He doesn't have ☐any / some☐ brothers.

: EXERCISES

A [ ] 안에서 알맞은 것을 고르시오.

1 [All / Every] the guests are welcome.

2 Would you like [some / any] more tea?

3 [Both / Each] baseball team has nine players.

4 I went to the store to buy some apples, but there weren't [some / any].

guest 명 손님

welcome
형 반가운, 환영 받는

player 명 선수

B 밑줄 친 부분을 어법에 맞게 고쳐 쓰시오.

1 All the students <u>was</u> in the auditorium.

2 Each <u>have to</u> bring a dessert to share.

3 Every <u>buildings</u> in the city is very classical.

4 Both of my brothers <u>is going to</u> study abroad.

auditorium 명 강당
dessert 명 후식, 디저트
share 동 나누다, 공유하다
classical 형 고전적인
study abroad
외국에서 공부하다

C 보기 에서 알맞은 부정대명사를 골라 대화를 완성하시오.

보기   both   some   one   every

1 A Is there any milk left?
   B Yes. There is _____ in the fridge.

2 A How often do you go camping?
   B I go camping _____ weekend.

3 A Which do you think is better, coffee or tea?
   B I think _____ are good.

4 A Is there a post office nearby?
   B Yes. There is _____ on Main Street.

fridge 명 냉장고
go camping 캠핑 가다
nearby 부 바로 이웃에,
바로 가까이에

D 우리말과 같은 뜻이 되도록 부정대명사와 주어진 단어를 이용하여 문장을 완성하시오.

1 그녀의 모든 돈은 옷을 사는 데 쓰였다. (her money, be)
   → _____ _____ _____ _____ used to buy her clothes.

2 내 자전거는 매우 낡았다. 그래서 나는 새 것을 살 것이다. (new)
   → My bike is very old, so I will buy _____ _____ _____.

3 나는 어린 시절의 사진을 한 장도 가지고 있지 않다. (have, photos)
   → I _____ _____ _____ _____ from my childhood.

4 그 호텔의 각 침실에는 욕실이 딸려 있다. (bedroom, have)
   → _____ _____ in the hotel _____ a bathroom.

UNIT 02 부정대명사 II

1. another 또 다른 하나, 또 하나

This pen is out of ink. Please give me **another**. 이 펜은 잉크가 다 됐어요. 다른 것을 주세요.

This skirt is not my style. Can you show me **another one**?
이 치마는 제 스타일이 아니에요. 다른 것을 보여 주실래요?

2. one, another, the other, the others

「one ~, the other …」 one ●→ the other	(둘 중) 하나는 ~, 나머지 하나는 … She bought two skirts. **One** is long, and **the other** is short. 그녀는 치마 두 개를 샀다. 하나는 길고, 나머지 하나는 짧다.
「one ~, another ~, the other」 ●→ one ●→ another ●→ the other	(셋 중) 하나는 ~, 또 다른 하나는 ~, 나머지 하나는 … He has three kids. **One** is two, **another** is six, and **the other** is ten. 그는 세 명의 아이가 있다. 한 명은 두 살, 또 다른 한 명은 여섯 살, 나머지 한 명은 열 살이다.
「one ~, the others …」 ●→ one ●●●→ the others	(여럿 중) 하나는 ~, 나머지 모두는 … She bought six apples. **One** was sweet, and **the others** were sour. 그녀는 여섯 개의 사과를 샀다. 하나는 달고, 나머지는 모두 시었다.

3. some, others, the others

「some ~, others …」 ●●●→ some ■■■■ ▲▲▲→ others	어떤 것[사람]들은 ~, 또 다른 것[사람]들은 … **Some** like novels, and **others** like poems. 어떤 사람들은 소설을 좋아하고, 또 다른 사람들은 시를 좋아한다.
「some ~, the others …」 ■■■■→ some ▲▲▲▲▲▲→ the others	어떤 것[사람]들은 ~, 나머지 모두는 There are fifty books on the shelf. **Some** are mine, and **the others** are my sister's. 책장에 50권의 책들이 있다. 일부는 내 것이고, 나머지 전부는 여동생 것이다.

4. each other (둘 사이에), one another (셋 이상 사이에) 서로

Greg and Jillian looked at **each other** for a moment.
Greg와 Jillian은 잠깐 동안 서로를 바라보았다.

Students are talking to **one another** about the test.
학생들은 서로 시험에 대해 이야기를 하고 있다.

> **Tips**
> each other는 둘 사이에,
> one another는 셋 이상 사이
> 에 주로 쓰지만, 종종 잘 구분
> 하지 않고 쓴다.

Check-up 우리말과 같은 뜻이 되도록 ☐ 안에서 알맞은 것을 고르시오.

1 수저를 떨어뜨렸어요. 다른 것을 가져다줄래요?

→ I dropped the spoon. Will you bring me another / other ?

2 나는 모자 세 개를 샀다. 하나는 파란색, 또 하나는 빨간색, 나머지 하나는 흰색이다.

→ I bought three caps. One is blue, another is red, and
  the other / the others is white.

: EXERCISES

A [   ] 안에서 알맞은 것을 고르시오.

1 I can do better next time. Please give me [another / the other] chance.

2 I have two sisters. One is a teacher, and [another / the other] is a police officer.

3 Fifty people work for the company. [One / Some] are hard-working, and others are lazy.

4 The boy got three presents. One is a bike, another is a toy robot, and [the other / other] is a puzzle book.

hard-working 형 근면한
lazy 형 게으른

B 밑줄 친 부분을 어법에 맞게 고쳐 쓰시오.

1 Ray and Phillip don't understand each others.

2 Barbara has three children, and she wants to have the other baby.

3 There are two questions here. One is easy, and another is difficult.

4 Tulips have many colors. Some are red, and the others are yellow.

understand 동 이해하다
tulip 명 튤립

C 보기 에서 알맞은 부정대명사를 골라 문장을 완성하시오.

보기   another   the others   the other   each other

1 My sister and I don't talk to _____ after a fight.

2 I don't like the color. Can you show me _____ one?

3 He invited ten friends to his party. Some came, and _____ didn't.

4 The girl drew three shapes. One is a circle, another is a square, and _____ is a star.

shape 명 모양
circle 명 원
square 명 네모

D 우리말과 같은 뜻이 되도록 부정대명사와 주어진 단어를 이용하여 문장을 완성하시오.

1 사람들은 서로를 존중해야 한다. (should, respect)

 → People _____ _____ _____ _____ .

2 제 차가 식었어요. 저에게 다른 것을 가져다주시겠어요? (bring)

 → My tea got cold. Could you _____ _____ _____ cup?

3 나는 애완견이 두 마리 있다. 한 마리는 푸들이고, 나머지 한 마리는 퍼그이다. (be)

 → I have two pet dogs. _____ _____ a poodle, and _____ _____ _____ a pug.

UNIT 03 재귀대명사

☆ **재귀대명사**: '~자신, ~자체'라는 뜻으로, 인칭대명사의 소유격이나 목적격에 −self(단수)/−selves(복수)를 붙인 형태이다.

1. 재귀용법: 동작의 대상이 주어 자신일 때 사용한다.

(1) 동사의 목적어

Louise <u>burned</u> **herself** while she was cooking. Louise는 요리를 하다가 화상을 입었다.

Did you <u>hurt</u> **yourself**? 다쳤니?

(2) 전치사의 목적어

Alice often talks <u>to</u> **herself**. Alice는 종종 혼잣말을 한다.

They should be proud <u>of</u> **themselves**. 그들은 스스로를 자랑스럽게 여겨야 한다.

2. 강조용법: 주어나 목적어를 강조하기 위해 사용한 경우로, 강조하는 말 바로 뒤 또는 문장의 맨 뒤에 위치하며 생략이 가능하다.

I **myself** fixed the broken computer. [주어 강조] 내가 직접 그 고장 난 컴퓨터를 고쳤다.

Did you see <u>the actress</u> **herself**? [목적어 강조] 네가 직접 그 여배우를 보았니?

3. 재귀대명사 관용 표현

by oneself (남의 도움 없이) 혼자서(alone), 홀로	for oneself (스스로를 위해) 혼자 힘으로
beside oneself 제정신이 아닌	in itself 본래, 그 자체로
between ourselves 우리끼리 이야기이지만	

My daughter traveled to Europe **by herself**. 내 딸이 홀로 유럽을 여행했다.

The boy solved the difficult problem **for himself**. 그 소년이 혼자 힘으로 그 어려운 문제를 풀었다.

Tips

「동사+재귀대명사」의 형태로 자주 쓰이는 동사
· enjoy oneself
즐거운 시간을 보내다
· hurt oneself 다치다
· kill oneself 자살하다
· teach oneself 독학하다
· introduce oneself
자기소개를 하다
· make oneself at home
편하게 하다
· speak[talk] to oneself
혼잣말하다
· help oneself to
~을 마음껏 먹다

Check-up 우리말과 같은 뜻이 되도록 [ ] 안에서 알맞은 것을 고르시오.

1 나는 그것을 혼자 해결할 수 있다.

→ I can do it by me / myself .

2 과자를 마음껏 드세요.

→ Please help you / yourself to the cookies.

3 Grace는 우리 부모님께 자신을 소개했다.

→ Grace introduced her / herself to my parents.

4 그것에 대해 아무에게도 말하지 마. 그건 우리끼리 이야기야.

→ Don't talk to anybody about it. It's between us / ourselves .

: EXERCISES

A [   ] 안에서 알맞은 것을 고르시오.

1 Did you make this soup [yours / yourself]?

2 I hurt [me / myself] when I played basketball.

3 If you believe in [your / yourself], you can do everything you want.

4 I need a partner for the party. I can't go to the party [beside / by] myself.

hurt (동) 다치다

believe in
~을 믿다, 신뢰하다

B 밑줄 친 부분이 생략 가능하면 O, 생략 가능하지 않으면 X표를 하시오.

1 The film <u>itself</u> is a lot of fun.

2 My parents built the house <u>themselves</u>.

3 They enjoyed <u>themselves</u> very much at the beach.

4 Welcome to my house. Please make <u>yourself</u> at home.

film (명) 영화; 필름

welcome (동) 환영하다

C 우리말과 같은 뜻이 되도록 빈칸에 알맞은 말을 쓰시오.

1 기린은 본래 온순한 동물이다.

→ The giraffe is a gentle animal _____ itself.

2 우리끼리 이야기이지만, Wilson은 정직하지 않다.

→ Just _____ ourselves, Wilson is not honest.

3 그 남자는 숲 속 오두막에서 혼자서 산다.

→ The man lives _____ himself in a cottage in the woods.

4 선수권 대회에서 우승했을 때 나는 들떠서 제 정신이 아니었다.

→ I was _____ myself with excitement when I won the
championship.

D 우리말과 같은 뜻이 되도록 재귀대명사와 주어진 단어를 이용하여 문장을 완성하시오.

1 George는 자기 자신을 천재라고 부른다. (call, a genius)

→ George _____ _____ _____ _____.

2 Wilson은 항상 자기 자신에 대해 이야기한다. (talk about)

→ Wilson _____ _____ _____ all the time.

3 아이들이 자신들의 방을 직접 꾸몄다. (decorate, rooms)

→ The kids _____ _____ _____ _____.

4 그 소년은 자신을 위해 혼자 힘으로 저녁을 요리했다. (cook, dinner)

→ The boy _____ _____ _____ _____.

: Review Test

[01-03] 빈칸에 들어갈 알맞은 것을 고르시오.

01

I lost my old camera. This is a new _____.

① it　　　　② one　　　③ another
④ other　　　⑤ the other

02

I have two sisters, and _____ of them enjoy reading books.

① any　　　② each　　　③ both
④ every　　⑤ some

03

We hurt _____ while we were playing football.

① we　　　② our　　　③ us
④ ours　　⑤ ourselves

04 빈칸에 공통으로 들어갈 말로 알맞은 것은?

· _____ student in school likes Ms. Lee.
· Sally and I go out for dinner _____ Friday night.

① some　　② any　　　③ both
④ every　　⑤ all

05 빈칸에 들어갈 말이 바르게 짝지어진 것은?

· Would you like _____ more tea?
· I tried to buy _____ tickets, but there weren't _____ left.

① some – some – some
② some – some – any
③ any – some – any
④ any – any – some
⑤ any – any – any

06 밑줄 친 부분 중 생략할 수 있는 것은?

① Take good care of <u>yourself</u>.
② I cut <u>myself</u> while I was shaving.
③ Adolf Hitler killed <u>himself</u>.
④ John said to <u>himself</u>, "I can do it."
⑤ I want to see my parents <u>themselves</u>.

[07-08] 우리말과 같은 뜻이 되도록 할 때 빈칸에 들어갈 말이 바르게 짝지어진 것을 고르시오.

07

어떤 사람들은 야구하는 것을 좋아하고, 또 다른 사람들은 농구하는 것을 좋아한다.
→ _____ like playing baseball, and _____ like playing basketball.

① One – the other　　② One – the others
③ Some – others　　　④ Some – the other
⑤ Some – the others

08

나는 삼촌이 두 명 있다. 한 명은 의사이고, 나머지 한 명은 조종사이다.
→ I have two uncles. _____ is a doctor, and _____ is a pilot.

① One – the other　　② One – another
③ One – others　　　④ Some – the other
⑤ Some – the others

09 밑줄 친 부분이 어법상 어색한 것은?

① <u>All the money are</u> gone.
② Do you have <u>any news</u> for me?
③ I have two children. <u>Both of them</u> like sports.
④ <u>Some of the trees</u> are dying because of the drought.
⑤ He <u>introduced himself</u> as our new English teacher.

[10-11] 밑줄 친 부분의 쓰임이 보기 와 같은 것을 고르시오.

10 보기 I made this pizza <u>myself</u>.

① Please help <u>yourself</u> to the donuts.
② My mom burned <u>herself</u> on the stove.
③ We can't carry these boxes <u>ourselves</u>.
④ Jason often calls <u>himself</u> a great warrior.
⑤ You should be ashamed of <u>yourselves</u>.

11 보기 Please have a seat, and make <u>yourself</u> at home.

① I <u>myself</u> fixed the broken radio.
② He taught <u>himself</u> English.
③ You should do your homework <u>yourself</u>.
④ She likes the movie <u>itself</u>, not the actor.
⑤ The kids cleaned the whole house <u>themselves</u>.

12 다음 대화 중 자연스럽지 <u>않은</u> 것은?

① A These shoes are too big. Do you have smaller ones?
  B Of course. What size do you want?
② A I don't like this color. Please show me another.
  B How about this blue one?
③ A How do you know each other?
  B We went to high school together.
④ A I heard you went on vacation. How was it?
  B We really enjoyed us during the vacation.
⑤ A What did you say? I couldn't hear you.
  B Never mind. I was just talking to myself.

13 다음 중 어법상 어색한 문장은?

① This pie is my favorite. Can I have other?
② Rick and I have truly understood each other for a long time.
③ Every person in the world has a different personality.
④ Some like pop music, and others like classical music.
⑤ He has three scarves. One is black, another is white, and the other is gray.

[14-15] 글을 읽고, 물음에 답하시오.

I have three friends from other countries. One is Mark, another is Noa, ❶ <u>other</u> is Antonio. ❷ <u>Each</u> comes from a different country. Mark is from England. He behaves ❸ <u>himself</u> like a gentleman, and (A) 그는 모든 일을 혼자 하는 것을 좋아한다. Noa comes from Japan. She is a very quiet and shy person, but she always cares about ❹ <u>others</u>. Antonio is from Brazil. He is outgoing. He enjoys meeting new people and visiting new places. Although they are all different from ❺ <u>one another</u>, they are good friends of mine.

14 밑줄 친 ❶~❺ 중 어법상 어색한 것은?

15 밑줄 친 (A)를 바르게 영작한 것은?

① he likes doing everything of himself
② he likes doing everything by himself
③ he likes doing everything in himself
④ he likes doing everything beside himself
⑤ he likes doing everything with himself

01 빈칸에 알맞은 대명사를 써 넣으시오.

(1) Samantha lost her cell phone yesterday, and she is looking for _____ now.

(2) I am not going to buy that expensive chair. I'll get a cheaper _____.

02 some과 any 중 빈칸에 공통으로 들어갈 말을 써 넣으시오.

· Would you like _____ coffee?

· _____ of the students passed the test, and the others didn't.

[03-04] 두 문장의 의미가 통하도록 빈칸에 알맞은 말을 써 넣으시오.

03 Brian likes Claire, and Claire likes Brian, too.

→ Brian and Claire like _____ _____.

04 We had a great time at the concert.

→ We enjoyed _____ at the concert.

[05-06] 우리말과 같은 뜻이 되도록 어법상 어색한 부분을 한 군데 찾아 바르게 고쳐 쓰시오.

05 Tom은 탁자 위에 있는 음식을 마음껏 먹었다.

→ Tom helped him to the food on the table.

_____

06 학교의 모든 학생이 그 수학 선생님을 좋아한다.

→ Both student in school likes the math teacher.

_____

07 보기에서 알맞은 단어를 골라 문장을 완성하시오.

[중복 사용 가능]

보기	one	some	the other
	others	another	the others

(1) We have many trees in the garden. _____ are tall, and _____ are small.

(2) I have two dreams. _____ is to be a comedian, and _____ is to be an astronaut.

(3) There are nine students in the classroom. Five of them are boys, and _____ are girls.

(4) We have three desserts. _____ is a cheesecake, _____ is a pudding, and _____ is an apple pie.

[08-10] 나의 가족을 소개하는 글이다. 우리말과 같은 뜻이 되도록 밑줄 친 단어를 배열하시오.

I have a large family: my grandparents, my parents, my twin brothers, my sister, and me. **08** (my grandparents, over, both, ninety, of, are). My father and mother like to talk to each other and share everything. My twin brothers are good at sports. One is a basketball player, and **09** (a, other, baseball player, is, the). My sister is really interested in her looks and often looks at herself in the mirror. **10** (one, love, us, of, very much, all, another).

08 나의 조부모님은 두 분 다 아흔이 넘으셨다.

→ _____

09 나머지 한 명은 야구 선수이다

→ _____

10 우리 모두는 서로를 매우 많이 사랑한다.

→ _____

Chapter 5

시제

현재완료

1. **현재완료의 쓰임:** 과거 한 시점에서 시작된 상태나 동작이 현재까지 영향을 미칠 때 사용한다.

  (1) 계속: 과거에 시작된 일이 현재까지 계속되는 것을 의미한다.

    She **has worked** here since she was twenty. 그녀는 20세 이후로 여기에서 일하고 있다.
    I **have studied** Spanish for three months. 나는 3개월 동안 스페인어를 공부해 왔다.

  (2) 경험: 과거부터 현재까지 있었던 경험을 의미한다.

    I **have read** the book before. 나는 전에 그 책을 읽은 적이 있다.
    Have you **been** to Europe? 너 유럽에 가본 적 있니?

  (3) 완료: 어떤 일이 현재에 막 완료되었음을 나타낸다.

    She **has** just **done** her homework. 그녀는 막 숙제를 마쳤다.
    Angela **has** not **finished** her report yet. Angela는 보고서를 아직 끝내지 못했다.

  (4) 결과: 과거에 일어난 일로 인해 생긴 결과가 현재까지 영향을 미침을 나타낸다.

    I **have lost** my passport. 나는 여권을 잃어버렸다. [현재 여권이 없다.]
    She **has gone** to New York. 그녀는 뉴욕에 갔다. [현재 여기에 없다.]

2. **부정문:** 「have+not/never+p.p. ～」

  She **has not met** him before. 그녀는 전에 그를 만난 적이 없다.
  I **have never been** abroad. 나는 한 번도 해외에 나가 본 적이 없다.

3. **의문문:** 「Have+주어+p.p. ～?」, 「의문사+ have + 주어+p.p. ～?」

  A **Have** you ever **played** tennis? 테니스를 쳐 본 적이 있나요?
  B Yes, I **have.** / No, I **haven't.** 네, 쳐 봤어요. / 아니요, 안 쳐 봤어요.

  A What **have** you **done**? 너 무슨 일을 한 거야?
  B I **haven't done** anything. 난 아무것도 안 했어.

> **Plus α**
>
> 「have been+to 장소」
> [경험] ～에 다녀온 적이 있다
>
> She **has been** to Australia.
> 그녀는 호주에 가본 적이 있다.
>
> 「have gone+to 장소」
> [결과] ～에 가고 없다
>
> She **has gone** to Australia.
> 그녀는 호주로 가 버렸다.

Check-up 우리말과 같은 뜻이 되도록 □ 안에서 알맞은 것을 고르시오.

1 나는 그를 몇 번 본 적이 있다.
  → I have │ see / seen │ him several times.

2 나는 한 번도 차를 운전해 본 적이 없다.
  → I │ have never driven / never have driven │ a car.

: EXERCISES

A [ ] 안에서 가장 알맞은 것을 고르시오.

1 I [had / have had] a terrible headache last night.

2 The movie [just begins / has just begun]. Please be quiet.

3 He [has gone / has been] to America. He is not here now.

4 Your hands are clean. [Have you washed / Do you wash] your hands already?

terrible
(형) 심한, 지독한; 끔찍한

headache (명) 두통

quiet (형) 조용한

wash one's hands
손을 씻다

B 주어진 단어를 현재완료형으로 바꿔 문장을 완성하시오.

1 Lucy is away on holiday now. She _____ to Greece. (go)

2 I'm really hungry. I _____ since breakfast. (eat / not)

3 I _____ to this house, so it's full of packed boxes.
(move / just)

4 Ann is back home from her vacation. She _____ to Hong Kong. (be)

be away on holiday
휴가 여행 중이다

Greece (명) 그리스

be back 돌아오다

be full of ~로 가득 차다

packed (형) 포장된

C 보기 에서 알맞은 것을 골라 현재완료형으로 바꿔 문장을 완성하시오.

보기   wear   sell   take   bake

1 I _____ her class several times.

2 Ryan _____ the same boots for years.

3 Mom _____ just _____ an apple pie. It smells delicious.

4 I'm sorry, but I can't lend you my car. I _____ it already.

several (형) 몇몇의

boot (명) 부츠

lend (동) 빌려주다

D 우리말과 같은 뜻이 되도록 주어진 단어를 이용하여 문장을 완성하시오.

1 Matt는 공항에 막 도착했다. (arrive at, just)

→ Matt _____ _____ _____ _____ the airport.

2 그녀는 두 시간 동안 여기에 있었다. (be)

→ She _____ _____ here for two hours.

3 우리 팀은 한 번도 경기에서 져 본 적이 없다. (lose, never)

→ Our team _____ _____ _____ a game.

4 그녀가 대학을 졸업한 이후로 나는 그녀와 함께 살고 있다. (live with)

→ I _____ _____ _____ _____ since she graduated from university.

UNIT 02 과거와 현재완료

1. 과거와 현재완료의 비교

(1) 과거: 현재와 상관없이 과거의 한 시점에서 발생한 동작이나 상태를 나타낸다.

Rachel **worked** for Town Bank. Rachel은 Town Bank에서 일했다.
[과거에 일했다는 사실에 초점, 현재 Town Bank에서 일하는지는 알 수 없음]

William Shakespeare **wrote** many great plays.
William Shakespeare는 위대한 극작품을 많이 썼다.

(2) 현재완료: 과거의 한 시점에서 발생한 일이나 동작이 현재까지 영향을 미치는 상태를 나타낸다.

Rachel **has worked** for Town Bank. Rachel은 Town Bank에서 일하고 있다.
[Town Bank에서 지금도 일하고 있음]

William is a writer. He **has written** many books. William은 작가이다. 그는 많은 책을 써 왔다.

2. 함께 쓰는 부사

(1) 과거: yesterday, last, ago, when 등 특정한 과거 시점을 나타내는 부사구와 함께 쓰인다.

The weather **was** very nice **last weekend**. 지난 주말에는 날씨가 정말 좋았다.

She **was** late for school **yesterday**. 그녀는 어제 학교에 지각했다.

(2) 현재완료

☆ 계속: for, since, so far 등과 함께 쓰인다.

The weather **has been** nice **since we arrived**. 우리가 도착한 이래로 좋은 날씨가 계속되고 있다.

It **has been** no problem **so far**. 지금까지는 아무 문제없다.

☆ 경험: before, never, ever, once, often 등

Have you **ever read** a story about Robin Hood? 너 로빈 후드에 관한 이야기를 읽은 적 있니?

I **have never seen** a polar bear myself. 나는 한 번도 북극곰을 직접 본 적이 없다.

☆ 완료: just, already, yet 등

They **have already made** up their mind. 그들은 이미 결정을 내렸다.

She **has just finished** doing the laundry. 그녀는 이제 막 빨래를 끝냈다.

Check-up 우리말과 같은 뜻이 되도록 ▢ 안에서 알맞은 것을 고르시오.

1 나는 지난해 이후로 그에게서 소식을 들은 적이 없다.

→ I didn't hear / haven't heard from him since last year.

2 Mathew와 Jason은 15년 동안 친구로 지내 왔다.

→ Mathew and Jason were / have been friends for fifteen years.

3 내가 그에게 전화를 걸었을 때, 그는 보고서를 쓰느라 바빴다.

→ He was / has been busy with writing a report when I called him.

: EXERCISES

A [   ] 안에서 가장 알맞은 것을 고르시오.

1 I [was / have been] to Florida twice.

2 The river [froze over / has frozen over] last month.

3 I [knew / have known] her since I was a little child.

4 Ted [took / has taken] a few pictures of the mountain yesterday.

freeze over 얼어붙다
(freeze–froze–frozen)

take pictures of
~의 사진을 찍다

B 밑줄 친 부분을 어법에 맞게 고쳐 쓰시오.

1 She has stayed here <u>since</u> an hour.

2 When <u>have you heard</u> from Mrs. Jones?

3 I <u>have lost</u> my keys, and I found them in the freezer.

4 Beethoven was a great musician. He <u>has composed</u> about 300 pieces of music.

hear from
~로부터 소식을 듣다

freezer (명) 냉장고, 냉동실

compose
(동) 작곡하다; 구성하다

C 주어진 단어를 이용하여 대화를 완성하시오.

1 A _____ you _____ the news about Jim and Sue? (hear)

   B Yes, I have. They _____ _____ last Sunday. (get married)

2 A _____ you _____ _____ to Prague? (ever / be)

   B Yes, I have. I _____ there two years ago, and I had a great time. (go)

3 A Do you know Alice's brother?

   B Not very well. I _____ _____ him several times, but I've never talked to him. (see)

get married 결혼하다
Prague (명) 프라하

D 우리말과 같은 뜻이 되도록 주어진 단어를 이용하여 문장을 완성하시오.

1 나는 Sarah와 저녁을 먹고 싶은데, 그녀는 이미 먹어버렸다. (eat, already)

   → I want to eat dinner with Sarah, but she _____ _____

   _____.

2 지금 9시인데, 그는 아직 집에 돌아오지 않았다. (come, home, yet)

   → It is nine o'clock now, but he _____ _____ _____

   _____.

3 그녀는 태어난 이래로 이 집에 살고 있다. (live in, since, be born)

   → She _____ _____ _____ this house _____

   _____ _____ _____.

UNIT 03 진행 시제

1. 진행 시제: 특정한 시점에서 진행 중인 행동을 나타낼 때 사용한다.

(1) 현재진행: 「am/are/is+-ing」 ~하고 있다, ~하는 중이다

I'm **waiting** for my friend in front of the library. 나는 도서관 앞에서 친구를 기다리고 있다.

Jean **is reading** an interesting book. Jean은 재미있는 책을 읽고 있다.

The telephone **is ringing.** 전화가 울리고 있다.

> **Plus α**
>
> 1 현재진행은 tonight, tomorrow 등과 같은 미래를 나타내는 부사구와 함께 쓰여 예정되어 있는 일정이나 계획을 나타내기도 한다.
>
> I'm **leaving** for Vancouver <u>tomorrow morning</u>. 나는 내일 아침 밴쿠버로 떠날 것이다.
> We **are going** on a picnic <u>this weekend</u>. 우리는 이번 주말에 소풍을 갈 것이다.
>
> 2 현재진행은 today, this week, this semester, this year와 같은 시간 표현과 함께 쓰여 최근에 일정 기간 지속되는 동작이나 상태를 나타내기도 한다.
>
> I'm **studying** biology <u>this semester</u>. 나는 이번 학기에 생물학을 공부하고 있다.

(2) 과거진행: 「was/were+-ing」 ~하고 있었다, ~하는 중이었다

When you called me last night, I **was sleeping.** 네가 어젯밤에 전화했을 때 나는 잠을 자고 있었다.

What **were** you **doing** when the accident happened? 사고가 났을 때 너는 무엇을 하고 있었니?

I **was watching** TV when Mom arrived home. 엄마가 집에 도착했을 때 나는 TV를 보고 있었다.

2. 진행형으로 쓰지 않는 동사: 소유, 지각, 감정, 인지를 나타내는 상태동사는 일반적으로 진행형으로 쓰지 않는다.

I **smell** something burning. 뭔가가 타는 냄새가 난다.

He **has** a big garden in his backyard. 그는 자신의 뒷마당에 큰 정원을 가지고 있다.

She **likes** riding her bike along the river. 그녀는 강을 따라서 자전거 타는 것을 좋아한다.

소유: belong to, have, own 등
지각: feel, hear, look, taste, smell 등
감정: like, love, hate, want 등
인지: believe, think, understand, know 등

> **Tips**
>
> 소유, 지각, 감정, 인지를 나타내는 상태동사도 동작의 의미를 나타내는 경우 진행형으로 만들 수 있다.
>
> The kid **is having** a great time at the circus.
> 그 아이는 서커스에서 좋은 시간을 보내고 있다.
>
> They **are having** dinner.
> 그들은 저녁을 먹고 있다.

Check-up 우리말과 같은 뜻이 되도록 ☐ 안에서 알맞은 것을 고르시오.

1 그들은 지금 소풍을 위해 음식을 준비하고 있다.

→ They prepared / are preparing food for a picnic now.

2 전화가 울렸을 때 그녀는 이메일을 쓰고 있었다.

→ She is writing / was writing an email when the phone rang.

: EXERCISES

A [ ] 안에서 알맞은 것을 고르시오.

1 Please be quiet! The baby [sleeps / is sleeping].

2 She [is cooking / was cooking] when he came in.

3 When the doorbell rang, I [am taking / was taking] a shower.

4 You'd better take an umbrella with you. It [rains / is raining] outside.

come in 들어오다

doorbell 초인종

ring ⑧ 울리다, 울려 퍼지다

take a shower
샤워를 하다

had better
~하는 편이 낫다

B 밑줄 친 부분을 어법에 맞게 고쳐 쓰시오.

1 Why are you <u>sit</u> all alone in the dark?

2 It was <u>snowed</u> when I woke up in the morning.

3 Let's open the window. This room <u>is smelling</u> bad.

4 Rochester <u>is having</u> a beautiful mansion near the lake.

all alone 홀로, 혼자서

wake up 일어나다

mansion ⑲ 대저택

C 보기 에서 알맞은 것을 골라 진행형으로 바꿔 쓰시오.

| 보기 | watch | come | read | practice |

1 Dad _____ home from his business trip tomorrow.

2 They _____ a tennis match on TV at that time.

3 Julie _____ hard for the piano competition these days.

4 While I _____ the newspaper, I found an interesting article.

practice ⑧ 연습하다

business trip 출장

competition
⑲ 경연, 대회

article ⑲ 기사

D 우리말과 같은 뜻이 되도록 주어진 단어를 이용하여 문장을 완성하시오.

1 갑자기 무슨 얘길 하고 있는 거니? (talk about)

→ What _____ _____ _____ _____ all of a sudden?

2 그 당시에 그는 과학 시험공부를 하고 있었다. (study for)

→ He _____ _____ _____ his science test at that time.

3 그들은 파티에서 즐거운 시간을 보내고 있다. (have a good time)

→ They _____ _____ _____ _____ at
the party.

4 엄마가 방문을 노크했을 때 나는 침대에서 쉬고 있었다. (take a rest)

→ I _____ _____ _____ _____ on the bed when
Mom knocked on the door.

[01-03] 빈칸에 들어갈 가장 알맞은 말을 고르시오.

01
> Rick _____ for me when I arrived at the airport.

① waits   ② is waiting
③ was waiting   ④ will wait
⑤ has waited

02
> Seth _____ in the hospital since last month.

① is   ② will be   ③ being
④ has been   ⑤ been

03
> Their wedding _____ in the Rose Garden last Sunday.

① takes place   ② took place
③ is taking place   ④ taking place
⑤ has taken place

[04-05] 빈칸에 들어갈 말이 바르게 짝지어진 것을 고르시오.

04
> · The couple moved to L.A. ten years _____.
> · I have lived in this place _____ twenty years.

① ago – for   ② before – for
③ ago – until   ④ before – since
⑤ ago – since

05
> · Tommy _____ you five times since this morning.
> · Tommy _____ you two hours ago.

① calls - called
② called – calls
③ called – has called
④ has called – called
⑤ has called – has called

06 우리말을 영어로 바르게 옮긴 것은?

> Clark은 산책하러 나가서 지금 집에 없다.

① Clark went out for a walk, so he wasn't home now.
② Clark goes out for a walk, so he isn't home now.
③ Clark has gone out for a walk, so he isn't home now.
④ Clark has been out for a walk, so he hasn't been home now.
⑤ Clark was going out for a walk, so he wasn't home now.

07 대화의 응답으로 알맞지 <u>않은</u> 것은?

> A How long have you worked for this company?
> B _____

① Since 2012.
② For more than three years.
③ I worked here two years ago.
④ I've worked here for five years.
⑤ It has been six years since I started working here.

08 밑줄 친 부분의 쓰임이 나머지와 <u>다른</u> 것은?

① Becky <u>has never ridden</u> a bike.
② I <u>have eaten</u> Indian food twice.
③ We <u>have been</u> to Japan several times.
④ My grandfather <u>has lived</u> there all his life.
⑤ She <u>has visited</u> the National Museum before.

09 보기 의 밑줄 친 부분과 쓰임이 <u>다른</u> 것은?

> 보기　Sam <u>has just written</u> his first book.

① The semester <u>has just ended</u>.
② I <u>haven't finished</u> my dessert yet.
③ Brian <u>has loved</u> her since his childhood.
④ He <u>has not done</u> his homework yet.
⑤ She <u>has already sent</u> all the invitations.

[10-11] 다음 중 어법상 <u>어색한</u> 것을 고르시오.

10 ① Are you listening to me?
② It is tasting bitter and sweet.
③ I'm looking for a used car.
④ Albert is having coffee with his coworkers.
⑤ He was painting the fence at that time.

11 ① She has never had her own car.
② I have been to Canada several times.
③ Has she returned from her vacation?
④ He has lost his passport, but he found it.
⑤ He has collected coins all his life.

12 다음 중 어법상 바른 문장은?

① When have you had a car accident?
② She has studied Chinese three years ago.
③ He enjoyed playing soccer in his childhood.
④ He was having an expensive car, and he was proud of it.
⑤ The company has produced this product since almost thirty years.

13 두 문장을 한 문장으로 바르게 나타낸 것은?

> Amy started to teach history two years ago.
> + She still teaches it.

① Amy is teaching history since two years ago.
② Amy was teaching history since two years ago.
③ Amy teaches history since two years.
④ Amy taught history since two years ago.
⑤ Amy has taught history for two years.

[14-15] 글을 읽고, 물음에 답하시오.

❶ <u>Have you ever been</u> to New York? It's my favorite place to go. I ❷ <u>have visited</u> there for the first time in 2000, and ❸ <u>since my first visit</u>, (A) 나는 그 도시와 사랑에 빠졌다. There are lots of places to visit and lots of things to do. ❹ <u>I've already been</u> there more than ten times. ❺ <u>I'm planning</u> to visit again next month. I can't wait!

14 밑줄 친 ❶~❺ 중 어법상 어색한 것은?

15 밑줄 친 (A)를 바르게 영작한 것은?

① I fall in love with the city
② I fallen in love with the city
③ I am falling in love with the city
④ I was falling in love with the city
⑤ I have fallen in love with the city

01 두 문장이 같은 뜻이 되도록 주어진 단어를 이용하여 문장을 완성하시오.

(1) He's going to move to a big city next year.

→ He _____ _____ to a big city next year. (move)

(2) She started to read a novel an hour ago, and she is still doing it.

→ She _____ _____ a novel for an hour. (read)

[02-03] 우리말과 같은 뜻이 되도록 주어진 단어를 이용하여 문장을 완성하시오.

02 우리는 10년 동안 서로 알고 지냈다. (know, ten years)

→ We _____ _____ each other _____ _____ _____.

03 나는 바다에서 수영을 해 본 적이 한 번도 없어. (swim, never)

→ I _____ _____ _____ in the ocean.

04 어법상 어색한 부분을 찾아 바르게 고쳐 쓰시오.

(1) When have you graduated from university?

_____

(2) When I arrived home, Mom is preparing dinner.

_____

[05-06] 우리말과 같은 뜻이 되도록 주어진 단어를 배열하시오.

05 그는 한 시간 전에 세차를 하고 있었다.
(was, his car, an hour, he, ago, washing)

→ _____

06 나는 일본어를 배운 적이 없다.
(have, Japanese, I, not, studied)

→ _____

07 주어진 단어를 이용하여 글을 완성하시오.

Mark _____ (start) his own business two years ago. His business _____ _____ (grow) to be successful since its opening, and he _____ _____ (decide) to open another shop.

08 주어진 단어를 이용하여 대화를 완성하시오.

A How long _____ _____ _____ (have, you) back pain?

B Since last Monday.

A What were you doing when you _____ (hurt) your back?

B I _____ _____ (carry) a box on my shoulder.

[09-10] 글을 읽고, 물음에 답하시오.

I love reading books. When I was young, Mom (A) (read) books to us every night. I really enjoyed listening to her reading. My parents often took me to the library near my house. (B) 그때 이후로, 나는 책을 일주일에 한 권씩 읽고 있다.

09 밑줄 친 (A)를 어법에 맞게 바꿔 쓰시오.

_____

10 밑줄 친 (B)를 주어진 단어를 이용하여 영작하시오.

_____

(read, since then, once a week)

Chapter 6

UNIT 01 can, may, will

☆ 조동사는 본동사를 도와주는 동사로, 추측, 가능, 허가, 부탁, 미래 등의 의미를 보충해 준다. 인칭이나 수에 따라 형태가 변하지 않고, 조동사 뒤에는 항상 동사원형이 온다.

1. 「can+동사원형」

(1) 능력, 가능 ~할 수 있다 [be able to+동사원형]
I **can play** the piano, but I **can't play** the violin. 나는 피아노는 칠 수 있지만, 바이올린은 연주할 수 없다.
→ I **am able to play** the piano, but I **am not able to play** the violin.
Can you **drive** a car? 너는 차를 운전할 수 있니?
→ **Are** you **able to drive** a car?

(2) 허가 ~해도 좋다 [may]
You **can leave** early if you want. 네가 원한다면 일찍 떠나도 좋다.
You **can use** my cell phone. 내 휴대 전화를 사용해도 좋다.

(3) 요청 ~해 줄래? ~해 주시겠어요?
Can you **help** me move this table? 내가 이 탁자 옮기는 것을 도와줄래?
Could you **tell** me the time? 시간을 좀 알려주시겠어요?

2. 「may+동사원형」

(1) 불확실한 추측 ~일지도 모른다
It **may rain** soon. 곧 비가 내릴지도 모른다.
She **may not come** to the party. 그녀는 파티에 오지 않을지도 모른다.

(2) 허가 ~해도 좋다
May I **sit** here? 여기에 앉아도 될까요?
You **may visit** me anytime. 너는 아무 때나 나를 방문해도 좋다.

3. 「will+동사원형」

(1) 예정, 의지 ~일 것이다, ~할 것이다
Clare **will not break** her promise. Clare는 자신의 약속을 어기지 않을 것이다.
Will the finals **take place** this Saturday? 결승전이 이번 주 토요일에 열릴 예정입니까?

(2) 요청 ~해 줄래? ~해 주시겠어요?
Will you **do** me a favor? 내 부탁 좀 들어줄래?
Would you **open** the door? 문을 열어 주시겠어요?

Plus α

can(능력, 가능)의 과거, 미래

1 과거: ~할 수 있었다
could, was[were] able to
When she was young, she **could**[was able to] swim well.
어렸을 때 그녀는 수영을 잘 할 수 있었다.

2 미래: ~할 수 있을 것이다
will be able to
Sam **will be able to** pass the test.
Sam은 그 시험에 통과할 수 있을 것이다.

Tips

1 요청을 나타내는 can, will 은 could, would를 사용 하면 더 정중한 표현이 된다.
2 may보다 약한 추측을 의 미할 때는 might를 사용 한다.
3 계획이나 가까운 미래를 나타내는 will은 be going to로 바꿔 쓸 수 있다.

Check-up 우리말과 같은 뜻이 되도록 ☐ 안에서 알맞은 것을 고르시오.

1 당신의 말이 잘 안 들려요. 좀 더 크게 말해 주시겠어요?
→ I [can't / won't] hear you. Could you speak louder?

2 저에게 조언을 좀 해 주시겠어요?
→ [Can / May] you give me some advice?

: EXERCISES

Answers / p.18

A [ ] 안에서 가장 알맞은 것을 고르시오.

1 [Can / May] you pass me the tissues?

2 He will [do / does] his best to win the game.

3 Brant [will can / will be able to] understand the situation.

4 I am able to [solve / solving] this problem by myself.

5 Please turn on the light. It's too dark. I [cannot / may not] see anything.

pass
(동) 건네주다; 지나가다

do one's best
최선을 다하다

situation (명) 상황

by oneself 혼자, 홀로

turn on ~을 켜다

B 밑줄 친 부분을 어법에 맞게 고쳐 쓰시오.

1 Will I have your name and address?

2 May you give me something to drink?

3 He wills be very happy to see you again.

4 When he was a boy, he can climb tall trees.

5 Mary is able using both hands equally well.

climb (동) 오르다

equally
(부) 똑같이, 동등하게

C 보기 에서 알맞은 조동사를 골라 대화를 완성하시오. [중복 사용 가능]

보기   will   can   may

1 A _____ I ask you something?
  B Sure. Go ahead.

2 A Where is Rick? I haven't seen him tonight.
  B He hasn't come home yet. He _____ be in his office now.

3 A I have two tickets to the concert this Friday. _____ you go
    with me?
  B Sure. I would love to.

go ahead
시작하다; 앞서 가다

tonight (부) 오늘 밤에

D 우리말과 같은 뜻이 되도록 조동사와 주어진 단어를 이용하여 문장을 완성하시오.

1 Sean이 그녀의 전화번호를 알지도 모른다. (know)
  → Sean _____ _____ her phone number.

2 Wilson 부인과 통화할 수 있을까요? (speak to)
  → _____ _____ _____ _____ Mrs. Wilson?

3 이번 주말에는 날씨가 화창할 것이다. (sunny)
  → The weather _____ _____ _____ this weekend.

4 Chad는 5개 국어를 할 수 있다. (speak)
  → Chad _____ _____ _____ _____ five languages.

UNIT 02 must, have to, should

1. 「must+동사원형」

(1) **의무, 필요** ~해야 한다 (=have to)

We **must[have to] protect** the environment. 우리는 환경을 보호해야 한다.

☆ 부정: 「must not+동사원형」 ~해서는 안 된다 [금지]

You **must not skip** your classes. 너는 수업을 빼먹으면 안 된다.

☆ 과거: 「had to+동사원형」 ~해야 했다

She **had to refuse** the offer. 그녀는 그 제안을 거절해야 했다.

☆ 미래: 「will have to+동사원형」 ~해야 할 것이다

He **will have to be** on time. 그는 제시간에 와야 할 것이다.

(2) **강한 추측** ~임이 틀림없다

She had a busy day. She **must be** tired.
그녀는 바쁜 하루를 보냈다. 그녀는 피곤함이 틀림없다.

Greg **must not know** the truth. Greg은 진실을 모르는 것이 틀림없다.

2. 「have to+동사원형」 ~해야 한다 [의무, 필요]

I **have to hand in** my report this afternoon. 나는 오늘 오후에 보고서를 제출해야 한다.

☆ 부정: 「don't have to+동사원형」 ~할 필요가 없다 [불필요]

She **doesn't have to attend** the meeting. 그녀는 그 회의에 참석할 필요가 없다.

3. 「should+동사원형」 ~해야 한다 [의무, 충고] (=ought to)

You **should[ought to] take** his advice. 너는 그의 충고를 따라야 한다.

We **should not be** late for school. 우리는 학교에 늦으면 안 된다.

> **Plus α**
>
> 1 부정적인 강한 추측에는 can't를 사용하며, '~일 리가 없다'라는 뜻이다.
>
>   I saw her in the library a minute ago. She **can't be** at home now. 나는 방금 전에 도서관에서 그녀를 보았어. 그녀는 지금 집에 있을 리가 없어.
>
> 2 불필요를 나타내는 don't have to는 need not 또는 don't need to로 바꿔 쓸 수 있다.
>
>   You **don't have to[need not/don't need to] answer** that question. 너는 그 질문에 대답할 필요가 없다.

Check-up 우리말과 같은 뜻이 되도록 ☐ 안에서 알맞은 것을 고르시오.

1 너는 거짓말을 하지 말아야 한다.

→ You ☐ don't have to / must not ☐ tell lies.

2 너는 금요일까지 이 책들을 도서관에 반납해야 할 것이다.

→ You ☐ will have to / will must ☐ return these books to the library by Friday.

3 Rory는 일주일 동안 학교에 오지 않았다. 매우 아픈 것이 틀림없다.

→ Rory hasn't come to school for a week. He ☐ has to / must ☐ be very sick.

: EXERCISES

A   [   ] 안에서 알맞은 것을 고르시오.

1   I'm allergic to seafood. I [must / must not] eat it.

2   We have enough time. We [have to / don't have to] hurry.

3   I heard that you helped my son. You [must / have to] be very kind.

4   The mid-term exams start next week. We [ought / should] prepare for them.

be allergic to
~에 알레르기가 있다

seafood 몡 해산물

hurry 동 서두르다

mid-term exam
중간고사

B   밑줄 친 부분을 어법에 맞게 고쳐 쓰시오.

1   Sam is a very nice person. You <u>must to meet</u> him.

2   Amy has several expensive cars. She <u>has to be</u> very rich.

3   I <u>have to not</u> get up early on Saturday to go to school.

4   If you want to get good grades, you <u>will must</u> study harder.

5   Yesterday, they <u>must wore</u> sunglasses because of the strong sunlight.

grade
몡 성적, 학점; 등급; 정도

sunlight 몡 햇빛

C   보기 에서 알맞은 말을 골라 대화를 완성하시오. [한 번씩만 쓸 것]

보기	had to	must	must not	don't have to

1   You _____ judge people by their looks.

2   It was really cold. I _____ wear a winter coat and a scarf.

3   You _____ take a taxi. I will give you a ride if you want.

4   The movie did well at the box office. It _____ be really good.

judge
동 판단하다 몡 판사

look 몡 겉모습, 외모; 보기

take a taxi 택시를 타다

give A a ride A를 태워주다

do well at the box
office 흥행에 성공하다

D   우리말과 같은 뜻이 되도록 주어진 단어를 배열하시오.

1   그는 수학을 잘하는 것이 틀림없어. (at, must, math, good, be)

→ He _____ .

2   너는 그들을 기다릴 필요가 없어. (have, wait for, don't, to, them)

→ You _____ .

3   너는 다시는 똑같은 실수를 하면 안 된다. (not, make, mistake, must, the same)

→ You _____ again.

4   길을 건널 때는 조심해야 한다. (be, should, careful, you)

→ _____ when you cross the street.

had better, used to, would like to

1. 「had better+동사원형」 ~하는 것이 좋겠다[조언, 충고]

You look pale. You **had better see** a doctor. 너 창백해 보여. 의사의 진찰을 받아보는 것이 좋겠어.

☆ 부정: 「had better not+동사원형」

I **had better not go out** in this cold weather. 나는 이런 추운 날씨에 외출을 안 하는 것이 좋겠다.

Tips

had better는 'd better로 줄여 쓰기도 한다.

You'd better take your umbrella with you. 우산을 가지고 가는 것이 좋겠다.

2. 「used to+동사원형」 ~하곤 했다, ~이었다[과거의 상태, 습관]

☆ used to는 과거의 반복되는 행동이나, 상태를 나타내며 과거의 반복되는 행동을 나타낼 경우에만 would로 바꾸어 쓸 수 있다.

Kelly **used to go** jogging every morning. [과거의 습관적인 행동] Kelly는 매일 아침 조깅을 하곤 했다.
→ Kelly **would go** jogging every morning.

He **used to have** a big house. [과거의 상태] 그는 큰 집을 소유했었다.
(X) He ~~would have~~ a big house.

> **Plus α**
>
> 1 used to의 부정문: 「didn't use to」, 「used not to」
>   She **didn't use to[used not to] exercise**, but she exercises often now.
>   그녀는 운동을 하지 않았지만, 지금은 자주 운동한다.
>
> 2 used to의 의문문: 「Did+주어+use to~?」
>   **Did** you **use to live** in London? 너는 런던에 살았니?

3. 「would like to+동사원형」 ~하고 싶다

I **would like to invite** you to my place. 너를 우리 집에 초대하고 싶다.

Would you like to see a movie with me tonight? 오늘 밤 저와 영화 보실래요?

Tips

would like to는 'd like to로 줄여 쓰기도 한다.

I'd like to see you today. 저는 오늘 당신을 뵙고 싶습니다.

Check-up 우리말과 같은 뜻이 되도록 ☐ 안에서 알맞은 것을 고르시오.

1 너는 오늘 밤에 집에 있는 게 좋겠다.
→ You had better / have better stay at home tonight.

2 우리는 당신에게 몇 가지 질문을 하고 싶습니다.
→ We would like ask / would like to ask you a few questions.

3 나는 어릴 때 TV를 많이 보곤 했다.
→ I used to watch / watching TV a lot when I was young.

: EXERCISES

A [ ] 안에서 알맞은 것을 고르시오.

1 I would like [book / to book] a room.

2 You [have / had] better listen to me carefully.

3 You [had better not / had not better] open the window.

4 Helen [used to / uses to] be very fat, but she is thin now.

5 There [used to / would] be a big park at the center of the town.

book ⑧ 예약하다
thin ⑲ 마른, 날씬한

B 밑줄 친 부분을 어법에 맞게 고쳐 쓰시오.

1 I <u>would like to reading</u> this book.

2 The theater <u>was used to be</u> an old hotel.

3 I <u>had better washing</u> my hands before dinner.

4 You <u>had not better call</u> him at this late hour.

theater ⑲ 극장
late ⑲ 늦은

C 보기 에서 알맞은 말을 골라 대화를 완성하시오.

보기	had better	used to	would like to

1 A How do you get to school?

B I _____ walk to school, but I take the subway these days.

2 A Are you ready to order?

B Yes. I _____ have a cheeseburger and orange juice.

3 A I will not eat dinner. I've gained too much weight.

B Don't skip meals. I think you _____ exercise more often.

order
⑧ 주문하다; 명령하다
gain weight 체중이 늘다
skip ⑧ 거르다; 빼먹다

D 우리말과 같은 뜻이 되도록 조동사와 주어진 단어를 이용하여 문장을 완성하시오.

1 나는 유럽을 여행하고 싶다. (travel)

→ I _____ _____ _____ _____ to Europe.

2 너는 생각을 바꾸는 것이 좋겠다. (change one's mind)

→ You _____ _____ _____ _____ _____.

3 너는 이렇게 늦은 시간에 밖에 나가지 않는 것이 좋겠다. (go out)

→ You _____ _____ _____ _____ _____ at this late hour.

4 우리 아버지께서는 대학에 다닐 때 농구 선수셨다. (be)

→ My father _____ _____ _____ a basketball player when he was in college.

: Review Test

[01-03] 빈칸에 들어갈 가장 알맞은 말을 고르시오.

01 I think I should wear glasses. I _____ see things clearly from a distance.

① won't ② can't
③ shouldn't ④ must not
⑤ had better not

02 The road is slippery with snow, so you _____ be careful when you walk.

① will ② can
③ must ④ don't have to
⑤ would like to

03 The car _____ be mine before I sold it to Jenny.

① would ② may ③ should
④ had better ⑤ used to

[04-05] 밑줄 친 부분과 바꾸어 쓸 수 있는 것을 고르시오.

04 We <u>must</u> wear a uniform when we go to school.

① can ② may ③ would
④ used to ⑤ have to

05 My grandmother <u>could</u> play five different musical instruments.

① didn't have to ② would like to
③ was able to ④ had better
⑤ need to

[06-07] 밑줄 친 부분의 의미가 나머지와 <u>다른</u> 것을 고르시오.

06 ① We <u>must</u> be quiet in the library.
② You <u>must</u> be kind to everyone at work.
③ He <u>must</u> practice hard to be a better player.
④ You <u>must</u> be very tired after your long flight.
⑤ He <u>must</u> wear a helmet when he ride a bike.

07 ① You <u>may</u> put your belongings here.
② There <u>may</u> be lots of people at the beach.
③ The movie <u>may</u> be based on a true story.
④ Rick <u>may</u> not pass the test because he hasn't studied enough.
⑤ She <u>may</u> know my brother. They went to the same college.

[08-09] 다음 중 어법상 <u>어색한</u> 문장을 고르시오.

08 ① Will you lend me your notebook?
② Do I have to tell him the bad news?
③ You had not better drink too much soda.
④ She doesn't have to prepare for dinner.
⑤ I used to eat a lot of chocolate, but not anymore.

09 ① You cannot park here.
② I would like to go on a trip to Egypt.
③ Mary will can arrive at the airport in time.
④ My brother may be at the gym right now.
⑤ You must not open this gift until your birthday.

10 대화의 빈칸에 들어갈 수 <u>없는</u> 말은?

A _____ you pass me the sugar, please?
B Of course. Here you are.

① Will ② May ③ Can
④ Would ⑤ Could

11 대화 중 자연스럽지 <u>않은</u> 것은?

① A Greg hasn't talked to me for a week.
　 B Really? He must be very angry with you.

② A I've waited for you for half an hour.
　 B I'm sorry. I promise I won't be late again.

③ A What can I do for you?
　 B I would like to exchange this sweater for a smaller one.

④ A May I have some more bread?
　 B No, thanks.

⑤ A Did you use to live with your grandparents?
　 B Yes, I did. But I live by myself now.

12 우리말을 영어로 옮긴 것 중 <u>어색한</u> 문장은?

① 파티에 뭘 입고 가야 하나요?
　→ What should I wear to the party?
② 제가 당신 옆에 앉아도 될까요?
　→ May I sit next to you?
③ 너는 어떤 것도 가져올 필요가 없다.
　→ You must not bring anything with you.
④ 내가 영어 에세이 쓰는 것을 좀 도와줄래?
　→ Will you help me with my English essay?
⑤ 발표하기 전에 연습을 하는 것이 좋겠어.
　→ I had better practice before I make a presentation.

13 빈칸에 들어갈 말이 바르게 짝지어진 것은?

· You _____ drive if you don't have a driver's license.
· I _____ travel to outer space someday.

① must – used to
② must not – used to
③ should – used to
④ must not – would like to
⑤ don't have to – would like to

[14-15] 글을 읽고, 물음에 답하시오.

Do you believe the saying "Change your thoughts and you ❶ can change your life"? If not, you ❷ had better believe it. It's true. (A) <u>나는 부정적으로 생각하곤 했다.</u> I complained a lot. One day, I got into a car accident and seriously hurt. I ❸ couldn't walk and ❹ <u>must</u> stay in the hospital for a month. While I was in the hospital, I saw many other patients and felt how lucky I was. After that, I started to thank for everything and my life has been totally changed. I ❺ <u>won't</u> complain again!

14 밑줄 친 ❶~❺ 중 어법상 어색한 것은?

15 밑줄 친 (A)를 바르게 영작한 것은?

① I used think negatively.
② I used to think negatively.
③ I used to thinking negatively.
④ I'm used to thinking negatively.
⑤ I'm used to think negatively.

[01-02] 두 문장이 같은 뜻이 되도록 문장을 완성하시오.

01 We can't live without water.

→ We _____ live without water.

02 We don't have to make a decision now.

→ We _____ make a decision now.

[03-04] 우리말과 같은 뜻이 되도록 주어진 단어를 이용하여 문장을 완성하시오.

03 그가 우리의 제안을 받아들이지 않을지도 모른다. (accept, offer)

→ He _____ .

04 너는 그 흰색 드레스를 입는 것이 좋겠어. (wear)

→ You _____ .

[05-06] 어법상 어색한 부분을 찾아 어법에 맞게 고쳐 쓰시오.

05 You will must explain about the project to the boss.

_____

06 My mother used being an English teacher.

_____

[07-08] 우리말과 같은 뜻이 되도록 주어진 단어를 배열하시오.

07 너는 여기에 애완동물을 데리고 오면 안 된다. (must, your pet, bring, not, here, you)

→ _____

08 제가 당신의 주소를 물어봐도 될까요? (I, ask, address, may, your)

→ _____

09 밑줄 친 우리말과 같은 뜻이 되도록 주어진 단어를 이용하여 대화를 완성하시오.

A (1) 저녁으로 무엇을 먹고 싶니?
B Could you make spaghetti for me?
A Of course. Did you have fun at school?
B Yes, I did. I played basketball with my classmates after school.
A (2) 그럼, 너 틀림없이 배가 많이 고프겠구나. But you'd better finish your homework before dinner.
B Okay, Mom.

조건 조동사를 이용할 것

(1) What _____ _____ _____

_____ _____ _____

_____ ? (have, for dinner)

(2) Then, _____ _____ _____

_____ _____ . (be, very, hungry)

10 초대장을 읽고, 우리말과 같은 뜻이 되도록 문장을 완성하시오.

Invitation
Olivia's 15th Birthday

Saturday May 1st
1:00 pm ~ 4:00 pm
Olivia's House

Please reply only if you will not attend.

(1) Olivia는 생일 파티에 친구들을 초대하고 싶다.

→ Olivia _____ _____ _____

_____ her friends to her birthday party.

(2) 너는 파티에 참석하지 않으려면 답신을 해야 한다.

→ You _____ _____ _____

if you will not attend.

Chapter 7

UNIT 01 원급 비교, 비교급, 최상급

1. 「A as+원급(형용사/부사)+as B」 A는 B만큼 …한

Jason can play soccer **as well as** Nick (can). Jason은 Nick만큼 축구를 잘할 수 있다.

Writing is **as interesting as** reading for me. 나에게 글쓰기는 책을 읽는 것만큼 재미있다.

2. 「A 비교급(형용사/부사)+than B」 A가 B보다 더 …한

A cheetah runs **faster than** a horse. 치타는 말보다 더 빨리 달린다.

London is **colder than** Paris in winter. 겨울에 런던이 파리보다 더 춥다.

Diamonds are **more expensive than** gold. 다이아몬드가 금보다 더 비싸다.

> **Plus α**
> 「A 비교급+than B」 A는 B보다 더 ~하다
> ➡ 「B not as[so]+원급+as A」 B는 A만큼 ~하지 않다
> ➡ 「B less+원급+than A」 B가 A보다 덜 ~하다
> His brother is **taller than** Robin. Robin의 형은 Robin보다 키가 크다.
> ➡ Robin is **not as[so] tall as** his brother (is). Robin은 형보다 키가 크지 않다.
> ➡ Robin is **less tall than** his brother. Robin은 형보다 키가 덜 크다.

3. 「the + 최상급」

(1) 「the+최상급+in+장소 또는 범위를 나타내는 명사」 ~에서 가장 …한

I ordered **the cheapest food** on the menu. 나는 메뉴 중 가장 싼 음식을 주문했다.

Ralph is **the most handsome boy** in school. Ralph는 학교에서 가장 잘생긴 소년이다.

Russia is **the biggest country** in the world. 러시아는 세계에서 가장 큰 나라이다.

(2) 「the+최상급+of+비교 대상이 되는 명사」 ~ 중에서 가장 …한

She is **the funniest** of my friends. 그녀는 내 친구들 중에서 가장 재미있다.

The physics test was **the most difficult** of all. 모든 시험 중에서 물리 시험이 가장 어려웠다.

> **Tips**
> 비교 대상은 동등한 형태가 와야 한다.
>
> **My sister's desk** is as big as **mine**.
> 내 여동생의 책상은 내 책상만큼 크다.
>
> **Writing** is as difficult as **speaking**.
> 글쓰기는 말하기만큼 어렵다.

> **Plus α**
> much, even, still, a lot, far 는 '훨씬'이라는 의미로 비교급을 강조한다.
>
> Brian is **much** <u>younger</u> than James.
> Brian은 James보다 훨씬 어리다.

Check-up 우리말과 같은 뜻이 되도록 ☐ 안에서 알맞은 것을 고르시오.

1 그의 여동생은 나만큼 날씬하다.
→ His sister is as ☐ thin / thinner ☐ as I am.

2 나는 우리 어머니보다 일찍 일어난다.
→ I get up ☐ earlier / earliest ☐ than my mother does.

3 태양은 태양계에서 가장 밝은 별이다.
→ The sun is the ☐ brighter / brightest ☐ star in the solar system.

: EXERCISES

A [ ] 안에서 알맞은 것을 고르시오.

1 Her hair is as [long / longer] as my hair.

2 This sofa is [more / most] comfortable than that one.

3 New York is [many / much] more crowded than Sydney.

4 The subway is the [faster / fastest] way to get around the city.

comfortable
⬛(형) 편안한, 편한

crowded
⬛(형) 복잡한, 붐비는

get around 돌아다니다

B 밑줄 친 부분을 어법에 맞게 고쳐 쓰시오.

1 Slow food is <u>healthy</u> than fast food.

2 Cameron works as <u>hardest</u> as you do.

3 I got a <u>very</u> better grade than Richard did.

4 This is the <u>more</u> delicious food in the restaurant.

slow food
슬로푸드 (천천히 시간을 들여
서 만들고 먹는 음식)

get a grade 성적을 받다

C 문장의 의미가 통하도록 주어진 단어를 이용하여 문장을 완성하시오.

1 This box is 20 kg. That box is 15 kg.

→ This box is _____ _____ that one. (heavy)

2 The red shirt is $20. The blue shirt is $20.

→ The red shirt is _____ _____ _____ the blue one.
(expensive)

3 Max is 168 cm tall. David is 172 cm tall. Chuck is 180 cm tall.

→ Chuck is _____ _____ of the three. (tall)

D 우리말과 같은 뜻이 되도록 주어진 단어를 이용하여 문장을 완성하시오.

1 그 정원은 축구 경기장만큼 넓다. (wide)

→ The garden is _____ _____ _____ a soccer field.

2 오늘은 어제보다 훨씬 따뜻하다. (warm, a lot)

→ Today is _____ _____ _____ _____.

3 사하라 사막이 세계에서 가장 큰 사막이다. (big, desert)

→ The Sahara is _____ _____ _____ in the world.

4 이 책이 저 책보다 더 흥미 있게 보인다. (interesting)

→ This book looks _____ _____ that one.

UNIT 02 비교급과 최상급 표현

1. 「배수사＋as＋원급＋as」 ～의 … 배 만큼 ～한/하게

His house is **three times as big as** my house (is). 그의 집은 내 집의 세 배만큼 크다.

The tower is **twice as tall as** the building (is). 그 탑은 그 건물의 두 배만큼 높다.

2. 「the＋비교급, the＋비교급」 ～하면 할수록 더 …하다

The more we smile, **the happier** we become. 우리는 많이 웃으면 웃을수록 더 행복해진다.

The more you spend time with her, **the more** you will like her.
그녀와 시간을 보내면 보낼수록, 너는 그녀를 더 좋아하게 될 것이다.

3. 「비교급＋and＋비교급」 점점 더 ～한/하게

More and more people are using the Internet. 점점 더 많은 사람들이 인터넷을 이용하고 있다.

The earth is getting **hotter and hotter** because of global warming.
지구 온난화 때문에 지구가 점점 더 더워지고 있다.

4. 「Which/Who＋비교급, A or B?」 A와 B 중 어떤 것이/누가 더 ～하니?

Which do you like **better, summer or winter?** 여름과 겨울 중 너는 어떤 것을 더 좋아하니?

Who is **taller, you or your sister?** 너와 언니 중 누가 더 키가 크니?

5. 「one of the＋최상급＋복수 명사」 가장 ～한 것 중 하나

Albert Einstein is **one of the most famous scientists.**
Albert Einstein은 가장 유명한 과학자 중 한 명이다.

The theater is **one of the oldest buildings** in town.
그 극장은 마을에서 가장 오래된 건물 중 하나이다.

6. 원급과 비교급을 이용한 최상급 표현

Mt. Everest is **the highest mountain** in the world. 에베레스트 산이 세계에서 가장 높다.

➡ **No other mountain** in the world is **higher than** Mt. Everest.

➡ **No other mountain** in the world is **as[so] high as** Mt. Everest.

➡ Mt. Everest is **higher than any other mountain** in the world.

➡ Mt. Everest is **higher than all the other mountains** in the world.

> **Plus α**
>
> twice와 half를 제외하고, 「배수사＋as＋원급＋as」는 「배수사＋비교급＋than」으로 바꿔 쓸 수 있다.
>
> His house is **three times as big as** my house.
>
> ➡ His house is **three times bigger than** my house.
> 그의 집은 내 집보다 세 배 크다.

Check-up 우리말과 같은 뜻이 되도록 ☐ 안에서 알맞은 것을 고르시오.

1 나는 점점 더 나아지고 있다. → I am getting better and ｜better / best｜.

2 그녀는 나보다 나이가 2배 많다. → She is ｜as twice / twice as｜ old as I am.

3 Sally와 Lisa 중 누가 더 인기가 많니? → Who is ｜more / most｜ popular, Sally or Lisa?

: EXERCISES

A [ ] 안에서 알맞은 것을 고르시오.

1 The older we grow, the [wise / wiser] we become.

2 Her car is [three / three times] as expensive as mine.

3 Which do you like [better / best], pizza or hamburger?

4 The Nile is longer than any other [river / rivers] in the world.

5 My English is getting [best and best / better and better] every day.

wise ⑲ 현명한
expensive ⑲ 비싼

B 밑줄 친 부분을 어법에 맞게 고쳐 쓰시오.

1 Sam ate <u>two</u> as much as I did.

2 It is getting <u>hard and hard</u> to get a job.

3 Paris is one of the most beautiful <u>city</u> in the world.

4 The more you exercise, the <u>healthy</u> you become.

get a job 취업하다
exercise
⑧ 운동하다; ⑲ 운동

C 두 문장이 의미가 통하도록 주어진 단어를 이용하여 문장을 완성하시오.

1 Simon has 20 books, and I have 10 books.

→ Simon has _____ I do. (twice)

2 Sue is more beautiful than any other girl in town.

→ No other girl in town is _____ Sue. (than)

→ No other girl in town is _____ Sue. (as)

3 When the weather gets hotter, we drink more water.

→ The hotter the weather gets, _____. (more)

D 우리말과 같은 뜻이 되도록 주어진 단어를 이용하여 문장을 완성하시오.

1 집이 크면 클수록 임대료는 더 비싸다. (big, high)

→ _____ _____ a house is, _____ _____ the rent is.

2 음악과 수학 중 너는 어떤 것을 더 좋아하니? (like)

→ _____ _____ _____ _____ _____, music or math?

3 인터넷 덕분에 세계가 점점 더 작아지고 있다. (small)

→ Thanks to the Internet, the world is getting _____ _____

_____.

4 그것은 세계에서 가장 아름다운 건물 중 하나이다. (beautiful)

→ It's _____ _____ _____ _____ _____

in the world.

: Review Test

[01-03] 빈칸에 들어갈 알맞은 말을 고르시오.

01
Saving money is as _____ as making money.

① important
② impotanter
③ importantest
④ more important
⑤ most important

02
Jason plays basketball _____ than Nicholas does.

① well
② most
③ much
④ better
⑤ best

03
London is the _____ city in England.

① busy
② busier
③ busiest
④ more busy
⑤ most busy

04 빈칸에 들어갈 수 없는 말은?

Winter this year will be _____ colder than winter last year.

① much
② even
③ a lot
④ very
⑤ far

05 대화의 빈칸에 들어갈 말이 바르게 짝지어진 것은?

A What do you think the best way to lose weight is?
B I think how much you eat is the most important thing. You know the more you eat, _____ you become.

① far
② fatter
③ the fatter
④ the fattest
⑤ the most fat

[06-07] 우리말을 영어로 바르게 옮긴 것을 고르시오.

06
그의 건강은 점점 더 좋아지고 있다.

① His health is getting the best.
② His health is getting well and well.
③ His health is getting best and best.
④ His health is getting good and good.
⑤ His health is getting better and better.

07
나의 가방은 그의 것의 세 배만큼 크다.

① My bag is three as big as his.
② My bag is three times as big as his.
③ My bag is as three times big as his.
④ My bag is three times bigger than him.
⑤ My bag is three times as bigger as his.

[08-09] 다음 중 어법상 어색한 문장을 고르시오.

08 ① I think camping is more exciting than fishing.
② I play the piano as well as she does.
③ The higher the mountain is, the harder it is to climb.
④ Mozart was one of the greatest composer in history.
⑤ More and more people are learning Korean.

09 ① Who is more famous, Jackson or Denis?
② I don't know as more people as he does.
③ I stayed at the cheapest hotel in the city.
④ Tom is much stronger than his brother is.
⑤ A hummingbird is lighter than any other bird in the world.

10 밑줄 친 부분을 바르게 고친 것으로 짝지어진 것은?

· Who studies <u>more hard</u>, Joanna or Ann?
· Today is one of the <u>most happier</u> days of my life.

① hardest – most happy   ② harder – happyest
③ harder – happyer   ④ harder – happiest
⑤ more harder – happiest

11 짝지어진 두 문장의 의미가 서로 같지 <u>않은</u> 것은?

① Iron is much more useful than gold.
   → Iron is even more useful than gold.
② My box is three times as heavy as yours.
   → My box is three times heavier than yours.
③ Casey and Carl both have 20 dollars.
   → Casey has as much money as Carl does.
④ Jake is more patient than I am.
   → Jake is as patient as I am.
⑤ No other planet in the solar system is bigger than Jupiter.
   → Jupiter is bigger than any other planet in the solar system.

12 다음 대화 중 어법상 자연스럽지 <u>않은</u> 것은?

① A Which do you like better, tea or coffee?
   B I like tea better.
② A Where should I buy a new computer?
   B Try shopping online. It's a lot cheaper.
③ A I met Jennifer the other day. She seems a really nice person.
   B Yes, she is. The best you know about her, the most you will like her.
④ A How large is Antarctica?
   B It is about twice as large as Australia.
⑤ A I'm getting fatter and fatter these days.
   B I think you need to do some exercise.

13 다음 중 어법상 올바른 문장은?

① Ray is the funnier guy of my friends.
② Sue is much most popular than Susan.
③ The situation is getting worst and worst.
④ My grandmother is four times old than me.
⑤ No other subject is more difficult than math.

[14-15] 글을 읽고, 물음에 답하시오.

Summer is coming, and it is getting ❶ <u>hotter and hotter</u>. When summer comes, we look for something cold to eat. What is ❷ <u>as colder as ice and as softer as snow</u>? It's ice cream. The history of ice cream may be ❸ <u>much older than</u> you think. It has been traced back to the 4th century B.C. This delicious dessert has been around for ❹ <u>more than</u> a thousand years. Its main ingredients are cream, sugar, and air. (A) 공기는 아이스크림의 가장 중요한 재료들 중 하나이다. Through the ages, many different flavors have been created. People love ice cream. In particular, kids seem to love it ❺ <u>more than anything else</u>.

14 밑줄 친 ❶~❺ 중 어법상 <u>어색한</u> 것은?

15 밑줄 친 (A)를 바르게 영작한 것은?

① The air is one of the important ingredients in ice cream.
② The air is one of the most important ingredients in ice cream.
③ The air is one of the most important ingredient in ice cream.
④ The air is as important as other ingredients in ice cream.
⑤ The air is the most important ingredient in ice cream.

[01-02] 표를 보고, 주어진 단어를 이용하여 문장을 완성하시오.

01

도시	Seoul	London	Moscow
기온 (℃)	9	12	5

→ Moscow is _____ _____ _____
of the three. (cold, city)

02

가족 구성원	Mom	Me
나이	45	15

→ My mom is _____ _____
_____ _____ _____ I am.
(three times, old)

[03-04] 두 문장이 같은 뜻이 되도록 빈칸에 알맞은 말을 쓰시오.

03 You will gain more weight as you eat more.

→ _____ _____ _____ _____,
the more weight you will gain.

04 The church is older than any other building
in town.

→ The church is _____ _____
_____ in town.

[05-06] 우리말과 같은 뜻이 되도록 주어진 단어를 이용하여
문장을 완성하시오.

05 Carrie는 점점 더 날씬해지고 있다. (slim)

→ Carrie is getting _____.

06 축구는 세계에서 가장 인기 있는 운동 중 하나이다.
(popular)

→ Soccer is _____
_____ in the world.

07 대화를 읽고, 밑줄 친 우리말과 같은 뜻이 되도록 문장을
완성하시오.

A Let's eat out.

B OK. Is there any restaurant you'd like to
go to?

A Actually, there are two restaurants.
(1) 너는 이탈리아 음식과 멕시코 음식 중 어느
것이 더 좋니?

B I like Italian better.

A Then, let's go to *La Cucina*!
(2) 그곳이 시내에서 가장 좋은 이탈리아 식당이야.

(1) _____,
Italian or Mexican?

(2) It is _____
downtown.

[08-10] 도표를 보고 주어진 단어를 이용하여 문장을 완성
하시오.

Book Title	Review	Year published	Pages	Number of copies sold
The Moon	★★★★★	2013	150	500,000
The Watchers	★★☆☆☆	2010	450	500,000
The Nightmare	★★★☆☆	1998	200	1,000,000

08 *The Moon* is his _____(late) book, and it
got the _____(many) stars in the reviews.

09 *The Watchers* is _____ _____
_____(three times, thick) than *The Moon*,
and it is _____ _____ _____
(popular) *The Moon*.

10 *The Nightmare* is _____ _____
(old) book of the three, but it is _____
_____ _____ (popular) book.

Chapter 8

접속사

시간, 이유, 결과 접속사

1. 시간을 나타내는 접속사

(1) when ～할 때 **while** ～하는 동안 **as** ～함에 따라, ～할 때

I enjoyed watching cartoons **when** I was young. 내가 어렸을 때 나는 만화 보는 것을 즐겼다.

While Helen was cooking dinner, she burned her hand.
Helen은 저녁을 하다가 손에 화상을 입었다.

As we get older, we become wiser. 우리는 나이가 들수록 더 현명해진다.

(2) before ～전에 **after** ～후에

I always read a book **before** I go to bed. 나는 항상 잠을 자기 전에 책을 읽는다.

What will you do **after** you graduate? 졸업을 한 후에 무엇을 할 거니?

(3) as soon as ～하자마자 **until[till]** ～할 때까지

As soon as he arrived home, he washed his hands. 그는 집에 도착하자마자 손을 씻었다.

The kids played basketball **until** it got dark. 아이들은 어두워질 때까지 농구를 했다.

2. 이유, 결과를 나타내는 접속사

(1) because, as, since ～이기 때문에

She went home early **because** she felt very tired.
그녀는 매우 피곤했기 때문에 집에 일찍 들어갔다.

As I'm a big fan of the actor, I see all of his movies.
나는 그 배우의 열혈 팬이어서 그의 영화는 모두 본다.

Since I don't know him well, I can't trust him. 나는 그를 잘 모르기 때문에 그를 신뢰할 수 없다.

(2) so ～해서 「**so ～ that** …」 너무 ～해서 …하다

I broke my tooth, **so** I went to the dentist. 나는 이가 부러져서 치과에 갔다.

The weather was **so** beautiful **that** we went on a picnic.
날씨가 너무 좋아서 우리는 소풍을 갔다.

Tips

1 시간을 나타내는 부사절에서는 현재 시제가 미래 시제를 대신한다.

I will call you when I finish the work. (O)
일이 끝나면 내가 너에게 전화할게

I will call you when I ~~will finish~~ the work. (X)

2 while은 '～인 반면에'라는 뜻으로 대조의 의미를 나타내기도 한다.

While Ann gets up early, her sister gets up late.
Ann은 일찍 일어나는 반면에 그녀의 여동생은 늦게 일어난다.

3 since는 '～이래로'라는 의미의 시간 접속사로 쓰이기도 한다.

It has been a year **since** I last saw you.
내가 너를 마지막으로 본 이후로 1년이 지났다.

Plus α

「because+주어+동사」
vs. 「because of+명사(구)」

Mia couldn't come **because** she had a cold.
Mia는 감기에 걸렸기 때문에 오지 못했다.

Mia couldn't come **because of** a cold.
Mia는 감기 때문에 오지 못했다.

Check-up 우리말과 같은 뜻이 되도록 ☐ 안에서 알맞은 것을 고르시오.

1 우리 어머니는 집안일을 할 때 노래를 부르신다.
→ My mother sings │ so / when │ she does housework.

2 나가기 전에 불을 꺼 주세요.
→ Please turn off the light │ before / while │ you go out.

3 그녀는 아파서, 아무것도 먹고 싶지 않았다.
→ │ Since / Until │ she was sick, she didn't want to eat anything.

: EXERCISES

A   [ ] 안에서 가장 알맞은 것을 고르시오.

1   Don't speak [while / so] you are eating.

2   What do you want to be [when / since] you grow up?

3   The computer is so expensive [that / because] I cannot buy it.

4   [As / Because] children grow, they learn to control their emotions.

5   I don't want to go out for dinner [after / because] I'm very tired now.

grow up 성장하다, 자라다
control
(동) 지배하다, 조절하다
(명) 지배, 통제
emotion (명) 감정

B   밑줄 친 부분을 어법에 맞게 고쳐 쓰시오.

1   It was Sunday, so I <u>stay</u> in bed until 10 am.

2   Traffic was terrible <u>because</u> the road construction.

3   Please call me when you <u>will arrive</u> at the airport.

4   I saw a car accident while I <u>am</u> driving home from work.

traffic (명) 교통(량)
terrible (형) 끔찍한, 심한
construction (명) 공사
accident (명) 사고

C   보기 에서 알맞은 접속사를 골라 문장을 완성하시오.

> 보기   as soon as   while   since   until

1   We'd better wait here _____ the rain stops.

2   There were a few visitors _____ you were away.

3   _____ I hung up the phone, it rang again.

4   _____ it was very noisy, I couldn't hear what he was saying.

visitor (명) 방문객, 손님
be away 부재중이다
hang up 전화를 끊다
ring (동) 울리다; 전화하다
noisy (형) 시끄러운

D   우리말과 같은 뜻이 되도록 주어진 단어를 이용하여 문장을 완성하시오.

1   Dean은 결혼할 때까지 부모님과 함께 살았다. (get married)

    → Dean lived with his parents _____ _____ _____

       _____.

2   오늘은 휴일이기 때문에 모든 은행이 문을 닫는다. (a holiday)

    → All the banks are closed _____ _____ _____

       _____ _____ today.

3   경기가 시작되기 전 그들은 준비 운동을 했다. (the game, start)

    → _____ _____ _____ _____, they did some

       warm-up exercises.

4   나는 배가 너무 고파서 식탁에 있는 것을 모두 먹었다. (hungry, eat, everything)

    → I was _____ _____ _____ _____

       _____ on the table.

UNIT 02 조건, 양보, 상관 접속사

1. 조건, 양보를 나타내는 접속사

(1) if 만약 ~한다면 **unless** 만약 ~하지 않는다면 [if ~ not]

If you practice hard, you will win the contest. 열심히 연습하면 너는 그 대회에서 우승할 것이다.

We will miss the bus **unless** we hurry. 서두르지 않으면 우리는 버스를 놓칠 것이다.

➡ We will miss the bus **if** we **don't** hurry.

(2) although, though, even though 비록 ~이지만, ~임에도 불구하고

Though/Although/Even though Eric is young, he is very thoughtful.
비록 Eric은 어리지만 매우 사려 깊다.

2. 상관 접속사: 두 개의 어구가 짝을 이루어 접속사 역할을 하는 것을 상관 접속사라고 한다.

(1) 「**not only A but also B**」 A뿐만 아니라 B도 (=B as well as A)

Christine is **not only** beautiful **but also** intelligent.

➡ Christine is intelligent **as well as** beautiful. Christine은 예쁠 뿐만 아니라 지적이다.

(2) 「**either A or B**」 A와 B 둘 중 하나

You should answer **either** yes **or** no to each question.
너는 각각의 질문에 예와 아니요 둘 중 하나로 답해야 한다.

(3) 「**both A and B**」 A와 B 둘 다

Both Isabel **and** Henry are very talented writers. Isabel과 Henry는 둘 다 재능 있는 작가이다.

(4) 「**neither A nor B**」 A와 B 둘 다 아닌

Jason is **neither** fat **nor** thin. Jason은 뚱뚱하지도 마르지도 않았다.

Tips

조건을 나타내는 부사절에서는 현재 시제가 미래 시제를 대신한다.

If I **go** to Paris, I'll visit the Louvre Museum. (O)
만약 파리에 가면 나는 루브르 박물관을 방문할 것이다.

If I ~~will go~~ to Paris, I'll visit the Louvre Museum. (X)

Plus α

☆ 「명령문+and」
~해라, 그러면 …할 것이다

Study hard, and you will pass the test.

➡ **If you study hard,** you will pass the test.
열심히 공부하면, 시험에 통과할 것이다.

☆ 「명령문+or」
~해라, 그렇지 않으면 …할 것이다

Leave now, or you will be late for school.

➡ **Unless you leave now,** you will be late for school.

➡ **If you don't leave now,** you will be late for school.
네가 지금 떠나지 않으면 학교에 늦을 것이다.

Check-up 우리말과 같은 뜻이 되도록 [ ] 안에서 알맞은 것을 고르시오.

1 Brian은 영국인 아니면 미국인일 것이다.
→ Brian may be [either / neither] British or American.

2 이 약을 복용해라, 그러면 나아질 것이다.
→ Take this medicine, [and / or] you will feel better.

3 서두르지 않으면 마지막 버스를 놓칠 것이다.
→ [If / Unless] you hurry, you will miss the last bus.

4 그는 매우 열심히 공부했음에도 불구하고, 시험에 떨어졌다.
→ [Though / Unless] he studied very hard, he failed the test.

: EXERCISES

A [ ] 안에서 가장 알맞은 것을 고르시오.

go for a walk
산책하러 가다

1 Their house was [either / neither] big nor small.

regularly (부) 규칙적으로

2 Walk fast, [and / or] we will be late for the movie.

stay healthy
건강을 유지하다

3 Rick went for a walk [although / so] it was raining.

catch a cold
감기에 걸리다

4 [If / Unless] you exercise regularly, you will stay healthy.

5 [If / Unless] you wear a warm coat, you will catch a cold.

B 밑줄 친 부분을 어법에 맞게 고쳐 쓰시오.

cowardly (형) 겁이 많은

1 I am not neither brave nor cowardly.

generous (형) 관대한

2 Mr. Collin is not rich but also generous.

do the dishes
설거지하다

3 If you will cook dinner, I will do the dishes.

4 Mom will be very angry unless you don't tell the truth.

C 두 문장의 의미가 통하도록 주어진 접속사를 이용하여 문장을 완성하시오.

press (동) 누르다

1 Mark was tired, and he was hungry, too. (both ~ and)

button (명) 단추; 버튼

→ Mark was _____.

get up late 늦잠을 자다

2 Press the button, and the door will open. (if)

→ _____, the door will open.

3 Go to bed now, or you will get up late tomorrow. (unless)

→ _____, you will get up late tomorrow.

4 She can play the violin and also play the cello. (not only ~ but also)

→ She can play _____.

D 우리말과 같은 뜻이 되도록 주어진 단어를 이용하여 문장을 완성하시오.

1 질문이 없으면 마치겠습니다. (have)

→ _____ _____ _____ any questions , I will call it a day.

2 모자를 써, 그러면 멋있어 보일 거야. (look)

→ Put on a hat, _____ _____ _____ _____ stylish.

3 나는 다리뿐만 아니라 팔도 다쳤다. (my arm, my leg)

→ I hurt _____ _____ _____ _____ _____

_____ _____.

4 나의 할머니는 95세임에도 불구하고 아주 건강하시다. (be)

→ _____ _____ _____ _____ 95 years old, she is very

healthy.

that, 간접의문문

1. 접속사 that이 이끄는 명사절은 문장에서 주어, 목적어, 보어 역할을 한다.

    (1) 주어 역할 ~라는 것은: that절이 문장에서 주어 역할을 할 경우, 보통 주어 자리에 가주어 it을 써 주고, that절을 문장 뒤로 보낸다.

      It is amazing **that** the audition winner is only ten years old.
      그 오디션 우승자가 겨우 열 살이라는 것이 놀랍다.

      It is not surprising **that** he entered Harvard University.
      그가 하버드 대학교에 입학한 것은 놀랄 일이 아니다.

    (2) 목적어 역할 ~라는 것을: 목적어절을 이끄는 that은 생략할 수 있다.

      She knows (**that**) her father loves her.
      그녀는 아버지가 자신을 사랑한다는 것을 알고 있다.

    (3) 보어 역할 ~라는 것(이다)

      The important thing is **that** she trusts him. 중요한 것은 그녀가 그를 신뢰한다는 것이다.

> **Plus α**
> 동격의 명사절을 이끄는 접속사 that: fact, truth, belief, idea, rumor, news, proof 등의 명사와 같이 쓰여, 앞에 있는 명사와 동일한 내용을 나타낸다.
>
> She didn't accept the fact **that** he was innocent.
> [the fact = he was innocent]
> 그녀는 그가 결백하다는 사실을 받아들이지 않았다.

2. 의문문이 문장의 일부로 들어간 문장을 간접의문문이라고 한다.

    (1) 의문사가 있는 문장의 간접의문문은 「의문사+주어+동사」의 어순으로 쓴다.

      Tell me. + What did you eat?
      ➡ Tell me **what you ate.** 나에게 무엇을 먹었는지 말해 줘.

    (2) 의문사가 없는 문장의 간접의문문은 「if/whether+주어+동사」의 어순으로 쓴다.

      I wonder. + Will she like my present?
      ➡ I wonder **if/whether she will** like my present. 나는 그녀가 내 선물을 좋아할지 궁금하다.

Check-up 우리말과 같은 뜻이 되도록 ☐ 안에서 알맞은 것을 고르시오.

1 네가 그녀를 모른다는 것은 이상한 일이다.
   → ☐ It / This ☐ is strange that you don't know her.

2 나는 그녀가 취직을 했는지 안 했는지 궁금하다.
   → I wonder ☐ if / that ☐ she got the job or not.

3 그가 올 건지 안 올 건지 나에게 말해 줄래?
   → Can you tell me ☐ that / whether ☐ he will come or not?

4 그녀가 대회에서 우승을 했다는 소식이 나를 행복하게 했다.
   → The news ☐ that / whether ☐ she won the contest made me happy.

: EXERCISES

A [ ] 안에서 알맞은 것을 고르시오.

1 It was true [that / if] she won a gold medal.

2 The rumor [that / if] he got married is not true.

3 Don't forget [that / whether] you should bring your camera.

4 I wonder [that / whether] she can finish her project on time or not.

win a gold medal
금메달을 따다
rumor 명 소문
get married 결혼하다
project
명 프로젝트, 사업, 기획된 일
on time 제때, 기한 내에

B 주어진 문장을 「It(가주어) ~ that(진주어)」 구문을 사용한 문장으로 바꿔 쓰시오.

1 That they need our help is certain.

→ It _____ .

2 That the driver survived the accident is a miracle.

→ It _____ .

3 That you remain calm during the interview is important.

→ It _____ .

certain
형 확실한, 틀림없는
survive 동 살아남다
miracle 명 기적
remain
동 여전히 ~하다, 지키다
calm 형 침착한, 차분한
interview 명 면접, 인터뷰

C 두 문장을 한 문장의 간접의문문으로 바꿔 쓰시오.

1 Can you tell me? + What is his name?

→ Can you tell me _____ ?

2 I wonder. + Where do they come from?

→ I wonder _____ .

3 Do you know? + Did they enjoy the party?

→ Do you know _____ ?

D 우리말과 같은 뜻이 되도록 주어진 단어를 이용하여 문장을 완성하시오.

1 그녀가 천재라는 것은 진실이다. (be, a genius)

→ It is true _____ _____ _____ _____ .

2 Lisa는 그녀가 운이 좋다고 생각한다. (think, be, lucky)

→ Lisa _____ _____ _____ _____ _____ .

3 나는 사람들이 내 의견에 동의할지 안 할지 궁금하다. (wonder, agree with)

→ I _____ _____ _____ _____ _____
_____ my opinion or not.

4 그녀는 자신의 아들이 경기에서 우승할 거라고 믿는다. (believe, win, the game)

→ She _____ _____ _____ _____ _____
_____ _____ _____ .

: Review Test

[01-03] 빈칸에 들어갈 알맞은 말을 고르시오.

01 Someone called you _____ you were out.

① that   ② if   ③ while
④ so   ⑤ unless

02 _____ you love your work, it is hard to succeed.

① Unless   ② That   ③ So
④ Since   ⑤ As

03 _____ I haven't met her, I've heard a lot about her.

① Unless   ② If   ③ That
④ When   ⑤ Although

04 빈칸에 들어갈 말로 알맞은 것을 <u>모두</u> 고르시오.

We didn't go to school _____ it was a holiday.

① as   ② since   ③ though
④ before   ⑤ because

05 빈칸에 공통으로 들어갈 말로 알맞은 것은?

· Either you _____ he is to blame for the mistake.
· Get up now, _____ you will miss your school bus.

① or   ② as   ③ so
④ and   ⑤ nor

[06-07] 두 문장의 의미가 통하도록 빈칸에 알맞은 말을 고르시오.

06 You can do anything if you don't give up.
→ You can do anything _____ you give up.

① since   ② unless   ③ because
④ although   ⑤ as soon as

07 He locked the door before he left the house.
→ He left the house _____ he locked the door.

① as   ② while   ③ when
④ after   ⑤ until

08 우리말을 영어로 옮긴 것 중 <u>어색한</u> 것은?

① 그녀는 생선과 고기 둘 다 먹지 않는다.
→ She eats neither fish nor meat.
② Bob은 배가 부를 때까지 먹고 또 먹었다.
→ Bob ate and ate until he was full.
③ 만약 네가 아프면 병원에 가는 게 좋겠다.
→ If you are sick, you had better see a doctor.
④ 그녀는 너무 바빠서 쇼핑하러 갈 시간이 없다.
→ She is so busy that she doesn't have time to go shopping.
⑤ 그는 그녀를 사랑하기 때문에 그녀가 행복하길 바란다.
→ He wants her to be happy, so he loves her.

[09-10] 밑줄 친 부분의 쓰임이 나머지와 <u>다른</u> 것은?

09 ① It is hard to believe <u>that</u> he is a lawyer.
② He was so happy <u>that</u> he sang loudly.
③ The problem is <u>that</u> I told him my secret.
④ She thinks <u>that</u> he dances very well.
⑤ He knows <u>that</u> she was born in Canada.

10 ① What were you doing <u>when</u> I called you?

② Time goes faster <u>when</u> I am having fun.

③ Be careful <u>when</u> you cross the street.

④ <u>When</u> I saw her, she gave me a big smile.

⑤ <u>When</u> did you move into your new house?

[11-12] 다음 중 어법상 <u>어색한</u> 것을 고르시오.

11 ① I wonder whether she likes me or not.

② I was late for work because heavy snow.

③ Let me know as soon as you get the email.

④ Both Betty and I enjoyed the trip.

⑤ Be positive, and you will be happy.

12 ① He is good at math as well as English.

② Either you or I should take care of our little sister.

③ If you will go with him, he will be very pleased.

④ Although she is young, she is able to speak three languages.

⑤ Not only Jane but also Steve will join the broadcasting club at school.

13 다음 대화 중 자연스럽지 <u>않은</u> 것은?

① A You look so tired.

  B I have no energy left. I ate neither breakfast nor lunch.

② A Will you tell me why Billy is so angry with me?

  B Unless he tells you himself, I won't tell you.

③ A Can you take out the trash before you go out?

  B I'm sorry. I will do it after I come back.

④ A What do you usually do on weekends?

  B I either read books or watch TV.

⑤ A Check the map, and you will get lost.

  B Don't worry. I think I know where it is.

[14-15] 글을 읽고, 물음에 답하시오.

Hi Angela,

I am writing this email to apologize to you. You may think ❶ <u>that</u> I stole your umbrella, but I didn't. ❷ <u>When</u> I left school, it was raining heavily. ❸ <u>So</u> I went back to the classroom and saw Jean. (A) <u>나는 그녀에게 여분의 우산이 있는지 궁금했다.</u> She said that she didn't have one, but there might be an extra in the classroom. ❹ <u>As</u> I looked around, I saw one on the floor. So I took it. I never thought that it was yours. I'm really sorry. From now on, I'll never take things, ❺ <u>if</u> I get the owner's permission. Please accept my apology.

Susan

14 밑줄 친 ❶~❺ 중 어법상 <u>어색한</u> 것은?

15 밑줄 친 (A)를 바르게 영작한 것은?

① I wondered if she had an extra umbrella.

② I wondered as she had an extra umbrella.

③ I wondered when she had an extra umbrella.

④ I wondered that she had an extra umbrella.

⑤ I wondered because she had an extra umbrella.

[01-02] 두 문장이 같은 뜻이 되도록 주어진 접속사를 이용하여 문장을 완성하시오.

01 Tell me the truth, and I will forgive you. (if)

→ _____, I will forgive you.

02 I have lost not only my wallet but also my cell phone. (as well as)

→ I have lost _____.

[03-04] 우리말과 같은 뜻이 되도록 주어진 단어를 이용하여 문장을 완성하시오.

03 너는 그 소문이 사실인지 아닌지 아니? (the rumor, be)

→ Do you know _____
_____ or not?

04 날씨가 너무 더워서 우리는 해변에 가기로 결정했다. (decide)

→ The weather was _____
_____ to go to the beach.

[05-06] 어법상 어색한 부분을 찾아 어법에 맞게 고쳐 쓰시오.

05 When you will see her, tell her to call me.

→ _____

06 She doesn't like neither the blue dress nor the red one.

→ _____

[07-08] 우리말과 같은 뜻이 되도록 주어진 단어를 배열하시오.

07 그와 그녀 둘 중 한 명이 그 기회를 얻게 될 것이다. (he, she, either, will, the chance, take, or)

→ _____

08 나는 약을 먹었음에도 불구하고 여전히 배가 아프다. (I, the medicine, although, took)

→ _____,
I still have a stomachache.

09 대화를 읽고, 밑줄 친 우리말과 같은 뜻이 되도록 문장을 완성하시오.

> A Hi, I'm sorry I'm late.
> B That's OK. Why are you late?
> A 나는 수업이 끝나자마자 출발했어. But there was a traffic jam.
> B It's better to take the subway at this time.
> A Yeah, you're right. By the way, have you ordered any food?
> B No, I haven't. Let's order.

조건 접속사와 주어진 단어를 이용할 것

→ I left _____ _____ _____
_____ _____ _____.
(finish, class)

10 도표를 읽고, 주어진 단어를 이용하여 문장을 완성하시오.

Name	Favorite Activities
Nick	Swimming, Bike riding
Michael	Playing computer games, Reading
Samuel	Watching movies, Cooking
Julia	Playing tennis, Rock Climbing
Robert	Running, Watching movies

(1) _____ Nick _____ Julia
_____ outdoor activities. (both, like)

(2) _____ Samuel _____ Michael
_____ playing sports. (neither, like)

(3) _____ _____ Samuel _____
_____ Robert _____ watching
movies. (not only, enjoy)

Chapter 9

관계사

관계대명사 I

☆ 관계대명사는 「접속사+대명사」의 역할을 하고, 관계대명사가 이끄는 절은 형용사처럼 앞에 나오는 명사를 수식한다. 관계대명사 절의 수식을 받는 명사를 선행사라고 한다.

선행사	사람	사물, 동물	사람, 사물, 동물
주격 관계대명사	who	which	that
목적격 관계대명사	who(m)	which	that
소유격 관계대명사	whose	whose	-

1. 주격 관계대명사 (who, which)

I have **a friend**. **+ She** studied abroad.
➡ I have a friend **who** studied abroad. 나는 외국에서 공부한 친구가 한 명 있다.
<u>사람 선행사</u> 「주격 관계대명사(주어 역할)+동사」

We stayed **in a room**. **+ It** was very big.
➡ We stayed <u>in a room</u> **which** was very big. 우리는 매우 큰 방에 묵었다.
사물 선행사 「주격 관계대명사(주어 역할)+동사」

2. 목적격 관계대명사 (who(m), which)

The phone call was from **a man**. **+ I** don't know **him**.
➡ The phone call was from <u>a man</u> **who(m)** I don't know.
사람 선행사 「목적격 관계대명사(목적어 역할)+주어+동사」
그 전화는 내가 모르는 남자에게서 걸려온 것이다.

This is **the movie**. **+ I** like **it** the best.
➡ This is <u>the movie</u> **which** I like the best. 이것이 내가 가장 좋아하는 영화다.
사물 선행사 「목적격 관계대명사(목적어 역할)+주어+동사」

3. 소유격 관계대명사 (whose)

I know **a boy**. **+ His** brother goes to Harvard University.
➡ I know <u>a boy</u> **whose** brother goes to Harvard University.
사람 선행사 「소유격 관계대명사(소유격 역할)+명사」
나는 형이 하버드 대학에 다니는 소년을 알고 있다.

Jennifer took care of **a cat**. **+ Its** leg was hurt.
➡ Jennifer took care of a cat **whose** leg was hurt. Jennifer는 다리를 다친 고양이를 돌봤다.
동물 선행사 「소유격 관계대명사(소유격 역할)+명사」

Tips

1 의문사 who
vs. 관계대명사 who

Do you know **who** the new teacher is?
너는 누가 새로 오신 선생님인지 아니? [who는 '누구'라는 뜻으로 know의 목적어절을 이끄는 의문사]

Do you know the woman **who** is singing?
너는 노래를 부르는 저 여자를 아니? [who는 선행사 the woman을 수식하는 관계대명사절을 이끄는 주격관계대명사]

2 주격, 목적격 관계대명사 who(m), which는 선행사에 관계없이 that으로 바꿔 쓸 수 있다.

Plus α

목적격 관계대명사는 전치사의 목적어로도 쓰인다.

This is **the company**.
+ My brother works for **it**.
➡ This is the company **which** my brother works for. [전치사의 목적어]
이곳이 우리 형이 일하는 회사다.

Check-up 우리말과 같은 뜻이 되도록 ☐ 안에서 알맞은 것을 고르시오.

1 나는 벽에 걸려 있는 저 사진을 좋아한다.
→ I like the picture [which / who] is on the wall.

2 네가 만나야 하는 사람이 한 명 더 있다.
→ There is one more person [which / whom] you should meet.

3 나는 이름이 Angelina인 소녀를 만났다.
→ I met a girl [who / whose] name was Angelina.

: EXERCISES

A [ ] 안에서 알맞은 것을 고르시오.

1 Kathy is my friend [which / who] I met in high school.

2 I saw a movie [which / who] was about music and love.

3 They are the couple [which / who] invited us to this party.

4 Have you seen the pictures [which / who] she took during the trip?

high school 고등학교
invite (동) 초대하다
during (전) ~동안

B 두 문장을 관계대명사를 이용하여 한 문장으로 만드시오.

1 Abbie is my friend. She lives in Australia.
→ Abbie is my friend _____ .

2 This is the girl. All of my classmates like her.
→ This is the girl _____ .

3 Harry is my friend. His hobby is bungee jumping.
→ Harry is my friend _____ .

4 Have you seen my sweater? My mother knitted it for me.
→ Have you seen my sweater _____ .

Australia
(명) 오스트레일리아, 호주
classmate (명) 급우
bungee jumping
번지점프
sweater (명) 스웨터
knit (동) 짜다, 뜨다

C 밑줄 친 부분을 어법에 맞게 고쳐 쓰시오.

1 The color <u>whom</u> I like most is violet.

2 Lola lives in the house <u>which</u> roof is red.

3 Do you have a friend <u>which</u> you can trust?

4 They are the children <u>which</u> live next door.

violet (명) 보라색
roof (명) 지붕
trust (동) 믿다
live next door
옆집에 살다

D 우리말과 같은 뜻이 되도록 관계대명사와 주어진 단어를 이용하여 문장을 완성하시오.

1 그는 박물관에서 일하는 사람이다. (a person, work)
→ He is _____ _____ _____ _____ at a museum.

2 너는 부모님이 음악가인 그 소년을 아니? (the boy)
→ Do you know _____ _____ _____ _____ are
musicians?

3 우리가 회의에서 만난 사람들은 매우 친절했다. (the people, meet)
→ _____ _____ _____ _____ in the
meeting were very friendly.

4 난 네가 지난달에 빌려간 책을 돌려주기를 원해. (the book, borrow)
→ I want you to return _____ _____ _____ _____
_____ last month.

UNIT 02 관계대명사 II

1. 관계대명사 that

(1) 선행사에 관계없이 주격 관계대명사와 목적격 관계대명사로 쓸 수 있다.

They're looking for an actress **that[who]** looks like Marilyn Monroe.
그들은 Marilyn Monroe를 닮은 여배우를 찾고 있다.

The woman **that[who(m)]** I met at the station was very kind.
내가 역에서 만난 여자는 매우 친절했다.

Do you like the book **that[which]** I gave you? 내가 너에게 준 책이 마음에 드니?

(2) 선행사가 「사람+동물」인 경우, 최상급, 서수, the only, the very, the same, the last 등의 수식을 받는 경우, –thing으로 끝나는 경우 주로 관계대명사 that을 쓴다.

Sam took <u>the first train</u> **that** leaves for Busan. Sam은 부산으로 떠나는 첫 기차를 탔다.

Rick is <u>the only friend</u> **that** I can rely on. Rick은 내가 의지할 수 있는 유일한 친구다.

Is there <u>anything</u> **that** you want to ask? 네가 묻고 싶은 게 있니?

2. 관계대명사의 생략

(1) 목적격 관계대명사

That is the movie **(which[that])** I <u>saw</u> several times. [saw의 목적어]
이것은 내가 여러 번 본 영화다.

This is the house **(which[that])** Sally lives <u>in</u>. [in의 목적어] 이곳은 Sally가 사는 집이야.

(2) 「주격 관계대명사+be동사」

The child **(who is)** reading a book is my sister. 책을 읽고 있는 저 아이가 내 여동생이다.

This is the poem **(which was)** written by my brother. 이것은 우리 오빠가 쓴 시이다.

3. 선행사를 포함하는 관계대명사 what

I know **what** you did last summer. 나는 네가 지난여름에 한 일을 알고 있다.
    = the thing that

<u>**What**</u> I want to know is the due date. 내가 알고 싶은 건 마감 날짜야.
= the thing that

Check-up   우리말과 같은 뜻이 되도록 ☐ 안에서 알맞은 것을 고르시오.

1 나는 네가 하는 말을 이해할 수 없어.
   → I don't understand ☐that / what☐ you said.

2 내 친구가 사 준 책을 읽고 있는 중이야.
   → I'm reading the book ☐that / what☐ my friend bought for me.

: EXERCISES

Answers / p.27

A [ ] 안에서 알맞은 것을 고르시오.

1 Have you seen the movie [that / what] I told you about?

2 Tell me [that / what] you want to be in the future.

3 I don't know the person [that / what] you are talking about.

4 This is the garden in [that / which] my mom planted roses.

in the future 미래에
talk about
　〜에 관해 이야기하다
plant 통 〜을 심다

B 밑줄 친 부분을 생략할 수 있으면 O, 생략할 수 없으면 X표 하시오.

1 I met a woman <u>who is</u> from Germany. _____

2 This is the house in <u>which</u> I was born. _____

3 The people <u>who</u> live upstairs are very kind. _____

4 Did you see the man <u>who</u> I was talking with? _____

Germany 명 독일
be born 태어나다
upstairs 부 위층에
talk with 〜와 이야기하다

C 주어진 문장을 관계대명사 what을 사용하여 다시 쓰시오.

1 Tell us the thing that you thought.

　→ Tell us _____ .

2 My parents didn't believe the words that I said.

　→ My parents didn't believe _____ .

3 We don't know the thing that we have to do next.

　→ We don't know _____ .

4 You should show me the things that you have in your pocket.

　→ You should show me _____ .

D 우리말과 같은 뜻이 되도록 주어진 단어를 알맞게 배열하여 문장을 완성하시오.

1 나는 초콜릿으로 만든 거라면 뭐든 좋아한다. (anything, chocolate, is, made of, that)

　→ I love _____ .

2 나는 스페인에서 보낸 첫 번째 밤을 기억한다. (in Spain, I, spent, the first night, that)

　→ I remember _____ .

3 산을 오르는 남자와 개를 보셨나요?
(the mountain, and, the dog, were climbing, that, the man)

　→ Did you see _____ ?

4 Anne은 내가 아는 가장 다정다감한 사람이다.
(I, known, the sweetest person, have, that, ever)

　→ Anne is _____ .

관계부사

☆ 관계부사는 「접속사＋부사」의 역할을 하고, 「전치사＋관계대명사」로 바꿔 쓸 수 있다. 관계부사가
  이끄는 절은 형용사처럼 앞에 나오는 명사를 수식하고 이 명사를 선행사라고 한다.

	선행사	관계부사	전치사＋관계대명사
시간	the time, the day, the year ...	when	at/on/in＋which
장소	the place, the house, the city ...	where	at/on/in＋which
이유	the reason	why	for which
방법	the way	how	in which

1. when: 선행사가 시간을 나타낼 때

I can't forget **the day**. ＋ We first met **on that day**.

➡ I can't forget **the day** <u>when[on which]</u> we first met. 나는 우리가 처음 만난 그날을 잊을 수 없어.

2. where: 선행사가 장소를 나타낼 때

This is **the room**. ＋ I always study **in the room**.

➡ This is **the room** <u>where[in which]</u> I always study. 여기가 내가 항상 공부하는 방이야.

3. why: 선행사가 이유를 나타낼 때

I know **the reason**. ＋ He didn't come to class **for that reason**.

➡ I know **the reason** <u>why[for which]</u> he didn't come to class.
  나는 그가 수업에 오지 않은 이유를 알고 있다.

4. how: 선행사가 방법을 나타낼 때

This is **the way**.＋Melissa makes a cake **in that way**.

➡ This is **the way in which** Melissa makes a cake.

➡ This is **how[the way]** Melissa makes a cake. 이것이 Melissa가 케이크를 만드는 방법이다.

> **Tips**
>
> 선행사 the way와 관계부사 how는 함께 쓸 수 없다.
>
> This is ~~the way how~~ Melissa makes a cake. (X)

Check-up 우리말과 같은 뜻이 되도록 ☐ 안에서 알맞은 것을 고르시오.

1 이것이 내가 그 퍼즐을 풀었던 방법이다.

  → This is │ how / where │ I solved the puzzle.

2 제발 나에게 그가 화난 이유를 말해 주세요.

  → Please tell me the reason │ how / why │ he is upset.

3 나는 밴쿠버에서 보냈던 시간이 그립다.

  → I miss the time │ when / why │ I stayed in Vancouver.

: EXERCISES

A [ ] 안에서 알맞은 것을 고르시오.

1 This is the theater [when / where] they usually perform.

2 Tomorrow is the day [when / where] I give a presentation.

3 Can you tell me [when / how] you prepared for the exam yesterday?

perform 동 공연하다
give a presentation 발표하다
prepare 동 준비하다

B 보기 에서 알맞은 관계부사를 골라 문장을 완성하시오.

보기   when   where   why   how

1 I don't understand the reason _____ you hate math.

2 2011 was the year _____ my father had surgery.

3 I usually ride my bike. This is _____ I relieve stress.

4 Is that the town _____ you were born and grew up?

surgery 명 수술
relieve 동 경감하다
grow up 성장하다

C 두 문장을 관계부사를 이용하여 한 문장으로 만드시오.

1 I love the hotel. We stayed in that hotel last summer.

→ I love the hotel _____ .

2 It is amazing to find out the way. They survived the tsunami in that way.

→ It is amazing to find out _____ .

3 Please tell me the reason. You were absent from the class for that reason.

→ Please tell me the reason _____ .

stay 동 묵다
find out 발견하다
survive 동 생존하다
tsunami 명 쓰나미
be absent from ~에 결석하다

D 우리말과 같은 뜻이 되도록 관계부사와 주어진 단어를 이용하여 문장을 완성하시오.

1 네가 떠나고 싶은 때를 말해줘. (want)

→ Tell me the time _____ _____ _____ to leave.

2 여기는 사람들이 자신의 사진을 올리는 웹사이트이다. (post)

→ This is the website _____ _____ _____ their photos.

3 그는 자신이 왜 우울한지 몰랐다. (be)

→ He doesn't know the reason _____ _____ _____ depressed.

4 면접관은 Lena에게 어떻게 영어 실력을 향상시켰는지 물었다. (improve)

→ The interviewer asked Lena _____ _____ _____ her English skills.

: Review Test

[01-02] 빈칸에 들어갈 알맞은 말을 고르시오.

01
I don't know the man _____ is smiling at me.

① who   ② whom   ③ whose
④ which   ⑤ what

02
Can you tell me _____ you saw last night?

① that   ② when   ③ where
④ whose   ⑤ what

03 빈칸에 들어갈 수 있는 것을 <u>모두</u> 고르시오.

They told the reporter _____ they survived the flood.

① how   ② who   ③ where
④ the way   ⑤ the way how

04 빈칸에 들어갈 말이 바르게 짝지어진 것은?

· Jane is the girl _____ I want to ask out.
· I don't know the reason _____ I keep failing the exam.

① who - how   ② whom - where
③ who - why   ④ whose - that
⑤ whom - which

05 밑줄 친 부분을 바르게 고친 것으로 알맞은 것을 <u>모두</u> 고르시오.

I bought a bag <u>whom</u> is made of leather.

① which   ② where   ③ who
④ that   ⑤ what

[06-07] 두 문장을 한 문장으로 만들 때, 빈칸에 들어갈 알맞은 말을 고르시오.

06
I know a woman. Her job is a programmer.
→ I know a woman _____ job is a programmer.

① who   ② whom   ③ which
④ whose   ⑤ what

07
Did you find the document? You were searching for it.
→ Did you find the document for _____ you were searching?

① who   ② when   ③ which
④ where   ⑤ that

08 밑줄 친 부분 중 생략할 수 <u>없는</u> 것은?

① He can get everything <u>that</u> he wants.
② Anne is the girl <u>who</u> Jack introduced to me.
③ The car <u>which</u> I want to buy is expensive.
④ The people <u>who</u> live upstairs are noisy.
⑤ My family liked the pie <u>that</u> I made.

09 밑줄 친 <u>that</u>의 쓰임이 어법상 <u>어색한</u> 것은?

① I have a friend <u>that</u> is studying art history.
② That is the watch <u>that</u> I really wanted to buy.
③ They are my friends with <u>that</u> I went camping.
④ The first thing <u>that</u> you should do is to call 911.
⑤ Do you know any experts <u>that</u> I can ask for advice?

10 밑줄 친 <u>what</u>의 쓰임이 나머지와 <u>다른</u> 것은?

① Tell me <u>what</u> you have in mind.
② <u>What</u> made you come here?
③ I don't know <u>what</u> you mean by that.
④ <u>What</u> you heard about him was not true.
⑤ You will never know <u>what</u> I gave up for you.

[11-12] 다음 중 어법상 <u>어색한</u> 문장을 고르시오.

11 ① It's the time when you can take a rest.
② The room where she took us was filled with books.
③ I don't know the reason why she can't work with us.
④ 2002 was the year when Korea held the World Cup.
⑤ Do you know any good cafes what we have great coffee?

12 ① I don't know the reason why she left.
② Do you remember the boy you met at the party?
③ The students are in the classroom are studying hard.
④ Jane arrived in Korea on the day when her sister left.
⑤ Can you tell me the place where you went on a trip?

13 우리말을 영어로 바르게 옮긴 것을 <u>모두</u> 고르시오.

여기가 내가 태어난 마을이다.

① This is the town in I was born.
② This is the town which I was born.
③ This is the town where I was born.
④ This is the town which I was born in.
⑤ This is the town in which I was born.

[14-15] 글을 읽고, 물음에 답하시오.

From childhood, the Wright brothers were always excited about things ___(a)___ flew. Their father knew it. So, one day, he gave them a toy ___(b)___ was called a helicopter. After they got the helicopter, they kept trying to make things like it. Even though they failed many times, they never gave up. They knew ___(c)___ they really wanted to make. (d) <u>그들은 마침내 최초로 비행기를 날린 사람들이 되었다.</u> Their invention changed their lives and ours.

14 빈칸 (a) ~ (c)에 들어갈 말이 바르게 짝지어진 것은?

	(a)		(b)		(c)
①	that	-	who	-	that
②	what	-	which	-	what
③	that	-	which	-	what
④	what	-	who	-	that
⑤	that	-	which	-	that

15 밑줄 친 (d)를 바르게 영작한 것은?

① They eventually became the first people that flew an airplane.
② They eventually became the first people whom flew an airplane.
③ They eventually became the first people which flew an airplane.
④ They eventually became the first people whose flew an airplane.
⑤ They eventually became the first people what flew an airplane.

[01-02] 빈칸에 알맞은 관계대명사를 넣어 대화를 완성하시오.

01 A Do you know the girl over there?

B Do you mean the one _____ is wearing a red hat?

02 A Did you bring the book _____ I lent you last Friday?

B Oh, I'm sorry. I haven't finished it yet. I'll finish it quickly.

[03-04] 두 문장을 관계대명사를 이용하여 한 문장으로 만드시오.

03 The roses are beautiful. They are growing in your garden.

→ The roses _____

_____ are beautiful.

04 I know a woman. Her husband is working in Brazil.

→ I know a woman _____

_____ in Brazil.

[05-06] 빈칸에 알맞은 관계부사를 넣어 대화를 완성하시오.

05 A Nick, do you remember the restaurant _____ we ate pasta the other day?

B Yes. It was downtown. I like that place.

06 A This cake is delicious! How did you make it?

B I can show you _____ I made it.

07 밑줄 친 ❶~❺ 중 어법상 어색한 것을 두 개 찾아 고쳐 쓰시오

> Dear Jill,
>
> ❶ I'm sending the picture who I took at the party. ❷ You look so happy in the picture. ❸ By the way, who is the man which is standing next to you? ❹ I can't remember him. ❺ If you have his email address, please send him the picture. I hope that you and he will like it.
>
> Love,
>
> *Jim*

_____

_____

[08-09] 우리말과 같은 뜻이 되도록 주어진 단어를 이용하여 문장을 완성하시오.

08 어제 우리가 시장에서 산 토마토는 신선했다. (the tomatoes, buy)

→ _____

at the market yesterday were fresh.

09 나에게 네가 기분이 안 좋은 이유를 말해 보렴. (the reason, why, be, not)

→ Tell me _____

_____ in a good mood.

10 우리말과 같은 뜻이 되도록 주어진 단어를 배열하시오.

(1) 나는 병원에서 성장해야 했던 소녀에 대한 영화를 보았다.
(in a hospital, had to, a girl, grow up, who)

→ I saw a movie about _____

_____.

(2) 그 금고를 어떻게 열었는지 말해 줄래?
(unlock, you, the safe, how)

→ Can you tell me _____

_____?

Chapter 10

분사

UNIT 01 현재분사, 과거분사

1. 분사의 형태와 의미

(1) 현재분사「동사원형+ing」: 능동(~하는, ~시키는)과 진행(~하고 있는)의 의미를 나타낸다.

a **boring** movie [능동] 지루한 영화   a **sleeping** baby [진행] 자고 있는 아기

(2) 과거분사「동사원형+ed」: 수동(~되는, ~당하는)과 완료(~한, ~해진)의 의미를 나타낸다.

bored students [수동] 지루해하는 학생들   **fallen** leaves [완료] 낙엽

2. 분사의 역할

(1) 명사 수식: 단독으로 쓸 때는 분사는 명사 앞에서, 수식어와 함께 쓸 때는 명사 뒤에서 명사를 수식한다.

He quickly walked past the <u>**barking** dog</u>. 그는 재빨리 짖고 있는 개를 지나쳐 걸었다.

Julian bought a <u>car **made in Germany**</u>. Julian은 독일에서 제조된 자동차를 샀다.

(2) 보어 역할

The museum remains **closed** on weekends. [주격보어] 박물관은 주말마다 문을 닫는다.

Sarah saw him **sitting** under a tree. [목적격보어] Sarah는 그가 나무 아래 앉아 있는 것을 보았다.

(3) 동사로 쓰인 분사

Jane **is cooking** dinner for the party. [진행 시제] Jane은 파티를 위해 저녁을 요리하고 있다.

The Eiffel Tower **was constructed** in 1889. [수동태] 에펠 타워는 1889년에 건설되었다.

I **haven't eaten** anything since this morning. [완료형] 나는 아침부터 아무것도 먹지 못했다.

3. 감정을 나타내는 분사: 명사가 감정을 느끼게 할 때는 현재분사를, 명사가 감정을 느낄 때는 과거분사를 쓴다.

amazing 놀라운 – amazed 놀란   boring 지루하게 하는 – bored 지루한

exiting 신나게 하는 – excited 신난   interesting 흥미로운 – interested 흥미를 느낀

shocking 충격적인 – shocked 충격 받은   surprising 놀라게 하는 – surprised 놀란

<u>The soccer game</u> was really **exciting**. 축구 경기는 정말 흥미진진했다.

<u>She</u> was very **excited** to hear the news. 그녀는 그 소식을 듣고 몹시 흥분했다.

Plus α

「관계대명사+be동사」의 생략: which is가 생략되면 분사로 a book을 수식한다.

She read a book (**which is**) **written in English**. 그녀는 영어로 쓰인 책을 읽었다.

Tips

현재분사 vs. 동명사

1 현재분사
- 명사수식(-ing+명사)
  a **sleeping** baby
  잠자는 아기
- 진행 시제(be+-ing)
  She **is writing** a book.
  그녀는 책을 쓰고 있는 중이다.
- 보어
  She sat **reading** a book.
  그녀는 책을 읽으며 앉아 있었다.
  [She ≠ reading a book]

2 동명사
- 명사의 용도(-ing+명사)
  a **sleeping** car 침대차
- 보어 역할(be+-ing)
  Her job **is writing** a book.
  그녀의 직업은 책을 쓰는 것이다.
  [her job = writing a book]

Check-up   우리말과 같은 뜻이 되도록 □ 안에서 알맞은 것을 고르시오.

1 그는 날아가는 새를 그리고 있다. → He is drawing a [flying / flown] bird.

2 깨진 창문을 봐. → Look at the [breaking / broken] window.

3 그는 감동적인 이야기를 많이 썼다. → He wrote many [touching / touched] stories.

4 나는 스포츠에는 흥미가 없다. → I am not [interesting / interested] in sports.

: EXERCISES

A [ ] 안에서 알맞은 것을 고르시오.

1 There is a girl [writing / written] a letter.

2 [Boiling / Boiled] eggs are my favorite food.

3 I love spaghetti [cooking / cooked] by my mom.

4 The girl [playing / played] the piano is my cousin.

5 I'm really [exciting / excited] about my trip to America.

boil (동) 삶다; 끓이다

cousin (명) 사촌

B 주어진 단어를 현재분사나 과거분사로 바꿔 문장을 완성하시오.

1 I have a kitten _____ Nina. (call)

2 My grandmother told me _____ news. (surprise)

3 The boy _____ on the sofa is my brother. (sit)

4 Look at the box _____ with a lot of chocolate. (fill)

5 These days, many Japanese students are _____ Korean. (learn)

kitten (명) 새끼 고양이

fill (동) 가득 채우다

C 주어진 단어를 알맞게 배열하여 문장을 완성하시오.

1 The police found _____. (stolen, a, car)

2 Moscow is _____ to visit. (city, interesting, an)

3 _____ is my brother, Dave. (on the grass, the boy, lying)

4 What is _____?
(in Switzerland, the language, spoken)

steal (동) 훔치다
(steal – stole – stolen)

grass (명) 잔디; 풀

lie (동) 눕다

Switzerland (명) 스위스

D 우리말과 같은 뜻이 되도록 주어진 단어를 이용하여 문장을 완성하시오.

1 한 남자가 그 잠긴 문을 열었다. (lock)

→ A man opened _____ _____ _____.

2 그 호텔의 서비스는 실망스러웠다. (be, disappoint)

→ The service at the hotel _____ _____.

3 학생들은 교장 선생님의 연설에 지루해했다. (be, bore)

→ _____ _____ _____ by the principal's speech.

4 첫 번째 줄에 앉아 있는 그 소녀가 내 여동생이다. (sit, in the first row)

→ _____ _____ _____ _____ _____

_____ is my sister.

UNIT 02 분사구문

☆ 분사구문은 「접속사+주어+동사」 형태의 부사절을 분사(동사원형+-ing)를 이용해 간단하게 만든 구문이다.

1. 분사구문 만드는 방법

When I was walking down the street, I met an old friend of mine.

　　① 　② 　　③

➡ **Walking** down the street, I met an old friend of mine.
길을 걸어가고 있을 때 나는 오랜 친구를 만났다.

① 부사절의 접속사를 생략한다.
② 부사절의 주어와 주절의 주어가 같을 경우 부사절의 주어 생략한다.
③ 부사절의 동사를 「동사+-ing」 형태로 바꾼다.

2. 분사구문의 의미

(1) 동시동작 : as, and ~하면서

Drinking a cup of coffee, I watched the movie. 커피를 마시면서 나는 영화를 보았다.
➡ As I was drinking a cup of coffee, I watched the movie.

(2) 시간 : when ~할 때 **while** ~하는 동안 **before** ~ 전에 **after** ~ 후에

Seeing me, she smiled and waved at me.
그녀가 나를 보았을 때, 그녀는 나에게 미소를 짓고 손을 흔들었다.
➡ When she saw me, she smiled and waved at me.

(3) 이유 : because, as, since ~이기 때문에

Feeling tired, she went home early. 피곤해서 그녀는 일찍 집에 갔다.
➡ Because she felt tired, she went home early.

(4) 조건 : if 만약 ~라면

Hurrying now, you can catch the train. 지금 서두르면 너는 기차를 탈 수 있다.
➡ If you hurry now, you can catch the train.

(5) 양보 : although, though, even though 비록 ~이지만, ~임에도 불구하고

(Although) **Living** alone, I don't feel lonely. 나는 혼자 살지만 외롭지 않다.
➡ Although I live alone, I don't feel lonely.

Plus α

분사구문의 부정은 분사 앞에 not 또는 never를 쓴다.

Not knowing what to do, he asked her for advice.
그는 무엇을 해야 할지 몰라서 그녀에게 조언을 부탁했다.

Plus α

「with+명사+분사」
'~한 채로', '~하면서'라는 의미로 동시동작을 나타낸다.

Jason was sitting on the chair **with his legs crossed**.
Jason은 다리를 꼰 채로 의자에 앉아 있었다.

She listened to me **with her eyes shining**.
그녀는 눈을 반짝거리면서 내 이야기를 들었다.

Check-up 우리말과 같은 뜻이 되도록 ☐ 안에서 알맞은 것을 고르시오.

1 그녀는 그 소식을 듣고 기쁨으로 미소를 지었다.

→ Hearing / Heard the news, she smiled with joy.

2 John은 열심히 일했지만, 여전히 그 일을 끝마칠 수 없었다.

→ Work / Working hard, John still couldn't finish the work.

3 나는 지갑을 잃어버려서 그녀에게 점심을 사줄 수 없었다.

→ To lose / Losing my wallet, I couldn't buy her lunch.

: EXERCISES

Answers / p.30

A [   ] 안에서 알맞은 것을 고르시오.

1 Jean hurt her leg [playing / played] tennis.

2 [Worn / Wearing] this dress, you will look beautiful.

3 [Look / Looking] out the window, she saw the sun rising.

4 [Being / Been] an outsider, I don't know much about their culture.

look out 밖을 보다
outsider 몡 외부인, 제3자
culture 몡 문화

B 두 문장의 의미가 통하도록 분사구문을 이용하여 문장을 완성하시오.

1 When he saw a dog, he ran away from it.

→ _____, he ran away from it.

2 Because she was sick, she didn't go to school.

→ _____, she didn't go to school.

3 If you take this train, you will arrive in Paris at five.

→ _____, you will arrive in Paris at five.

run away (from)
(~에서) 달아나다
arrive 몽 도착하다

C 주어진 접속사를 이용하여 두 문장의 의미가 통하도록 부사절을 완성하시오.

1 Being poor, they are always happy. (although)

→ _____, they are always happy.

2 Saving the file, she turned off the computer. (after)

→ _____, she turned off the computer.

3 Singing and dancing, we had a great time at the party. (as)

→ _____, we had a great time at the party.

save
몽 저장하다; 저축하다
turn off 끄다

D 우리말과 같은 뜻이 되도록 주어진 단어를 이용하여 분사구문을 완성하시오.

1 오른쪽으로 돌면 시청이 보일 거예요. (turn, right)

→ _____ _____, you will find the city hall.

2 그녀를 기다리는 동안 나는 잡지를 읽었다. (wait for)

→ _____ _____ _____, I read a magazine.

3 할 일이 없었기 때문에 나는 하루 종일 심심했다. (have, nothing to do)

→ _____ _____ _____ _____, I felt bored all day.

4 작지만 그 방은 쾌적하고 편안하다. (be, small)

→ _____ _____, the room is pleasant and comfortable.

: Review Test

[01-03] 빈칸에 들어갈 알맞은 말을 고르시오.

01 She is trying to soothe her _____ baby.

① cry ② cries ③ crying
④ cried ⑤ to cry

02 They found a box _____ with gold and jewels.

① fill ② fills ③ filled
④ filling ⑤ to fill

03 _____ close to his school, he is on time.

① Live ② Lives ③ Lived
④ Living ⑤ To live

[04-05] 빈칸에 들어갈 말이 바르게 짝지어진 것을 고르시오.

04 The news is really _____. They will be _____ to hear it.

① surprise – shock
② surprised – shocked
③ surprised – shocking
④ surprising – shocked
⑤ surprising – shocking

05 History class is _____ because I'm not _____ in history.

① bored – interesting
② bore – interested
③ boring – interesting
④ boring – interested
⑤ boring – interest

[06-07] 밑줄 친 부분을 분사구문으로 바꿔 쓸 때 가장 알맞은 것을 고르시오.

06 Because I got up late, I missed my school bus.

① Get up late
② Got up late
③ To get up late
④ Getting up late
⑤ Being got up late

07 As he drove along the coast, he enjoyed the beautiful view.

① Drive along the coast
② Drove along the coast
③ To drive along the coast
④ Driving along the coast
⑤ Being driving along the coast

[08-09] 밑줄 친 부분을 부사구로 바꿔 쓸 때 가장 알맞은 것을 고르시오.

08 Dressing warmly, she still felt cold.

① Since she dressed warmly
② As she dressed warmly
③ When she dressed warmly
④ Though she dressed warmly
⑤ Because she dressed warmly

09 Taking this bus, you can get to the central station.

① If you take this bus
② As you take this bus
③ While you take this bus
④ Though you take this bus
⑤ Because you take this bus

[10-11] 밑줄 친 부분의 쓰임이 나머지와 <u>다른</u> 것을 고르시오.

10 ① I saw a boy <u>stealing</u> my bike.

② Greg sat <u>watching</u> the sun setting.

③ Her job is <u>taking</u> care of sick people.

④ He is looking for his <u>missing</u> daughter.

⑤ Look at the monkey <u>swinging</u> in the tree.

11 ① <u>Being</u> tired, he finished work early.

② <u>Being</u> sick, she didn't go to see a doctor.

③ <u>Being</u> friendly, you will make a lot of friends.

④ <u>Being</u> beautiful, she is popular among boys in school.

⑤ <u>Being</u> thin looks good, but being healthy is better.

[12-13] 다음 중 어법상 <u>어색한</u> 것을 고르시오.

12 ① She felt bored with the movie.

② His idea sounds amazed to me.

③ The girl waiting for me over there is Lilly.

④ We saw dolphins jumping out of the water.

⑤ The jeans worn by Dennis are very expensive.

13 ① Knowing not the answer, he kept silent.

② Listening to classical music, she studied math.

③ Having no time, I can't go on a vacation this year.

④ Talking to Jacob, you will know he is a good person.

⑤ Being young, she knows how to help people in need.

[14-15] 글을 읽고, 물음에 답하시오.

(A) <u>When I saw a shooting star</u>, I quickly made a wish. I know it's just a superstition. I won't get ❶ <u>disappointing</u> even though my wish won't come true. Here are some more superstitions. To find a four-leaf clover is to find good luck. ❷ <u>Opening</u> an umbrella in the house will bring you bad luck. If you catch a ❸ <u>falling</u> leaf in autumn, you will not catch a cold all winter. If your right ear itches, someone is ❹ <u>speaking</u> well of you. Superstition may not be true, but these superstitions are ❺ <u>interesting</u> to know.

* superstition 미신

14 밑줄 친 (A)를 분사구문으로 바르게 옮긴 것은?

① See a shooting star

② Saw a shooting star

③ Seeing a shooting star

④ Seen a shooting star

⑤ Sees a shooting star

15 밑줄 친 ❶~❺ 중 어법상 바르지 <u>않은</u> 것은?

[01-02] 분사를 이용하여 두 문장을 한 문장으로 바꿔 쓰시오.

01 They have adopted a dog. It is called Aurora.

→ They have adopted a dog _____.

02 The man is my uncle, Jim. He is dancing with my sister.

→ The man _____ is my uncle, Jim.

[03-04] 두 문장의 의미가 통하도록 분사구문을 이용하여 문장을 완성하시오.

03 As she said hello, she sat next to me in class.

→ _____, she sat next to me in class.

04 Because I was surprised at the news, I couldn't say a word.

→ _____, I couldn't say a word.

[05-06] 어법상 <u>어색한</u> 부분을 찾아 바르게 고쳐 쓰시오.

05 His hobby is reading books writing in Spanish.

→ _____

06 Seeing the barked dog, the boy hid behind his mother.

→ _____

[07-08] 우리말과 같은 뜻이 되도록 주어진 단어를 배열하시오.

07 나는 전에 저기 서 있는 남자를 본 적이 있다. (standing, seen, the man, have, over there)

→ I _____ before.

08 시간은 충분했지만, 그는 보고서를 시간 내에 끝내지 못했다. (enough time, he, finish, couldn't, having)

→ _____ _____ his report in time.

[09-10] 주어진 단어와 분사를 이용하여 밑줄 친 우리말과 같은 뜻이 되도록 대화를 완성하시오.

A **09** <u>저기서 밝게 미소 짓고 있는 그 소녀는 누구니?</u>
B She is a new student, Kelly.
A What is she like?
B She is easygoing and friendly.
A Will you introduce me to her?
B Sure. **10** <u>그녀를 만나면 너는 그녀를 아주 좋아하게 될 거야.</u>

09 Who is _____ _____ over there? (smile, brightly)

10 If _____, you will like her very much. (meet)

Chapter 11

수동태

UNIT 01 능동태와 수동태

1. 능동태와 수동태

☆**능동태**: 주어가 동작이나 행위의 주체가 될 때 사용하며, 「주어+동사+목적어」의 형태로 '~가 …한다'라는 의미이다.

A lot of people **love** soccer. 많은 사람들이 축구를 사랑한다.

☆**수동태**: 주어가 동작이나 행위를 당하거나 영향을 받을 때 사용하며, 「be동사+p.p. (+by 행위자)」 의 형태로 '~가 …당하다, 받다, 되어진다'라는 의미이다.

Soccer **is loved by** a lot of people. 축구는 많은 사람들에 의해 사랑 받는다.

2. 「by + 행위자」 생략: 행위자가 일반인이거나 중요하지 않은 경우, 그리고 분명하지 않은 경우에는 「by+행위자」를 생략한다.

The Internet **is used** all over the world. 인터넷은 전 세계에서 사용된다.

The church **was built** in 1820. 그 교회는 1820년에 지어졌다.

His bag **was stolen** in the library. 그의 가방은 도서관에서 도둑맞았다.

3. 수동태의 시제

(1) 현재: 「am/are/is +p.p. (+by 행위자)」

Many people drink coffee. 많은 사람들이 커피를 마신다.
➡ Coffee **is drunk** by many people.

(2) 과거: 「was/were+p.p. (+by 행위자)」

Kate broke the window. Kate가 창문을 깼다.
➡ The window **was broken** by Kate.

(3) 미래: 「will+be+p.p. (+by 행위자)」

Michael Bay will direct the movie. Michael Bay가 그 영화를 감독할 것이다.
➡ The movie **will be directed** by Michael Bay.

(4) 진행: 「be동사+being+p.p. (+by 행위자)」

My grandmother is making a cheesecake. 우리 할머니는 치즈 케이크를 만들고 있다.
➡ A cheesecake **is being made** by my grandmother.

Check-up 우리말과 같은 뜻이 되도록 ☐ 안에서 알맞은 것을 고르시오.

1 이 웹사이트는 많은 사람들의 방문을 받는다.
→ This website visits / is visited by many people.

2 그 가방은 유명한 예술가에 의해 디자인되었다.
→ The bag designed / was designed by a famous artist.

3 우리 아버지가 그 벽을 페인트칠하고 있다.
→ My father is painting / is painted the walls.

: EXERCISES

Answers / p.32

A [ ] 안에서 알맞은 것을 고르시오.

1 Ruth [hit / was hit] by the ball.

2 This computer is [be used / being used] now.

3 Stephen King [writes / is written] horror novels.

4 Rosa [cleans / is cleaned by] the windows every week.

5 The next World Cup [will hold / will be held] in Korea.

horror
형 공포를 느끼게 하는

hold
동 열다, 개최하다; 잡다

B 밑줄 친 부분을 어법에 맞게 고쳐 쓰시오.

1 The city hall is <u>rebuilding</u> now.

2 The final game <u>will played</u> on Saturday.

3 The gate <u>is be locked</u> at 9 pm every day.

4 The picture <u>was paint</u> by Vincent van Gogh.

city hall 시청

rebuild
동 다시 세우다, 재건하다

final game 결승전

lock 동 잠기다, 잠그다

C 능동태 문장을 수동태 문장으로 바꿔 쓰시오.

1 Donald is driving a limousine.

→ A limousine _____ .

2 Jane will post the letter.

→ The letter _____ .

3 Many teenagers read this magazine.

→ This magazine _____ .

4 The Wright Brothers invented the airplane.

→ The airplane _____ .

limousine 명 리무진

post 동 발송하다, 부치다
명 우편물, 우편

teenager 명 십대

invent 동 발명하다

D 우리말과 같은 뜻이 되도록 주어진 단어를 이용하여 문장을 완성하시오.

1 이 커피는 코스타리카에서 재배된다. (grow)

→ This coffee _____ _____ in Costa Rica.

2 'Imagine'이라는 노래는 John Lennon에 의해 작곡되었다. (compose)

→ The song 'Imagine' _____ _____ _____ John Lennon.

3 그 도둑은 곧 경찰에게 잡힐 것이다. (catch)

→ The thief _____ _____ _____ by the police soon.

4 그 복사기는 지금 수리 중입니다. (repair)

→ The photocopier _____ _____ _____ now.

여러 가지 수동태

1. 수동태의 부정문과 의문문

(1) 부정문: 「be동사+not+p.p. (+by 행위자)」

The room **was not cleaned** by Alex. 그 방은 Alex가 청소한 것이 아니다.

(2) 의문문: 「be동사+주어+p.p. (+by 행위자) ~?」

Are oranges **grown** in California? California에서 오렌지가 재배되나요?

2. 조동사 수동태: 「조동사+be+p.p. (+by 행위자)」

The construction **should be finished** by late April. 그 공사는 4월 말까지 끝나야 한다.

Smoking **must not be allowed** in public places. 흡연은 공공장소에서 허용되어서는 안 된다.

3. 4문형 수동태와 5문형 수동태

(1) 4문형 수동태: 목적어가 두 개인 4문형은 두 가지의 수동태 문장을 만들 수 있다. 직접목적어를 주어로 수동태 문장을 만들 경우 간접목적어 앞에 전치사를 쓴다.

Jim gave her a box of chocolate. Jim이 그녀에게 초콜릿 한 상자를 주었다.
　　　　간접목적어　　　직접목적어

→ **A box of chocolate** was given **to** her by Jim. [직접목적어가 주어]

→ **She** was given a box of chocolate by Jim. [간접목적어가 주어]

(2) 5문형 수동태: 목적어가 수동태 문장의 주어가 되며 목적격보어는 그대로 쓴다.

Her friends call **her** Queen Bee. 그녀의 친구들은 그녀를 여왕벌이라고 부른다.

→ **She** is called Queen Bee by her friends.

My parents allowed **me** to keep a pet. 우리 부모님은 내가 애완동물 기르는 것을 허락하셨다.

→ I was allowed to keep a pet by my parents.

Tips

간접목적어 앞에 쓰는 전치사

- **to**: give, show, bring, send, lend, tell, teach 등 대부분의 동사
- **for**: buy, get, make, cook 등
- **of**: ask

Plus α

☆ 지각동사, 사역동사 문장의 수동태:
목적격보어가 분사인 경우는 그대로 쓰고, 동사원형인 경우 to부정사로 바꿔 쓴다. 지각동사 문장의 경우 현재분사로도 바꿔 쓸 수 있다.

My sister always makes me **laugh**.
➜ I am always made to laugh by my sister.
내 여동생은 나를 항상 웃게 만든다.

Ethan saw a stranger **talk** to Jane.
➜ A stranger was seen to talk[talking] to her by Ethan.
Ethan은 낯선 사람이 Jane에게 말을 거는 것을 보았다.

Check-up 　우리말과 같은 뜻이 되도록 [　] 안에서 알맞은 것을 고르시오.

1 그 책은 영어로 쓰이지 않았다.

　→ The book | was not written / did not be written | in English.

2 이웃사람이 경찰을 불렀을지도 모른다.

　→ The police | be might called / might be called | by the neighbor.

3 그 멋진 스웨터는 우리 할머니가 나에게 만들어 준 것이다.

　→ The nice sweater was made | for / to | me by my grandmother.

4 아이들이 웃는 소리가 들렸다.

　→ The children were heard | laugh / to laugh |.

: EXERCISES

A [   ] 안에서 알맞은 것을 고르시오.

1 [Does / Is] this coat made in Korea?

2 Pets [did not / are not] allowed in the hotel.

3 Rick was asked [to be / be] quiet by his teacher.

4 The report [must finished / must be finished] by Friday.

5 A bunch of flowers was sent [for / to] her by a stranger.

allow
(동) 허용하다, 허락하다
bunch (명) 다발, 묶음

B 밑줄 친 부분을 어법에 맞게 고쳐 쓰시오.

1 Passengers will <u>serve</u> beverages.

2 The letter was written <u>for</u> me.

3 The picture <u>did</u> not painted by Picasso.

4 She was seen <u>talk</u> on the phone.

passenger (명) 승객
beverage (명) 음료

C 능동태 문장을 수동태 문장으로 바꿔 쓰시오.

1 Greg didn't tell the lie.

→ The lie _____ .

2 Drivers must obey traffic laws.

→ Traffic laws _____ .

3 Mr. Roy teaches us science.

→ Science _____ .

→ We _____ .

4 The boy found the gift box empty.

→ The gift box _____ .

driver (명) 운전자
obey
(동) (법 등을) 따르다; 복종하다
traffic (명) 교통
empty (형) 빈

D 우리말과 같은 뜻이 되도록 주어진 단어를 이용하여 문장을 완성하시오.

1 나에게 장학금이 수여되었다. (give)

→ A scholarship _____ _____ _____ me.

2 어제 내 비행기는 지연되지 않았다. (delay)

→ My flight _____ _____ _____ yesterday.

3 그 결과가 내일 발표될 것이다. (announce)

→ The result _____ _____ _____ tomorrow.

4 나는 의사에게 운동을 권유 받았다. (advise, exercise)

→ I _____ _____ _____ _____ by the doctor.

UNIT 03 주의해야 할 수동태

1. 동사구 수동태: 동사구는 하나의 동사로 취급한다.

She will **take care of** my cat while I'm away. 내가 없는 동안 그녀가 고양이를 돌봐줄 것이다.
➡ My cat will **be taken care of** by her while I'm away.

A lot of people **look up to** Nelson Mandela. 많은 사람들이 Nelson Mandela를 존경한다.
➡ Nelson Mandela **is looked up to** by a lot of people.

2. 수동태로 쓰지 않는 동사

(1) happen, appear, disappear, seem, look 등 목적어를 갖지 않는 자동사

The sun **appeared** over the horizon. 태양이 지평선 위로 나타났다.
(X) The sun ~~was appeared~~ over the horizon.

(2) have, resemble, cost, belong to 등과 같이 소유나 상태를 나타내는 동사

Edward **resembles** his father in many ways. Edward는 많은 면에서 그의 아버지와 닮았다.
(X) His father ~~is resembled by~~ Edward in many ways.

3. by 이외의 전치사를 이용하는 수동태: 대개 「by+행위자」로 나타내지만, by 이외의 전치사를 쓰는 경우도 있다.

be covered with[in] ~로 덮여 있다	be known to+명사 ~에게 알려지다
be interested in ~에 흥미가 있다	be known to+동사원형 ~로 알려져 있다
be pleased with ~로 기뻐하다	be known as ~로서 알려져 있다
be satisfied with ~에 만족하다	be known for ~로 유명하다
be filled with[be full of] ~로 가득 차다	be known by ~로 알 수 있다
be surprised at ~에 놀라다	be made of ~로 만들어지다(재료의 물리적 변화)
be worried about ~을 걱정하다	be made from ~로 만들어지다(재료의 화학적 변화)
be tired of ~에 싫증나다	be disappointed with[in, at, about] ~에 실망하다
be tired from ~ 때문에 지치다	

Her good deed **was known to** the whole world. 그녀의 선행은 온 세상에 알려졌다.
I **am satisfied with** my exam results. 나는 내 시험 결과에 만족한다.

Check-up 우리말과 같은 뜻이 되도록 ☐ 안에서 알맞은 것을 고르시오.

1 그 발명가는 사람들에게 비웃음을 샀다.
→ The inventor was ⏎laughed by / laughed at by⏎ people.

2 탁자 위에 있는 잔에 물이 채워져 있다.
→ The glass on the table is filled ⏎by / with⏎ water.

3 우리 할머니께서 내 꿈에 나타나셨다.
→ My grandmother ⏎appeared / was appeared⏎ in my dream.

: EXERCISES

A 밑줄 친 부분을 바르게 고치시오.

1 The meeting <u>was put off</u> the boss.

2 A strange thing <u>was happened</u> last night.

3 We <u>were surprised in</u> his unexpected visit.

4 A lot of animals <u>are run over</u> speeding cars.

strange 형 이상한; 낯선
unexpected
형 뜻밖의, 예기치 않은
visit 명 방문
speeding 형 과속의

B 보기 에서 알맞은 말을 골라 문장을 완성하시오. [한 번씩만 쓸 것]

| 보기 | in | with | about | of |

1 This shirt is made _____ cotton.

2 He is worried _____ his sick father.

3 All the furniture was covered _____ dust.

4 She is not really interested _____ pop music.

cotton 명 면
furniture 명 가구
dust 명 먼지
pop music 대중음악

C 능동태 문장을 수동태 문장으로 바꿔 쓰시오.

1 Emma will take care of my baby.

→ My baby _____ .

2 He looks down on his colleagues.

→ His colleagues _____ .

3 He asked for my personal information.

→ My personal information _____ .

colleague 명 동료
ask for ~에 대해 묻다
personal
형 개인적인, 개인의

D 우리말과 같은 뜻이 되도록 주어진 단어를 이용하여 문장을 완성하시오.

1 서재는 오래된 책들로 가득 차 있었다. (fill)

→ The study _____ _____ _____ old books.

2 비 때문에 콘서트가 연기되었다. (put off)

→ The concert _____ _____ _____ because of the rain.

3 우리는 그의 공연에 실망했다. (disappoint, with)

→ We _____ _____ _____ his performance.

4 Silvia는 조부모님에 의해 길러졌다. (bring up)

→ Silvia _____ _____ _____ _____ her grandparents.

: Review Test

[01-03] 빈칸에 들어갈 알맞은 말을 고르시오.

01 The newspaper is _____ every morning.

① deliver　　② delivers　　③ delivering
④ delivered　　⑤ to deliver

02 The cell phone was bought _____ me by my father.

① with　　② for　　③ by
④ of　　⑤ to

03 The girl was heard _____ the piano by him.

① play　　② plays　　③ to play
④ played　　⑤ being play

[04-05] 빈칸에 공통으로 들어갈 말로 알맞은 것을 고르시오.

04 · Mr. Smith is pleased _____ his students' performance.
· The room was filled _____ the aroma of green tea.

① to　　② at　　③ of
④ from　　⑤ with

05 · This song is known _____ people of all ages.
· A diamond ring was given _____ Mary.

① to　　② at　　③ of
④ from　　⑤ with

[06-07] 대화의 빈칸에 들어갈 말이 바르게 짝지어진 것을 고르시오.

06 A Wow, these pictures are great. Who took all the pictures?
B They were taken _____ my father. He is very interested _____ taking pictures.

① at – by　　② in – of　　③ by – in
④ with – of　　⑤ from – with

07 A Was the new bike bought _____ you by your parents?
B No. My aunt gave it to me for my birthday. I was very pleased _____ the gift.

① at – about　　② to – with　　③ by – from
④ of – by　　⑤ for – with

[08-09] 다음 중 어법상 어색한 것을 고르시오.

08 ① The secret must be kept by us.
② Harry is worried in his health.
③ He was seen to walk down the street.
④ The letter was written to him by Sarah.
⑤ The baseball stadium is being built now.

09 ① Does English spoken in South Africa?
② He was not expected to win the game.
③ My dog will be looked after by my neighbor.
④ The concert will be held on Friday.
⑤ A few questions were asked of me by the teacher.

[10-11] 우리말을 영어로 바르게 옮긴 것을 고르시오.

10 그 메시지는 엉뚱한 사람에게 보내졌다.

① The message was sent to the wrong person.
② The message was sent of the wrong person.
③ The message was sent for the wrong person.
④ The message sent the wrong person.
⑤ The message sent to the wrong person.

11 그녀는 젊은 과학자들에게 존경을 받는다.

① She looks up to young scientists.
② She looks up to by young scientists.
③ She is looked up by young scientists.
④ She is looked up to young scientists.
⑤ She is looked up to by young scientists.

12 다음 대화 중 자연스럽지 <u>않은</u> 것은?

① A Are you going to paint the house by yourself?
  B Yes, I am. It will be painted green.
② A Whose car is this? It looks expensive.
  B It is belonged to by my uncle.
③ A Was a gold medal given to the winner?
  B No. The winner received a trophy.
④ A Why didn't you come to Olivia's party?
  B I was not invited to it.
⑤ A I was advised to drink a lot of water by my doctor.
  B He's right. You should drink at least eight glasses of water a day.

13 다음 중 어법상 옳은 문장은?

① The puzzle will solve by Brian.
② Jake is resembled actor Jim Carrey.
③ The flowers didn't be watered by Peter.
④ Jonathan was not satisfied by his grade.
⑤ She was made to go to bed early last night.

[14-15] 글을 읽고, 물음에 답하시오.

Last night, my mother ❶ was surprised in the messy house. The floor ❷ was covered with dust and mud, and the sink ❸ was filled with dirty dishes. She cleaned the house, but we didn't help her. This morning, a family meeting ❹ was held by my mother. She said that she ❺ was disappointed with us, and she wanted us to share the housework. Now, the housework is divided up evenly. Mother will do all the cooking and the dishes. Father will vacuum the house and do the laundry. (A) I should take care of our pet dog and clean the bathroom.

14 밑줄 친 ❶~❺ 중 어법상 <u>어색한</u> 것은?

15 밑줄 친 (A)를 수동태 문장으로 바꾼 것 중 알맞은 것은?

① Our pet dog should take care of by me
② Our pet dog should take care by me
③ Our pet dog should be taken care by me
④ Our pet dog should be taken care of me
⑤ Our pet dog should be taken care of by me

: 서술형 평가

[01-02] 능동태 문장을 수동태 문장으로 바꿔 쓰시오.

01 My father is washing the car.

→ The car _____ .

02 I heard her singing on the stage.

→ She _____ .

[03-04] 우리말과 같은 뜻이 되도록 주어진 단어를 이용하여 문장을 완성하시오.

03 내 우산이 강한 바람에 의해 부러졌다.
(break, strong wind)

→ My umbrella _____

_____ .

04 James가 그 집에서 나오는 것이 목격되었다.
(see, come, out of)

→ James _____

_____ the house.

[05-06] 어법상 <u>어색한</u> 부분을 찾아 어법에 맞게 고쳐 쓰시오.

05 She was made wake up early in the morning.

→ _____

06 The rumor about the boss was told of me by Karen.

→ _____

[07-08] 우리말과 같은 뜻이 되도록 주어진 단어를 배열하시오.

07 등록비는 신용카드로 지불될 수 있다.
(be, can, credit card, by, paid)

→ The registration fee _____

_____ .

08 우리는 경기 결과에 실망했다.
(with, of the game, disappointed, were, the result)

→ We _____ .

09 밑줄 친 우리말과 같은 뜻이 되도록 주어진 단어를 이용하여 대화를 완성하시오.

> A (1) 영화 'Fantasy'가 곧 개봉될 거야. I have been looking forward to it.
> B I watched the preview of the movie. (2) 나는 뛰어난 컴퓨터 그래픽에 매우 깊은 인상을 받았어.
> A How come you went to the preview?
> B I applied for preview tickets, and I was chosen.
> A Really? You were lucky.

조건 수동태를 사용할 것

(1) The movie *Fantasy* _____ _____ _____ soon. (release)

(2) I _____ _____ _____ _____ the excellent computer graphics. (impress)

10 학교 교칙을 읽고, 의미가 통하도록 주어진 단어를 이용하여 문장을 완성하시오.

> **School Rules**
> · Be polite.
> · Be respectful.
> · Listen to others.
> · Look after things properly.
> (1) · Keep the school clean and tidy.
> (2) · Follow teachers' instructions.
> (3) · Do not use cell phones in class.

조건 수동태를 사용할 것

(1) The school _____

_____ . (should)

(2) Teachers' instructions _____

_____ by students. (must)

(3) Cell phones _____

_____ in class. (shouldn't)

Chapter 12

가정법, 일치, 화법

01 가정법 과거, 가정법 과거완료

1. 가정법 과거: 현재 사실을 반대로 가정하거나 실현 가능성이 없는 상황을 가정할 때 쓴다.

☆ 「If+주어+동사의 과거형, 주어+조동사의 과거형+동사원형」 만약 ~라면 …할 텐데

If you **were** here, we **would do** lots of things together.
네가 여기 있다면 우리는 많은 것을 함께 할 수 있을 텐데.

◀ As you aren't here, we don't do lots of things together.

If it **were** spring now, we **could see** a lot of flowers. 지금이 봄이라면 많은 꽃을 볼 수 있을 텐데.

◀ As it isn't spring now, we can't see a lot of flowers.

Tips

가정법의 if절에서 be동사는 주어의 인칭이나 수에 관계없이 were를 쓰지만, 구어체에서는 was를 쓰기도 한다.

If it **were[was]** sunny, we **could go** for a picnic.
날씨가 화창하면 우리는 소풍을 갈 수 있을 텐데.

> **Plus α**
>
> 1 단순 조건: 실현 가능성이 있음을 나타낸다.
>   **If** you **leave** now, you **can catch** the train. 지금 떠나면, 기차를 탈 수 있을 거야.
>
> 2 가정법 과거: 실현 가능성이 없는 상황이나 현재 사실의 반대를 가정한다.
>   **If** you **left** now, you **could catch** the train. 지금 떠난다면, 그 기차를 탈 수 있을 텐데.

2. 가정법 과거완료: 과거 사실을 반대로 가정할 때 쓴다.

☆ 「If+주어+had p.p., 주어+조동사의 과거형+have p.p.」 만약 ~였다면 …했을 텐데

If you **had left** earlier, you **wouldn't have been** late.
네가 더 빨리 출발했더라면 늦지 않았을 텐데.

◀ As you didn't leave earlier, you were late.

If I **had studied** harder, I **could have gotten** a higher score.
내가 공부를 더 열심히 했더라면 더 높은 점수를 받았을 텐데.

◀ As I didn't study harder, I couldn't get a higher score.

Check-up 우리말과 같은 뜻이 되도록 ☐ 안에서 알맞은 것을 고르시오.

1 내가 너라면 그에게 진실을 말할 텐데.
→ If I [am / were] you, I would tell him the truth.

2 내가 시간이 있었다면 할머니께 전화를 했을 텐데.
→ If I [had / had had] time, I would have called my grandmother.

3 너에게 펜이 있으면 하나 빌려 줄래?
→ If you [have / had] a pen, can you lend me one?

: EXERCISES

A   [ ] 안에서 알맞은 것을 고르시오.

1   If I [go / went] to Paris, I will visit the Louvre.

2   If you are tired, you [can / could] go home and rest.

3   If Lisa knew your phone number, she [will / would] call you.

4   If you [had / had had] more time, I would have asked you to stay longer.

B   주어진 단어를 이용하여 문장을 완성하시오.

1   If it _____ sunny, we would go hiking. (be)

2   If your parents heard the news, they would _____ happy. (be)

3   If you _____ your best, you would have won the competition. (do)

4   If we _____ more money, we would have traveled around Europe. (have)

C   두 문장의 의미가 통하도록 문장을 완성하시오.

1   As I am not rich, I can't buy an expensive car.

    → If I _____ , I _____ .

2   As Jamie is not tall enough, he cannot ride a roller coaster.

    → If Jamie _____ , he _____ .

3   As I forgot your phone number, I couldn't call you.

    → If I _____ , I _____ .

D   우리말과 같은 뜻이 되도록 주어진 단어를 이용하여 문장을 완성하시오.

1   그들이 서둘렀다면, 비행기를 놓치지 않았을 텐데. (hurry, miss)

    → If they _____ _____ , they _____ _____ _____ the flight.

2   Henry가 책 읽는 것을 좋아한다면, 독서클럽에 가입할 텐데. (like, join)

    → If Henry _____ reading books, he _____ _____ the reading club.

3   내가 물을 무서워하지 않는다면, 너랑 수영하러 갈 텐데. (be afraid of, go swimming)

    → If I _____ _____ _____ water, I _____ _____ _____ with you.

I wish, as if

1. I wish

(1) 「I wish+가정법 과거」 ∼하면 좋을 텐데

: 현재에 이루기 힘든 소망이나 현재 사실에 대한 유감 등을 표현한다.

I wish I **had** a girlfriend. 나에게 여자 친구가 있다면 좋을 텐데.
← I'm sorry I don't have a girlfriend.
I wish my grandparents **were** alive. 우리 조부모님께서 살아계시면 좋을 텐데.
← I'm sorry my grandparents aren't alive.

(2) 「I wish+가정법 과거완료」 ∼했다면 좋을 텐데

: 과거에 이루지 못한 사실에 대한 유감 등을 표현한다.

I wish you **had passed** the test. 네가 시험에 통과했으면 좋을 텐데.
← I'm sorry you didn't pass the test.
I wish I **had bought** the tickets. 내가 그 표를 샀으면 좋을 텐데.
← I'm sorry I didn't buy the tickets.

2. as if [as though]

(1) 「as if+가정법 과거」 마치 ∼인 것처럼

: 현재 사실에 반대되는 내용을 가정한다.

He talks **as if** he **were** a doctor. 그는 마치 자신이 의사인 것처럼 말한다.
← In fact, he isn't a doctor.
James acts **as if** he **had** a girlfriend. James는 마치 여자 친구가 있는 것처럼 행동한다.
← In fact, he doesn't have a girlfriend.

(2) 「as if+가정법 과거완료」 마치 ∼했던 것처럼

: 과거 사실에 반대되는 내용을 가정한다.

She talks **as if** she **hadn't seen** me. 그녀는 마치 나를 보지 못했던 것처럼 말한다.
← In fact, she saw me.
He acts **as if** he **had heard** the story before. 그는 전에 그 이야기를 들었던 것처럼 행동한다.
← In fact, he didn't hear the story before.

Plus α

1 「as if+가정법 과거」
마치 ∼인 것처럼
[현재 사실에 대한 반대를 가정할 때 사용]

He talks **as if** he **knew** the truth.
그는 마치 진실을 아는 것처럼 말한다.
← In fact, he doesn't know the truth.

2 「as if+직설법 현재」
마치 ∼인 것처럼
[실제로 그런지 아닌지 모를 때 사용]

He talks **as if** he **knows** the truth.
그는 마치 진실을 아는 것처럼 말한다.
← We don't know whether he knows the truth or not.

Check-up 우리말과 같은 뜻이 되도록 ☐ 안에서 알맞은 것을 고르시오.

1 그가 여기 우리와 함께 있으면 좋을 텐데.
→ I wish he │ is / were │ here with us.

2 그가 밤새 게임을 하지 않았다면 좋을 텐데.
→ I wish he │ didn't play / hadn't played │ computer games all night.

3 그는 마치 답을 아는 것처럼 말하지만, 답을 모른다.
→ He talks as if he │ knows / knew │ the answer, but he doesn't.

: EXERCISES

Answers / p.35

A [ ] 안에서 알맞은 것을 고르시오.

1 I wish he [were / had been] in Korea now.

2 I wish I [bought / had bought] the skirt yesterday.

3 She acts as if she [lived / had lived] in New York, but she didn't.

4 He acts as if he [knew / had known] everything about me, but he doesn't.

buy 동 구매하다
skirt 명 치마
New York 뉴욕

B 주어진 단어를 이용하여 문장을 완성하시오.

1 I wish I _____ a sister or a brother. (have)

2 I wish I _____ how to ski when I was young. (learn)

3 He looks as if he _____ a ghost, but he didn't. (see)

4 She acts as if she _____ a middle school student, but she isn't. (be)

ski 동 스키 타다
ghost 명 귀신
middle school 중학교

C 두 문장의 의미가 통하도록 문장을 완성하시오.

1 I'm sorry today is Monday.
→ I wish today _____ .

2 I'm sorry I didn't bring an umbrella.
→ I wish I _____ .

3 In fact, Sue is not a millionaire.
→ Sue acts as if she _____ .

4 In fact, Jack hasn't traveled alone.
→ Jack talks as if he _____ .

Monday 명 월요일
bring 동 가져오다
umbrella 명 우산
millionaire 명 백만장자
alone 부 홀로

D 우리말과 같은 뜻이 되도록 주어진 단어를 이용하여 문장을 완성하시오.

1 나를 아기처럼 대하지 마세요. (as if, be)
→ Don't treat me _____ _____ _____ _____ a baby.

2 내가 고등학교 때 공부를 더 열심히 했다면 좋을 텐데. (wish, study)
→ I _____ _____ _____ _____ harder in high school.

3 내가 독일어를 유창하게 말할 수 있다면 좋을 텐데. (wish, can, speak)
→ I _____ _____ _____ _____ German fluently.

4 그들은 오랫동안 서로를 알아온 것처럼 행동하지만, 아니었다. (act, as if, know)
→ They _____ _____ _____ _____ _____ _____ each other for a long time, but they haven't.

UNIT 03 시제 일치

1. 시제 일치: 주절의 시제에 따라 종속절의 시제가 달라진다.

주절	종속절
현재	모든 시제
과거	과거, 과거완료

(1) 주절의 시제가 현재일 때, 종속절에는 모든 시제가 다 올 수 있다.

I **think** you **did** a good job. 나는 네가 잘했다고 생각해.

I **think** you **are doing** a good job. 나는 네가 잘하고 있다고 생각해.

I **think** you **will do** a good job. 나는 네가 잘할 거라고 생각해.

(2) 주절의 시제가 과거일 때, 종속절에는 주로 과거와 과거완료가 온다.

I **thought** you **were doing** a good job. 나는 네가 잘하고 있다고 생각했어.

I **thought** you **had done** a good job. 나는 네가 잘했다고 생각했어.

2. 시제 일치의 예외

(1) 일반적인 진리나 격언, 과학적인 사실은 항상 현재 시제로 쓴다.

The book **said** that water **boils** at 100℃. 그 책에는 물이 100도에서 끓는다고 쓰여 있었다.

My mother **told** me that action **speaks** louder than words.
우리 어머니가 나에게 말보다 행동이 중요하다고 말씀하셨다.

(2) 역사적 사실은 항상 과거 시제로 쓴다.

My teacher **said** that Hangul **was created** by Sejong the Great.
우리 선생님은 한글이 세종대왕에 의해 창제되었다고 말씀하셨다.

I **learned** that Leonardo da Vinci **painted** the *Last Supper*.
나는 Leonardo da Vinci가 「최후의 만찬」을 그렸다고 배웠다.

(3) 과거의 상황이나 행동이 현재에도 계속될 때는 현재와 과거 시제 모두 쓸 수 있다.

My sister **told** me that she **studies**[studied] art history nowadays.
내 여동생이 나에게 요즘 미술사 공부를 한다고 말했다.

Rebecca **said** her father **is**[was] a teacher. Rebecca는 자신의 아버지가 교사라고 말했다.

Plus α

과거에서 바라본 미래는 조동사 will의 과거 would를 사용하여 나타낸다.

She **thought** Joey **would come** back by eight.
그녀는 Joey가 여덟 시까지 돌아올 거라고 생각했다.

Tips

시간이나 조건이 부사절에서는 미래 시제 대신 현재 시제를 사용한다.

I **will call** you **when** I **get** there.
내가 그곳에 도착하면 전화할게.

Anne **will inform** us if she **has** a clue.
단서가 있으면 Anne이 우리에게 알려줄 거야.

> **Check-up** 우리말과 같은 뜻이 되도록 ☐ 안에서 알맞은 것을 고르시오.

1 나는 네가 Sally를 좋아하는 것을 알고 있어.

→ I know that you ⃞like / liked⃞ Sally.

2 나는 네가 Sally를 좋아했다는 것을 알고 있었어.

→ I knew that you ⃞like / liked⃞ Sally.

: EXERCISES

Answers / p.36

A   [ ] 안에서 알맞은 것을 고르시오.

1   We learned that the earth [is / was] round.

2   Rick thought that he [meets / had met] Carol before.

3   I believe that my daughter [goes / went] to the library last Friday.

4   My teacher told me Alfred Bernhard Nobel [invented / had invented] dynamite.

> the earth 지구
> round (형) 둥근
> invent (동) 발명하다
> dynamite (명) 다이너마이트

B   주어진 단어를 이용하여 문장을 완성하시오.

1   I'll tell him when he _____ back to the office. (come)

2   Do you know that the Korean War _____ in 1953? (end)

3   We knew that the World Cup _____ every four years. (take place)

4   Back then, people didn't believe that the earth _____ around the sun. (go)

> office (명) 사무실
> the Korean War 한국 전쟁
> the World Cup 월드컵
> back then 그때 당시에
> go around ~의 주위를 돌다

C   주절의 시제를 과거 시제로 바꿔 문장을 완성하시오.

1   We know that bad news travels fast.

    → We knew that bad news _____.

2   I think that I won't miss the shuttle bus.

    → I thought that I _____.

3   They say that they are glad to get the postcard.

    → They said that they _____.

4   Many people don't know World War I broke out in 1914.

    → Many people didn't know World War I _____.

> shuttle bus 순환버스
> World War I 제1차 세계대전
> break out 발발하다

D   우리말과 같은 뜻이 되도록 주어진 단어를 이용하여 문장을 완성하시오.

1   나는 네가 부지런한 학생이었다고 생각해. (think, be)

    → I _____ that you _____ a diligent student.

2   우리 할머니가 나에게 시간은 금이라고 말씀하셨다. (tell, be)

    → My grandmother _____ me that time _____ gold.

3   선생님은 아홉 시에 수업이 시작한다고 말씀하셨다. (say, start)

    → The teacher _____ that the class _____ at 9.

4   나는 Nelson Mandela가 2013년 12월 5일에 돌아가셨다고 들었다. (hear, pass away)

    → I _____ that Nelson Mandela _____ _____ on December 5, 2013.

1. 직접화법과 간접화법

☆ **직접화법**: 다른 사람의 말을 큰따옴표(" ")를 사용하여 그대로 전달하는 것

Kelly said, "I'm happy." Kelly가 "나는 행복해"라고 말했다.

☆ **간접화법**: 다른 사람의 말을 전달하는 사람의 입장에서 바꾸어 전달하는 것

Kelly **said (that) she was** happy. Kelly는 자신이 행복하다고 말했다.

2. 평서문의 화법 전환

Rick <u>said to me</u>, "<u>I</u> <u>am doing</u> <u>my</u> laundry <u>now</u>."
①   ②③ ④   ⑤   ⑤

➡ Rick **told me (that)** <u>**he was doing his**</u> laundry **then**.

    Rick은 내게 그때 빨래하는 중이었다고 말했다.

① 전달동사를 적절하게 바꿔 준다. (say → say, said to → said to / told)

② 쉼표(,)와 큰따옴표(" ")를 생략하고 접속사 that을 쓴다. (이때 that은 생략 가능하다.)

③ that절의 주어를 전달자에 따라 적절하게 바꿔 준다.

④ that절의 동사를 전달 동사에 따라 적절하게 바꿔 준다.

⑤ that절의 대명사와 부사를 적절하게 바꿔 준다.

Tips 〈화법 전환 시 함께 바뀌는 부사와 지시대명사〉

직접화법　　→　　간접화법

ago → before	this → that	next~ → the following~
these → those	today → that day	last~ → the previous ~
now → then[at that time]	yesterday → the day before [the previous day]	
here → there[the following day]	tomorrow → the next day[the following day]	

Tips

화법 전환 시 시제 변경: 전달동사가 현재일 때는 그대로 쓰고, 과거일 때는 과거 또는 과거완료로 바꿔 준다.

Paul **says**, "I **miss** you."
➡ Paul **says** that he **misses** me.
  Paul은 나를 보고 싶다고 말한다.

Paul **said**, "I **missed** you."
➡ Paul **said** that he **(had) missed** me.
  Paul은 나를 보고 싶었다고 말했다.

3. 의문문의 화법 전환

(1) 의문사가 있는 경우: 전달동사를 ask로 바꾸고, 「의문사+주어+동사」 어순으로 쓴다.

Julia **said to** me, "**What is this**?"
➡ Julia **asked** me **what that was.** Julia가 나에게 그것이 무엇이냐고 물었다.

(2) 의문사가 없는 경우: 전달동사를 ask로 바꾸고, 「if/whether +주어+동사」 어순으로 쓴다.

Nick **said to** me, "**Are you ready**?"
➡ Nick **asked** me if / whether I was ready. Nick이 나에게 준비가 되었는지 물었다.

Check-up　우리말과 같은 뜻이 되도록 ☐ 안에서 알맞은 것을 고르시오.

1 Chris는 다이어트 중이라고 말했다.

  → Chris said, "I am / was on a diet."

2 Laura는 나에게 Tom을 봤다고 말했다.

  → Laura told me that she sees / saw Tom.

: EXERCISES

A   [ ] 안에서 알맞은 것을 고르시오.

1   Greg told me that I [look / looked] tired at that time.

2   David asked me [if / that] I bought the school uniform.

3   Daniel asked her when [did she arrive / she arrived] there.

4   Alice said that she [moves / moved] to California in 1997.

tired ⑧ 피곤한

school uniform 교복

move to ~로 이주하다

B   직접화법 문장을 간접화법 문장으로 바꿔 쓰시오.

1   Fred said, "I'm heading downtown."

    → Fred said _____ .

2   Ron said to me, "What did you bring for the party?"

    → Ron asked me _____ .

3   Thomas said to me, "Will you stay home today?"

    → Thomas asked me _____ .

head ⑧ 향하다

downtown ⑨ 시내로, 번화가에

stay home 집에 머무르다

C   남겨진 메시지를 전달하는 문장을 완성하시오.

> 1   "I got your message." - Anne
> 2   "I will be back in an hour." - Mark
> 3   "Can you stop by?" - Sally

1   Anne told me _____ my message.

2   Mark told me _____ in an hour.

3   Sally asked me _____ .

get one's message
~의 메시지를 받다

be back 돌아오다

stop by 들르다

D   우리말과 같은 뜻이 되도록 주어진 단어를 배열하시오.

1   나는 그에게 어디에 갔었냐고 물었다. (where, been, asked, he, him, had)

    → I _____ .

2   Eric은 내게 그 스카프가 내 것이냐고 물었다. (if, was, me, mine, the scarf, asked)

    → Eric _____ .

3   Sarah는 그날 나를 방문할 거라고 말했다. (that, that day, would, said, me, she, visit)

    → Sarah _____ .

4   Rachel은 그때 도서관에 가는 중이라고 말했다.
    (then, she, told, was going to, that, the library, me)

    → Rachel _____ .

[01-03] 빈칸에 들어갈 알맞은 말을 고르시오.

01

If I _____ rich, I would study abroad.

① am　　　　② be　　　　③ have been
④ were　　　⑤ had been

02

I wish I _____ the contest, but I didn't.

① win　　　　② won　　　　③ had won
④ will win　　⑤ have won

03

He said that Jane Austen _____ *Emma*.

① writes　　　② wrote　　　③ has written
④ had written　⑤ was writing

[04-05] 대화의 빈칸에 들어갈 알맞은 말을 고르시오.

04

A Why don't we go shopping tonight?
B I'd love to, but I'm too busy. If I _____ time, I would go with you.

① have　　　　② had　　　　③ would have
④ have had　　⑤ had had

05

A I'm sorry that the Dodgers lost.
B If it _____ a home game, the Dodgers would have won.

① is　　　　　② were　　　　③ have been
④ had been　　⑤ would have been

06 빈칸에 공통으로 들어갈 알맞은 말은?

· Jay asked _____ you would come to see her.
· _____ you had done your best, you would have passed the test.

① that　　　　② if　　　　③ what
④ whether　　⑤ when

07 문장의 빈칸에 들어갈 알맞은 표현은?

If I see her, I _____.

① will send your love to her
② could have brought her
③ had gone with her
④ would give her a hug
⑤ would have said to thank you for coming

[08-09] 우리말을 영어로 바르게 옮긴 것을 고르시오.

08 나는 10 더하기 10이 20이라는 것을 배웠다.

① I learn that 10 and 10 makes 20.
② I learn that 10 and 10 made 20.
③ I learned that 10 and 10 made 20.
④ I learned that 10 and 10 makes 20.
⑤ I learned that 10 and 10 had made 20.

09 그가 아프지 않다면 우리와 함께 등산할 수 있을 텐데.

① If he is not sick, he could go hiking with us.
② If he were not sick, he could go hiking with us.
③ If he has not been sick, he could go hiking with us.
④ If he had not been sick, he could have gone hiking with us.
⑤ If he had not been sick, he could go hiking with us.

10 두 문장의 뜻이 통하도록 빈칸에 들어갈 말이 바르게 짝지어진 것은?

> As he didn't visit me, I couldn't give him the book.
> → If he _____ me, I _____ him the book.

① visit - could give

② visited - could have given

③ visited - gave

④ had visited - could give

⑤ had visited - could have given

11 다음 두 문장의 의미가 서로 <u>다른</u> 것은?

① If I had her phone number, I could call her.
  → As I don't have her phone number, I cannot call her.

② If you hadn't brought your umbrella, you would have been wet.
  → As you didn't bring your umbrella, you were wet.

③ If he were not rich, he could not buy a car.
  → He is rich, so he can buy a car.

④ If I hadn't been too busy, I would have hung out with them.
  → As I was too busy, I didn't hang out with them.

⑤ If she knew about it, she would tell me.
  → She doesn't know about it, so she doesn't tell me.

12 다음 문장 중 어법상 <u>어색한</u> 것은?

① George asked her if she enjoyed learning Spanish.

② She told me she couldn't sleep at all.

③ Joan asked me whether did I finish reading the book.

④ Tom asked me who I was dating.

⑤ Jen told me that she wanted to see me.

13 빈칸에 들어갈 말이 바르게 짝지어진 것은?

> I live in Seoul, and my cousin lives in New York. If we _____ closer, we _____ each other more often.

① live – can see

② live – could see

③ lived – could see

④ lived – can see

⑤ had lived – could have seen

[14-15] 글을 읽고, 물음에 답하시오.

It was sunny and bright. The wind was blowing softly. I was sitting in the sun with my eyes closed. My pet dog, Lucky, was sitting next to me. Suddenly, I heard my mom ❶ call my name. I realized that today ❷ was house cleaning day. Yesterday, my mom told us that we ❸ would clean the whole house and clean our own bedrooms. And she also asked me ❹ that I would clean the garage. Now, I have to clean my room and the garage. I envy Lucky very much. (A) 만약 내가 Lucky라면, 어떤 것도 청소하지 않을 텐데. I'd better start cleaning before my mother ❺ finds me.

14 밑줄 친 ❶~❺ 중 어법상 <u>어색한</u> 것은?

15 밑줄 친 (A)를 바르게 영작한 것은?

① If I am Lucky, I won't clean anything.

② If I were Lucky, I won't clean anything.

③ If I were Lucky, I wouldn't clean anything.

④ If I had been Lucky, I wouldn't clean anything.

⑤ If I had been Lucky, I wouldn't have cleaned anything.

[01-02] 우리말과 같은 뜻이 되도록 주어진 단어를 이용하여 문장을 완성하시오.

01 내가 러시아어를 유창하게 할 수 있으면 좋을 텐데.
(wish, can, speak)

→ I _____
Russian fluently.

02 네가 좀 더 일찍 말했으면 네 숙제를 도와줄 수 있었을 텐데. (tell, can, help)

→ If you _____ me earlier,
I _____ you with
your homework.

03 두 문장의 의미가 통하도록 가정법 문장을 완성하시오.

(1) He didn't try hard, so he didn't reach his goal.
→ If he _____,
he _____.

(2) As I don't live near my grandparents, I can't visit them often.
→ If I _____,
I _____.

(3) I'm sorry that you didn't win first prize.
→ I wish you _____.

(4) In fact, he is not a reporter.
→ He acts as if he _____.

04 대화의 빈칸에 알맞은 말을 써 넣으시오.

A Who called while I was out?
B It was John. He asked me _____
you had invited Kelly to the party.

05 밑줄 친 (a), (b), (c)를 어법에 맞게 바꿔 쓰시오.

· If I (a) (have) wings like a bird, I would fly everywhere.
· If I miss the last train, I (b) (will, take) a taxi.
· I miss you a lot. I wish you (c) (be) here with us.

(a) _____ (b) _____ (c) _____

[06-07] 두 문장의 의미가 통하도록 간접화법 문장을 완성하시오.

06 Tom said, "I am behind my schedule."

→ Tom said _____
_____.

07 The clerk said to me, "Which color do you like better?"

→ The clerk asked me _____
_____.

[08-10] 보기 에서 알맞은 말을 골라 우리말과 같은 뜻이 되도록 문장을 완성하시오.

보기   break out   freeze   go

08 나는 물이 0℃ 이하에서 언다고 배웠다.

→ I learned that water _____
below zero.

09 그는 나에게 매일 아침 산책을 간다고 말했다.

→ He told me that he _____ for
a walk every morning.

10 우리 선생님이 우리에게 세계 2차 대전이 1939년에 발발했다고 말했다.

→ My teacher told us that the Second World
War _____ in 1939.

이것이 THIS IS 시리즈다!

THIS IS GRAMMAR 시리즈

▷ 중·고등 내신에 꼭 등장하는 어법 포인트 분석 및 총정리

강남인강
강의교재

THIS IS READING 시리즈

▷ 다양한 소재의 지문으로 내신 및 수능 완벽 대비

강남인강
강의교재

THIS IS VOCABULARY 시리즈

▷ 주제별로 분류한 교육부 권장 어휘

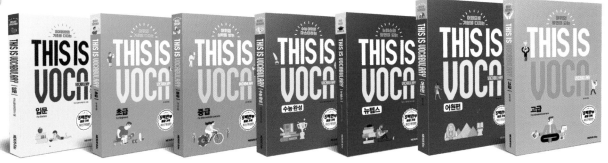

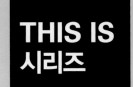
THIS IS GRAMMAR 시리즈
Starter 1~3   영어교육연구소 지음 | 205×265 | 144쪽 | 각 권 12,000원
초·중·고급 1·2   넥서스영어교육연구소 지음 | 205×265 | 250쪽 내외 | 각 권 12,000원

THIS IS READING 시리즈
Starter 1~3   김태연 지음 | 205×265 | 156쪽 | 각 권 12,000원
1·2·3·4   넥서스영어교육연구소 지음 | 205×265 | 192쪽 내외 | 각 권 10,000원~13,000원

THIS IS VOCABULARY 시리즈
입문   넥서스영어교육연구소 지음 | 152×225 | 224쪽 | 10,000원
초·중·고급·어원편   권기하 지음 | 152×225 | 180×257 | 344쪽~444쪽 | 10,000원~12,000원
수능 완성   넥서스영어교육연구소 지음 | 152×225 | 280쪽 | 12,000원
뉴텝스   넥서스 TEPS연구소 지음 | 152×225 | 452쪽 | 13,800원

LEVEL CHART

	초1	초2	초3	초4	초5	초6	중1	중2	중3	고1	고2	고3

VOCA

초등필수 영단어
1–2 · 3–4 · 5–6학년용

The VOCA + (플러스) 1~7

THIS IS VOCABULARY
입문 · 초급 · 중급

THIS IS 고급 · 어원 · 수능 완성 · 뉴텝스

WORD FOCUS
중등 종합 5000 · 고등 필수 5000 · 고등 종합 9500

Grammar

초등필수 영문법 + 쓰기
1~2

OK Grammar 1~4

This Is Grammar Starter
1~3

This Is Grammar
초급~고급 (각 2권: 총 6권)

Grammar 공감 1~3

Grammar 101 1~3

Grammar Bridge 1~3 (NEW EDITION)

The Grammar Starter, 1~3

한 권으로 끝내는 필수 구문 1000제

구사일생
(구문독해 Basic) 1~2

구문독해 204 1~2 (개정판)

고난도 구문독해 500

그래머 캡처 1~2

[특급 단기 특강]
어법어휘 모의고사

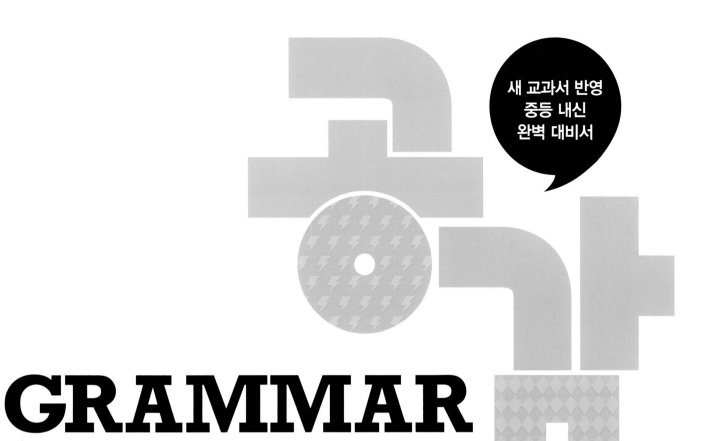

GRAMMAR

넥서스영어교육연구소 지음

Workbook

Level 2

NEXUS Edu

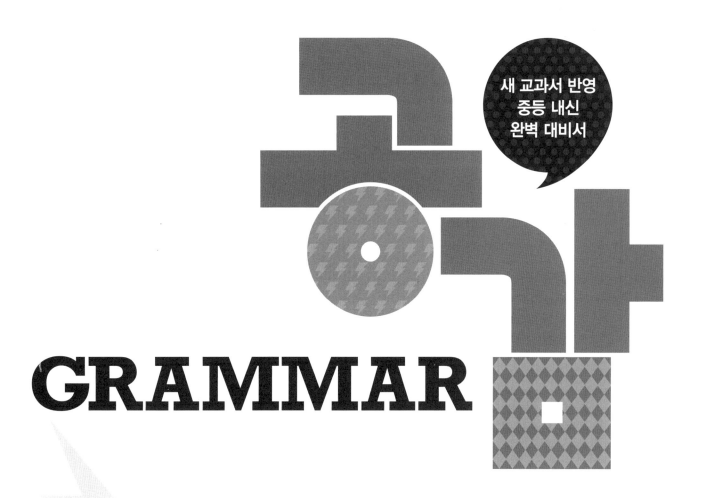

GRAMMAR

Workbook

Level 2

NEXUS Edu

UNIT 01 감각동사, 수여동사

A 보기 에서 동사를 골라 어법에 맞게 고쳐 쓰시오.

| 보기 | taste | smell | sound | feel |

1 Lavender _____ great.

2 This fabric _____ rough.

3 This medicine _____ bitter.

4 Your voice _____ strange over the phone.

B 보기 에서 알맞은 단어를 골라 문장을 완성하시오.

| 보기 | sweet | my English teacher | chocolate | generous |

1 This tea tastes like _____.

2 The old lady looks _____.

3 All kinds of candies taste _____.

4 The man looks like _____.

C 두 문장이 같은 뜻이 되도록 문장을 완성하시오.

1 Can you lend me a red pen?

→ Can you lend a red pen _____ _____?

2 She will bring us some food.

→ She will bring some food _____ _____.

3 I would like to ask a favor of you.

→ I would like to ask _____ _____ _____.

4 Will you get me a glass of warm water?

→ Will you get a glass of warm water _____ _____?

5 Mrs. Brown teaches basic dance steps to us.

→ Mrs. Brown teaches _____ _____ _____ _____.

6 Paul bought his girlfriend a white shirt.

→ Paul bought a white shirt _____ _____ _____.

7 My mom always makes a healthy meal for us.

→ My mom always makes _____ _____ _____.

D 우리말과 같은 뜻이 되도록 주어진 단어를 이용하여 문장을 완성하시오.

1 그 영화는 재미있어 보인다. (interesting)

→ The movie _____ _____ .

2 그들은 친절한 사람들처럼 보인다. (kind)

→ They _____ _____ _____ _____ .

3 그 진주목걸이는 진짜 같아 보인다. (real)

→ The pearl necklace _____ _____ .

4 이 식당의 스테이크는 맛이 좋다. (good)

→ The steak in this restaurant _____ _____ .

5 그녀는 나에게 요리하는 방법을 가르쳐 주었다. (teach)

→ She _____ _____ how to cook.

6 선생님이 그에게 어려운 질문을 했다. (ask, difficult, question)

→ The teacher _____ _____ _____ _____ .

7 Linda는 그녀의 반 친구들에게 카드를 만들어 주었다. (make, cards, her classmates)

→ Linda _____ _____ _____ _____ _____ .

E 우리말과 같은 뜻이 되도록 주어진 단어를 배열하시오.

1 이 샴푸는 복숭아 향이 난다. (smells, peaches, like)

→ This shampoo _____ .

2 이 담요는 아주 부드러운 느낌이 난다. (soft, really, feels)

→ This blanket _____ .

3 Louise는 나에게 좋은 조언을 해 주었다. (advice, me, gave, good)

→ Louise _____ .

4 그녀는 어린 소녀처럼 보였다. (looked, young, a, like, girl)

→ She _____ .

5 Ross가 나에게 내 전화번호를 물었다. (me, my phone number, asked)

→ Ross _____ .

6 그녀는 책 몇 권을 자신의 친구에게 빌려 주었다. (her friend, books, some, lent, to)

→ She _____ .

7 우리 할머니는 종종 나에게 자신의 그림들을 보여 주신다. (often, her, me, shows, paintings)

→ My grandmother _____ .

3

동사＋목적어＋명사/형용사/to부정사

A 보기 에서 알맞은 말을 골라 문장을 완성하시오.

> 보기   successful   a genius   warm   the new class president

1 His friends call him _____.

2 Students elected Herriot _____.

3 His honesty and diligence made him _____.

4 These gloves will keep your hands _____ in cold weather.

B 보기 에서 알맞은 동사를 골라 어법에 맞게 고쳐 쓰시오.

> 보기   sit down   taste   buy   do

1 I asked Jonathan _____ a little Kimchi.

2 What do you want me _____ at the market?

3 Mom told me _____ my homework before dinner.

4 He ordered Jeff _____ and keep calm in class.

C 밑줄 친 부분을 어법에 맞게 고쳐 쓰시오.

1 A good diet keeps you <u>healthily</u>.

2 He asked me <u>came</u> to his birthday party.

3 My parents want me <u>take</u> care of my brother.

4 Every student found Mr. Brown's class <u>difficulty</u>.

5 That news made him <u>famously</u> all over the world.

6 My sister doesn't allow me <u>playing</u> on the computer.

D 우리말과 같은 뜻이 되도록 주어진 단어를 이용하여 문장을 완성하시오.

1 나는 그에게 집에 있으라고 말했다. (tell, stay)

→ I told _____ _____ _____ home.

2 시민들이 그를 시장으로 선출했다. (elect, mayor)

→ The citizens _____ _____ _____.

3 그의 어머니는 그를 잠시 혼자 내버려 두었다. (leave, alone)

→ His mother _____ _____ _____ for a while.

4 의사 선생님이 나에게 물을 많이 마시라고 권하셨다. (advise, drink)

→ The doctor _____ _____ _____ _____ a lot of water.

5 그녀는 자신의 아들을 유명한 야구 선수로 만들었다. (make, famous)

→ She _____ _____ _____ _____ _____ _____.

6 미술관은 사람들이 사진을 찍는 것을 허용하지 않는다. (allow, take pictures)

→ The gallery _____ _____ _____ _____ _____.

7 사람들은 그녀가 인기 있는 작가가 될 거라고 예상하지 않았다. (expect, be)

→ People _____ _____ _____ _____ _____ a popular writer.

E 우리말과 같은 뜻이 되도록 주어진 단어를 배열하시오.

1 방을 청소할 때는 창문을 열어 두어라. (the windows, leave, open)

→ _____ when you clean your room.

2 Alex가 나에게 자기와 결혼해 달라고 했다. (to, asked, him, marry, me)

→ Alex _____.

3 Kim은 나에게 긍정적이 되라고 조언했다. (positive, me, advised, be, to)

→ Kim _____.

4 도서관에서는 아이들이 조용히 하도록 해 주세요. (the children, keep, quiet)

→ _____ in the library.

5 그녀는 그가 정말 매력 있다는 것을 알게 되었다. (him, found, attractive, very)

→ She _____.

6 그는 나에게 건강을 위해 채소를 더 많이 먹으라고 말했다. (eat, to, me, told, more vegetables)

→ He _____ for my health.

7 우리 부모님은 내가 Penny네 집에서 외박하는 것을 허락하지 않으신다. (sleep over, to, allow, me, don't)

→ My parents _____ at Penny's house.

UNIT 03 동사＋목적어＋동사원형／–ing

A 주어진 단어를 이용하여 문장을 완성하시오.

1 Did you hear him _____? (sing)

2 I will have him _____ your computer. (repair)

3 They saw Joshua _____ on the stage. (act)

4 The boys helped me _____ trees. (plant)

5 I let her _____ with her friends in the playground. (play)

6 That noise made Henry _____ in the early morning. (wake up)

7 My mother had me _____ a book to my younger sister. (read)

B 보기 에서 동사를 골라 어법에 맞게 문장을 완성하시오.

[1~5]

| 보기 | burn | sing | relieve | shake | play |

1 His mother let the boy _____ the cello.

2 The fresh air helps me _____ stress.

3 People felt the ground _____ a little bit.

4 Mom smelled the bread _____ in the oven.

5 The audience listened to the singer _____ her hit songs.

[6~10]

| 보기 | erase | know | play | fall | talk |

6 I heard him _____ in his sleep.

7 Sandra saw snow _____ from the sky.

8 Her teacher had her _____ the blackboard.

9 She watched children _____ ice hockey.

10 The campaign makes people _____ about air pollution.

C 우리말과 같은 뜻이 되도록 주어진 단어를 이용하여 문장을 완성하시오.

1 그 실수로 인해 나는 실망감을 느꼈다. (make, feel)

→ That mistake _____ _____ _____ disappointed.

2 우리 선생님은 주말마다 나에게 책을 읽도록 시킨다. (have, read)

→ My teacher _____ _____ _____ a book every weekend.

3 아버지께서 나로 하여금 남동생의 숙제를 도와주게 했다. (let, help)

→ Dad _____ _____ _____ with my brother's homework.

4 Ann은 자신의 아기가 벽에 무언가를 그리고 있는 것을 보았다. (see, draw)

→ Ann _____ _____ _____ _____ something on the wall.

5 나는 누군가 내 이름을 부르는 소리를 들었다. (call)

→ I _____ _____ _____ my name.

6 이 웹사이트는 네가 보고서에 필요한 정보를 찾는 데 도움이 될 것이다. (help, find)

→ This website will _____ _____ _____ information for your report.

7 Carrie는 자신의 여동생에게 엄마의 생신 파티를 위한 케이크를 사 오도록 시켰다. (have, buy)

→ Carrie _____ _____ _____ _____ a cake for Mom's birthday party.

D 우리말과 같은 뜻이 되도록 주어진 단어를 배열하시오.

1 Henry는 멀리서 개가 짖는 것을 들었다. (a dog, barking, heard)

→ Henry _____ in the distance.

2 이 종이를 복사해 주시겠어요? (to, these papers, you, copy, get)

→ Can I _____ ?

3 바람이 그 사진을 벽에서 떨어지게 했다. (fall, made, the picture)

→ The wind _____ off the wall.

4 나는 누군가가 나를 응시하고 있는 것을 느꼈다. (me, someone, felt, staring at)

→ I _____ .

5 Emily는 엄마가 쿠키를 만들고 있는 것을 보았다. (cookies, her mom, making, watched)

→ Emily _____ .

6 나는 어젯밤 9시쯤에 유리가 깨지는 소리를 들었다. (breaking, heard, glass)

→ Last night, about 9 pm, I _____ .

7 Jina는 남동생이 자신의 자전거를 이용하도록 허락해 주었다. (her bike, let, use, her brother)

→ Jina _____ .

명사적 쓰임

A 보기 에서 알맞은 단어를 골라 to부정사로 바꿔 문장을 완성하시오.

> 보기   take   forget   stay up   win

1 It is difficult for me _____ late.

2 She wishes _____ the bad memory.

3 Our team expected _____ the semi-final.

4 Her only hobby is _____ pictures of flowers.

B 두 문장이 같은 의미가 되도록 문장을 완성하시오.

1 To live without air is impossible.

   → _____ is impossible _____.

2 To go to bed early is a good habit.

   → _____ is a good habit _____.

3 To upgrade your computer is necessary.

   → _____ is necessary _____.

4 To take care of my baby sister is not easy.

   → _____ is not easy _____.

5 To learn a foreign language is very useful.

   → _____ is very useful _____.

6 To eat a lot of sweets is bad for your teeth.

   → _____ is bad for your teeth _____.

7 I know how to bake cookies.

   → I know _____.

8 Steve couldn't decide what to do next.

   → Steve couldn't decide _____.

9 Please let me know where I should get off.

   → Please let me know _____.

10 I didn't know when I should call her back.

   → I didn't know _____.

C 우리말과 같은 뜻이 되도록 보기 에서 알맞은 단어를 골라 「의문사 + to부정사」로 바꿔 문장을 완성하시오.

보기　write　stay　buy　catch　press　put

1 나는 언제 버튼을 눌러야 할지 모르겠다.
→ I don't know _____ the button.

2 이 코트를 어디에 놓아야 하는지 알려주시겠어요?
→ Can you tell me _____ this coat?

3 Stella는 여행하는 동안 어디서 머무를지 결정하지 못했다.
→ Stella couldn't decide _____ during her trip.

4 그 다섯 살 난 소녀는 벌써 어떻게 글을 쓰는지 안다.
→ The five-year-old girl already knows _____.

5 나는 Tony의 생일 선물로 무엇을 사야 할지 결정하지 못했다.
→ I couldn't decide _____ for Tony's birthday.

6 우리 아버지께서 나에게 어떻게 물고기를 잡는지 가르쳐주셨다.
→ My father taught me _____ fish.

D 우리말과 같은 뜻이 되도록 주어진 단어를 이용하여 문장을 완성하시오.

1 언제 시작하는지 말씀해 주세요. (start)
→ Please tell me _____ _____ _____.

2 나는 첫차를 놓치고 싶지 않다. (miss, the first train)
→ I don't want _____ _____ _____ _____.

3 그녀는 스페인 어를 어떻게 하는지 모른다. (speak, Spanish)
→ She doesn't know _____ _____ _____.

4 이 호수에서 수영하는 것은 안전하지 않다. (swim, in this lake)
→ It is not safe _____ _____ _____ _____.

5 그들은 올해 5월에 결혼하기로 결정했다. (get married, this May)
→ They decided _____ _____ _____ _____.

6 내 직업은 집과 다른 건물을 설계하는 것이다. (design, houses and other buildings)
→ My job is _____ _____ _____.

7 그는 그 정치가로부터 돈을 받는 것을 거절했다. (accept, the money, from the politician)
→ He refused _____ _____ _____ _____ _____ _____.

9

UNIT 02 형용사적 쓰임

A 주어진 단어를 이용하여 문장을 완성하시오.

1 It is _____ _____ _____ goodbye. (say, time)

2 I have _____ _____ _____ you. (tell, nothing)

3 We have _____ _____ _____ _____. (keep, a promise)

4 She bought _____ _____ _____ _____ during her trip. (read, a book)

5 It will give me _____ _____ _____ _____ a better job. (find, a chance)

6 Can you give me _____ _____ _____ _____? (drink, cold, something)

7 There are _____ _____ _____ _____ _____ on TV.
(watch, lots of programs)

B 보기 와 같이 문장을 바꿔 쓰시오.

> 보기   She has many friends. She talks to them.
> → She has <u>many friends to talk to.</u>

1 I have a cup of hot water. I'll drink it.

→ I have _____.

2 I have several problems. I worry about them.

→ I have _____.

3 The old lady has a walking stick. She uses it.

→ The old lady has _____.

4 My twin sons have some great toys. They play with them.

→ My twin sons have _____.

5 The couple have three kids. They take care of them.

→ The couple have _____.

6 Brenda bought a dress. She will wear it on her birthday.

→ Brenda bought _____ on her birthday.

C 두 문장이 같은 의미가 되도록 to부정사를 이용하여 문장을 완성하시오.

1 We should obey the law.

→ We _____ _____ _____ the law.

2 He is going to come here tomorrow.

→ He _____ _____ _____ here tomorrow.

3 The musician was destined to die young.

→ The musician _____ _____ _____ young.

4 Nothing could be seen in the dark room.

→ Nothing _____ _____ _____ _____ in the dark room.

5 If you intend to buy a house, you should save some more money.

→ If you _____ _____ _____ a house, you should save some more money.

D 우리말과 같은 뜻이 되도록 주어진 단어를 이용하여 문장을 완성하시오.

1 Stella는 다음 주에 시험을 보기로 되어 있다. (take, tests)

→ Stella is _____ _____ _____ next week.

2 너는 여섯 시까지 집에 돌아와야 한다. (be back, home)

→ You are _____ _____ _____ _____ by six.

3 Sue는 신고 다닐 편한 신발이 필요하다. (wear, comfortable shoes)

→ Sue needs _____ _____ _____ _____.

4 나는 너에게 보여 줄 사진을 많이 가지고 있다. (show, many pictures)

→ I have _____ _____ _____ _____ you.

E 우리말과 같은 뜻이 되도록 주어진 말을 알맞게 배열하시오.

1 냉장고에 먹을 것이 있나요? (something, there, eat, to, is)

→ _____ in the refrigerator?

2 나는 거기에 가는 길을 알고 있다. (the way, get, know, to, there)

→ I _____.

3 그들은 머무를 호텔을 찾고 있다. (looking for, a hotel, are, stay at, to)

→ They _____.

4 Jacob은 함께 놀 많은 친구를 사귀었다. (play, many, to, made, friends, with)

→ Jacob _____.

UNIT 03 부사적 쓰임

A 보기 에서 알맞은 동사를 골라 to부정사로 바꿔 문장을 완성하시오.

| 보기 | help | win | be | eat | watch |

1 This food is not safe _____.

2 Jefferson lived _____ over a hundred.

3 Jenny must be kind _____ poor people.

4 He turned on the TV _____ a tennis match.

5 She was pleased _____ first place in the contest.

B 보기 와 같이 문장을 바꿔 쓰시오.

> I'm studying hard to get good grades.
> 보기 → I'm studying hard in order to get good grades.
> → I'm studying hard so as to get good grades.

1 I went to Russia to learn ballet.

→ _____

→ _____

2 I exercise not to put on weight.

→ _____

→ _____

3 Mom bought some oranges to make juice.

→ _____

→ _____

4 He wrote down the phone number not to forget it.

→ _____

→ _____

5 They called the Chinese restaurant to book a table.

→ _____

→ _____

C 우리말과 같은 뜻이 되도록 주어진 말을 이용하여 문장을 완성하시오.

1 그렇게 하다니 그는 무례한 게 틀림없다. (do, rude)

→ He must be _____ _____ _____ so.

2 이 복사기는 이용하기 어렵다. (use, difficult)

→ This copy machine _____ _____ _____ _____.

3 그녀는 산책을 하기 위해 공원에 간다. (take a walk)

→ She goes to the park _____ _____ _____ _____.

4 슬픈 소식을 들어 매우 유감입니다. (hear, the sad news)

→ I'm so sorry _____ _____ _____ _____ _____.

5 Roan은 정보를 찾으려고 인터넷을 검색했다. (find, some information)

→ Roan searched the Internet _____ _____ _____ _____.

6 소녀는 자라서 유명한 패션모델이 되었다. (be, a famous fashion model)

→ The girl grew up _____ _____ _____ _____.

D 우리말과 같은 뜻이 되도록 주어진 단어를 배열하시오.

1 그 산은 오르기 힘들다. (climb, hard, is, to)

→ The mountain _____.

2 그는 최선을 다했지만, 결국 실패했다. (his best, fail, only, tried, to)

→ He _____, _____.

3 나는 선물을 받아서 정말 기뻤다. (the gift, very, to, happy, receive)

→ I was _____.

4 Dave는 저녁을 먹으려고 식탁을 차렸다. (dinner, set, to, the table, have)

→ Dave _____.

5 Martine이 안부를 전하기 위해 나에게 전화했다. (say hello, me, called, to)

→ Martine _____.

6 그 제의를 거절하다니 그녀가 현명한 건지도 모른다. (the offer, refuse, wise, to)

→ She may be _____.

13

UNIT 04 의미상의 주어, too ~ to, enough to

A 주어진 단어를 이용하여 빈칸에 알맞은 의미상의 주어를 쓰시오.

1 It is fun _____ to go on a picnic. (I)

2 It was wise _____ to tell the truth. (he)

3 It is necessary _____ to study hard. (we)

4 It is generous _____ to understand me. (they)

5 It was careless _____ to take the wrong bus. (you)

6 It was easy _____ to find the National Museum. (we)

7 It was impossible _____ to climb the mountain. (she)

8 It was polite _____ to hold the door open for me. (he)

B 두 문장이 같은 뜻이 되도록 문장을 완성하시오.

1 He ran too fast for me to catch up.

→ He ran _____ with him.

2 The book is too hard for me to understand.

→ The book is _____ it.

3 The problem is so complicated that he can't explain it.

→ The problem is _____ .

4 The children were so excited that they couldn't stay calm.

→ The children were _____ .

5 He was rich enough to buy her a car.

→ He was _____ .

6 Mandy is slim enough to wear skinny jeans.

→ Mandy is _____ .

7 Rick is so brave that he can catch a thief.

→ Rick is _____ .

8 She is so patient that she can endure the pain.

→ She is _____ .

C 우리말과 같은 뜻이 되도록 주어진 단어를 배열하시오.

1 내가 그 일을 하는 것은 어렵다. (for, to, the work, do, me, hard)

→ It is _____.

2 선생님께 말대답을 하다니 그가 무례했어. (him, rude, of, answer back, to)

→ It was _____ to the teacher.

3 그 학교는 아이들이 걸어가기엔 너무 멀다. (walk to, for, far, to, children, too)

→ The school is _____.

4 그녀가 그 시험에 통과하는 것은 중요하다. (for, to, the exam, pass, important, her)

→ It is _____.

5 똑같은 실수를 저지르다니 너는 부주의했구나. (the same, careless, you, of, make, to, mistake)

→ It was _____.

6 Sean은 너무 수줍음을 타서 자신의 의견을 말하지 못한다. (give, too, to, shy, opinions, his)

→ Sean is _____.

7 그녀는 운전면허증을 딸 만큼 충분히 나이가 들었다. (get, a driver's license, to, enough, old)

→ She is _____.

D 우리말과 같은 뜻이 되도록 주어진 단어를 이용하여 문장을 완성하시오.

1 이 강은 수영하기에 너무 깊다. (swim in, deep)

→ This river is _____ _____ _____ _____ _____.

2 그가 일찍 일어나는 것은 불가능하다. (get up, he, impossible)

→ _____ is _____ _____ _____ _____ _____ early.

3 그녀는 그 집을 살 만큼 충분히 부유하다. (buy, rich)

→ She is _____ _____ _____ _____ the house.

4 그는 그 책을 반납해야 할 필요가 있다. (return, he, necessary)

→ _____ is _____ _____ _____ _____ the book.

5 그는 아파서 아무것도 먹을 수가 없었다. (eat, sick)

→ He was _____ _____ _____ _____ anything.

6 그녀는 가수가 될 만큼 충분히 노래를 잘한다 (be, well)

→ She sings _____ _____ _____ _____ a singer.

UNIT 01 동명사의 쓰임

A 주어진 동사를 동명사로 바꿔 문장을 완성하시오.

1 Harry avoids _____ his friend, Sally. (meet)

2 Her plan is _____ the work in a week. (finish)

3 He is not good at _____ his feeling. (express)

4 The little boy is afraid of _____ to the dentist. (go)

5 _____ how to swim is my goal this year. (learn)

6 Many children like _____ on computers. (play)

7 I take a shower after _____ every morning. (exercise)

B 두 문장의 의미가 통하도록 보기 와 같이 바꿔 쓰시오.

> 보기 My aunt designs clothes. It is her job.
> → My aunt's job is <u>designing clothes</u>.

1 I want to travel around the world. It is my dream.

→ My dream is _____.

2 Sarah listens to classical music. She enjoys it.

→ Sarah enjoys _____.

3 Jason draws cartoons. He is interested in it.

→ Jason is interested in _____.

4 Don't eat too much. It is bad for your health.

→ _____ is bad for your health.

5 I can't get up early. It is difficult.

→ _____ is difficult for me.

6 I play baseball with friends. It is my favorite thing to do.

→ My favorite thing to do is _____.

7 Wash your hands before a meal. It is a good habit.

→ _____ is a good habit.

C 우리말과 같은 뜻이 되도록 동명사와 주어진 단어를 이용하여 문장을 완성하시오.

1 아침을 먹는 것은 하루를 시작하는 좋은 방법이다. (be, eat, breakfast)

→ _____ _____ _____ a good way to start the day.

2 볼륨을 좀 줄여 주시겠어요? (mind, turn down, the volume)

→ Would you _____ _____ _____ _____ _____?

3 그녀는 전공을 바꾸려고 생각 중이다. (think about, change)

→ She _____ _____ _____ _____ her major.

4 그에 대해 생각하는 것은 나를 미소 짓게 만든다. (think of, make)

→ _____ _____ _____ _____ me smile.

5 그는 사람들과 예술에 관해 얘기하는 것을 좋아한다. (love, talk to)

→ He _____ _____ _____ people about art.

6 Patty의 꿈은 초등학생들에게 영어를 가르치는 것이다. (be, teach, English)

→ Patty's dream _____ _____ _____ to school children.

7 블로그를 쓰는 것은 내 친구들 사이에서 인기가 있다. (be, write, blogs)

→ _____ _____ _____ popular among my friends.

D 우리말과 같은 뜻이 되도록 주어진 단어를 배열하시오.

1 다시 해봐도 소용없다. (no, trying, is, again, it, use)

→ _____

2 나는 파티에 가고 싶지 않다. (to, don't, the party, going, feel like)

→ I _____.

3 Jason은 그녀를 보고 웃지 않을 수 없었다. (laughing at, couldn't, her, help)

→ Jason _____.

4 이번 주말에 캠핑하러 가고 싶니? (do, go, want, camping, you, to)

→ _____ this weekend?

5 그 소식을 듣고, 그는 기뻐서 펄쩍 뛰었다. (the news, hearing, on)

→ _____, he jumped for joy.

6 Sam은 자신의 면접을 준비하느라 바빴다. (preparing for, job interview, busy, his, is)

→ Sam _____.

7 일이 끝난 후에 저녁 먹으러 나가는 것이 어때? (going out, how about, for dinner)

→ _____ after work?

UNIT 02 동명사와 to부정사

A 주어진 단어를 알맞은 형태로 바꿔 문장을 완성하시오.

1 I gave up _____ on diets. (go)

2 It began _____ heavily. (rain)

3 Carrie avoids _____ my eyes. (meet)

4 He hopes _____ the test this time. (pass)

5 My children hate _____ carrots. (eat)

6 Sean finished _____ his living room wall. (paint)

7 Kerry decided _____ the truth to her parents. (tell)

8 The students practiced _____ musical instruments. (play)

B 보기 에서 알맞은 단어를 골라 어법에 맞게 바꿔 문장을 완성하시오.

[1~4]

보기	move	do	talk about	know

1 I want _____ more about Monica.

2 They plan _____ to another country.

3 She doesn't mind _____ the housework.

4 My grandfather kept _____ his childhood.

[5~8]

보기	make	feed	read	solve

5 I forgot _____ my dog, and I fed him again.

6 Rick tried _____ the math problem, but he couldn't.

7 Would you stop _____ that noise? I can't concentrate.

8 I remember _____ the book last year, and it was very boring.

C 두 문장의 의미가 통하도록 보기 와 같이 바꿔 쓰시오.

> 보기
> Remember that you should lock the door when you leave.
> → Remember to lock the door when you leave.

1 Ray wanted to take a rest, so he stopped.

→ Ray stopped _____.

2 I forgot that I borrowed fifty dollars from Brenda.

→ I forgot _____.

3 She decided not to play tennis because of her injury.

→ She stopped _____.

4 Remember that you should call me tomorrow morning.

→ Remember _____.

5 Don't forget that you should bring your passport with you.

→ Don't forget _____.

6 I remember that I watched the movie with Raymond last Friday.

→ I remember _____.

D 우리말과 같은 뜻이 되도록 주어진 단어를 이용하여 문장을 완성하시오.

1 패스트푸드를 그만 먹어. 그것은 네 건강에 나빠. (stop, eat)

→ _____ _____ _____ _____. It is bad for your health.

2 자기 전에 양치질을 하는 거 잊지 마. (forget, brush one's teeth)

→ Don't _____ _____ _____ _____ _____ before you go to bed.

3 그들은 콘서트를 취소하기로 합의했다. (agree, cancel, the concert)

→ They _____ _____ _____ _____ _____.

4 나는 스키니 진을 한번 입어 보았다. (try, put on, the skinny jeans)

→ I _____ _____ _____ _____ _____ _____.

5 그는 여자 친구와 쇼핑하러 가는 것을 좋아한다. (like, go, shop)

→ He _____ _____ _____ with his girlfriend.

6 그녀는 게으른 사람들과 같이 일하는 것을 싫어한다. (hate, work with, lazy)

→ She _____ _____ _____ _____ _____ _____.

7 그 과학자는 날 수 있는 자동차를 발명하려고 노력하고 있다. (try, invent)

→ The scientist is _____ _____ a flying car.

UNIT 03 동명사 vs. 현재분사

A   보기 에서 알맞은 단어를 골라 동명사나 현재분사로 바꿔 문장을 완성하시오.

[1~4]   보기   play   bark   walk   ride

1 She enjoyed ＿＿＿＿＿＿＿ horses.

2 His favorite hobby is ＿＿＿＿＿＿ chess.

3 I walked quickly past the ＿＿＿＿＿＿ dog.

4 The old man cannot walk without a ＿＿＿＿＿＿ stick.

[5~8]   보기   fry   go   sleep   run

5 ＿＿＿＿＿＿＿ out alone at night is dangerous.

6 Her dream is ＿＿＿＿＿＿ her own company.

7 Mom bought a pot, a kettle, and a ＿＿＿＿＿＿ pan.

8 I found a cat ＿＿＿＿＿＿ under the kitchen table.

B   두 문장이 같은 뜻이 되도록 밑줄 친 부분을 보기 와 같이 바꿔 쓰시오.

[1~3]   보기   The girl put on her <u>shoes for dancing</u>.
             → The girl put on her <u>dancing shoes</u>.

1 Does the store have <u>a space for parking</u>?

   → Does the store have ＿＿＿＿＿＿＿＿＿＿＿＿＿＿＿?

2 She went to <u>the room for fitting</u> to try the skirt on.

   → She went to ＿＿＿＿＿＿＿＿＿＿＿＿ to try the skirt on.

3 I bought <u>a bag for sleeping</u> for my camping trip.

   → I bought ＿＿＿＿＿＿＿＿＿＿＿＿ for my camping trip.

[4~6]   보기   The man is very talented. He is <u>playing the piano</u>.
             → The man <u>playing the piano</u> is very talented.

4 The girl is my classmate. She is <u>waving at me</u>.

   → The girl ＿＿＿＿＿＿＿＿＿＿＿＿ is my classmate.

5 The monkey is mine. It is <u>dancing on the street</u>.

   → The monkey ＿＿＿＿＿＿＿＿＿＿＿＿ is mine.

6 The boy is my nephew. He is <u>waiting for the train</u>.

   → The boy ＿＿＿＿＿＿＿＿＿＿＿＿ is my nephew.

C 우리말과 같은 뜻이 되도록 주어진 단어를 이용하여 문장을 완성하시오.

1 **(1)** 그는 새 세탁기 사기를 원한다. (wash)

→ He wants to buy _____ _____ _____ _____ .

(2) Eric은 욕조에서 옷을 빨고 있다. (wash)

→ Eric _____ _____ his clothes in the bath.

2 **(1)** 그 남자는 흡연실을 찾고 있다. (smoke)

→ The man is looking for _____ _____ _____ .

(2) 나는 금연 표지판 밑에서 담배를 피우고 있는 한 남자를 보았다. (smoke)

→ I saw _____ _____ _____ under the No Smoking sign.

3 **(1)** 그 소년들은 헤엄치는 물고기를 보고 있다. (swim)

→ The boys are watching _____ _____ .

(2) 그 저택은 뒤뜰에 수영장이 한 개 있다. (swim)

→ The mansion has _____ _____ _____ in its backyard.

4 **(1)** 우리 거실에 큰 탁자가 한 개 놓여 있다. (live)

→ We have a big round table in the _____ _____ .

(2) 황제 펭귄은 남극에 사는 동물이다. (live)

→ An emperor penguin is _____ _____ _____ in Antarctica.

D 우리말과 같은 뜻이 되도록 주어진 말을 알맞게 배열하시오.

1 잠자는 아이를 깨우지 마라. (baby, the, wake, sleeping)

→ Don't _____ .

2 빛나는 별들을 봐. (shining, stars, the)

→ Look at _____ .

3 엄마는 낯선 사람과 얘기 중이다. (talking, the, stranger, to, is)

→ Mom _____ .

4 그 대기실은 환자들로 붐볐다. (crowded, the, room, was, waiting)

→ _____ with patients.

5 나는 수영복으로 갈아입어야 한다. (my, suit, change into, swimming)

→ I need to _____ .

6 너를 보며 미소 짓고 있는 여자가 누구니? (you, smiling, at, the woman)

→ Who is _____ ?

7 당신은 탈의실에서 이 치마를 입어 볼 수 있습니다. (fitting, this skirt, the, room, in)

→ You can try on _____ .

UNIT 01 부정대명사 I

A 보기 에서 알맞은 대명사를 골라 대화를 완성하시오. (한 번씩만 쓸 것)

보기	both	one	all	it	each

1 A Which dress looks better on me?

　B I think the white _____.

2 A You should not force your ideas on other people.

　B _____ person has his or her own ideas.

3 A How many sisters do you have?

　B I have two sisters, and _____ are college students.

4 A How was the test? Do you think you did well on it?

　B It was a piece of cake. _____ the questions were easy.

5 A What did you get from your parents for your birthday?

　B They gave me a watch, and I really like _____.

B 문장의 빈칸에 any 또는 some을 써 넣으시오.

1 Do you have _____ brothers or sisters?

2 I want to stay longer, but I have _____ work to do.

3 I wanted to drink some milk but there isn't _____ left.

4 Sandy went to the movie with _____ of her friends.

C 밑줄 친 부분을 어법에 맞게 고쳐 쓰시오.

1 All the seats in the theater is taken.

2 Each of the members have one vote.

3 Every boys enjoyed seeing the circus.

4 There is a bag on the desk. One is mine.

5 I'm looking for a house. I need it with a garden.

D 우리말과 같은 뜻이 되도록 부정대명사와 주어진 단어를 이용하여 문장을 완성하시오.

1 네 볼에 크림이 조금 묻었다. (have, cream)

→ You ＿＿＿＿＿＿ ＿＿＿＿＿＿ ＿＿＿＿＿＿ on your cheek.

2 주말에 무슨 계획이라도 있니? (have, plans)

→ ＿＿＿＿＿ ＿＿＿＿＿ ＿＿＿＿＿ ＿＿＿＿＿ ＿＿＿＿＿ for this weekend?

3 그들 모두는 고등학교 학생이다. (them, be)

→ ＿＿＿＿＿＿ ＿＿＿＿＿＿ ＿＿＿＿＿＿ ＿＿＿＿＿＿ high school students.

4 나는 매주 토요일에 할아버지와 체스를 둔다. (Saturday)

→ I play chess with my grandfather ＿＿＿＿＿ ＿＿＿＿＿.

5 각각의 후보자는 응답할 기회를 갖는다. (candidate, have)

→ ＿＿＿＿＿＿ ＿＿＿＿＿ ＿＿＿＿＿ an opportunity to respond.

6 그는 컴퓨터가 고장 나서 새 것을 사야 한다. (buy, new)

→ His computer is broken down, so he should ＿＿＿＿＿ ＿＿＿＿＿ ＿＿＿＿＿ ＿＿＿＿＿.

7 그 선수들은 둘 다 대회에서 우승하기를 원한다. (both, the players)

→ ＿＿＿＿＿ ＿＿＿＿＿ ＿＿＿＿＿ ＿＿＿＿＿ ＿＿＿＿＿ to win the contest.

E 우리말과 같은 뜻이 되도록 주어진 단어를 배열하시오.

1 이 셔츠는 너무 커요. 더 작은 것이 있나요? (smaller, you, have, one, do, a)

→ This shirt is too big. ＿＿＿＿＿＿＿＿＿＿＿＿＿＿＿＿＿

2 각각의 아이는 다른 꿈을 가지고 있다. (child, has, dream, each, different, a)

→ ＿＿＿＿＿＿＿＿＿＿＿＿＿＿＿＿＿＿＿＿＿＿＿

3 나의 여동생은 둘 다 수영을 잘 한다. (my sisters, swimming, are, both, of, good at)

→ ＿＿＿＿＿＿＿＿＿＿＿＿＿＿＿＿＿＿＿＿＿＿＿

4 나는 도서관에서 책을 몇 권 빌렸다. (books, checked out, the library, some, from)

→ I ＿＿＿＿＿＿＿＿＿＿＿＿＿＿＿＿＿＿＿＿.

5 나는 Jason으로부터 어떤 편지도 받지 못했다. (from Jason, didn't, any, letters, receive)

→ I ＿＿＿＿＿＿＿＿＿＿＿＿＿＿＿＿＿＿＿＿.

6 우리 모두는 그 독서클럽의 회원이다. (of the book club, the members, us, of, all, are)

→ ＿＿＿＿＿＿＿＿＿＿＿＿＿＿＿＿＿＿＿＿＿＿＿

7 모든 학생은 자신의 점심을 가지고 왔다. (brought, his or her, student, every, own lunch)

→ ＿＿＿＿＿＿＿＿＿＿＿＿＿＿＿＿＿＿＿＿＿＿＿

UNIT 02 부정대명사 II

A 보기 에서 알맞은 말을 골라 문장을 완성하시오. (한 번씩만 쓸 것)

[1~5]

> 보기   the other   the others   one another   another   others

1 Three puppies are chasing _____.

2 This knife is not clean. Give me _____ one.

3 I have two cars. One is gray, and _____ is white.

4 There are balls of many different colors. Some are blue, and _____ are red.

5 There are thirty students in the class. Some students solved the problem, and _____ didn't.

[6~10]

> 보기   another   each other   the other   others   the others

6 The man and the woman are smiling at _____.

7 The little boy has a lot of toys, but he wants _____ toy car.

8 Many people like sports. Some like baseball, _____ like soccer.

9 Dean left the party early. Some people saw him, and _____ didn't see him.

10 I bought three gifts. One is for my mom, another is for my dad, and _____ is for my brother.

[11~15]

> 보기   the others   the other   each other   some   another

11 I should leave now. I hope we see _____ soon.

12 Ten students took the test. _____ passed the test, and the others failed.

13 He has three pets. One is a dog, _____ is a hamster, and the other is a parrot.

14 They arranged to meet at six. Only one of them came on time; _____ were late.

15 I have two bad habits. One is biting my fingernails, and _____ is shaking my legs.

B 우리말과 같은 뜻이 되도록 주어진 단어를 이용하여 문장을 완성하시오.

1 이 햄버거가 맛있네요. 하나 더 먹을 수 있을까요? (have)

→ This hamburger is delicious. Can I _____ _____ ?

2 사람들은 어려움이 생기면 서로 돕는다. (help)

→ People _____ _____ _____ when they are in trouble.

3 저 집에는 다섯 명이 산다. 몇 명은 아침을 먹고, 나머지 모두는 아침을 거른다. (eat, skip)

→ Five people live in that house. _____ _____ breakfast, and _____
_____ _____ it.

4 우리 할머니는 정원에 많은 꽃을 가꾼다. 일부는 장미고, 또 다른 일부는 카네이션이다. (be)

→ My grandmother grows many flowers in her garden. _____ _____ roses, and
_____ _____ carnations.

5 나는 오늘 아침에 우연히 친구를 두 명 만났다. 한 명은 Ryan이었고 나머지 한 명은 Jane이었다. (be)

→ I ran into two friends this morning. _____ _____ Ryan, and _____
_____ _____ Jane.

6 Brown 씨는 아들이 세 명 있고. 한 명은 미국에 살고, 다른 한 명은 독일에 살고, 나머지 한 명은 중국에 산다. (live)

→ Mrs. Brown has three sons. _____ _____ in the USA, _____ _____ in
Germany, and _____ _____ _____ in China.

C 우리말과 같은 뜻이 되도록 주어진 말을 알맞게 배열하시오.

1 너희 두 사람은 서로 어떻게 만났니? (did, meet, the two of, each other, you)

→ How _____ ?

2 가고 싶지만, 그날은 다른 약속이 있어요. (another, on, have, appointment, that day)

→ I'd love to go, but I _____ .

3 어떤 사람들은 그의 의견에 찬성했고, 나머지 모두는 찬성하지 않았다.

(agreed with, the others, his idea, some, didn't, and)

→ _____

4 많은 사람들이 그 영화를 보았다. 일부는 좋아했고, 또 다른 일부는 싫어했다. (didn't, liked, others, some, it, and)

→ Lots of people saw the movie. _____

5 나는 네 명의 형제자매가 있다. 한 명은 언니이고, 나머지 모두는 남동생이다.

(a sister, is, and, the others, one, brothers, are)

→ I have four siblings. _____

6 나는 책 두 권을 읽었다. 하나는 재밌었고, 다른 하나는 지루했다. (interesting, was, boring, the other, was,
one, and)

→ I read two books. _____

UNIT 03 재귀대명사

A 빈칸에 알맞은 재귀대명사를 쓰시오.

1 A snake sometimes bites _____.

2 I introduced _____ to the audience.

3 We seated _____ at the outdoor table.

4 You have to take care of _____ during the trip.

5 My mother burned _____ while she was ironing.

6 My brother cut _____ when he was sharpening a pencil.

7 Tom enjoyed _____ very much at the Halloween party last Friday.

B 보기 에서 알맞은 표현을 골라 대화를 완성하시오.

[1~4] 보기 by oneself   talk to oneself   help oneself to   hurt oneself

1 A Be careful. You can _____.

   B Thank you. I didn't see the warning sign.

2 A _____ the food. I made it for you.

   B Thanks. It looks really delicious.

3 A I'm sorry, I didn't hear you. What did you say?

   B Oh, never mind. I was just _____.

4 A It's getting dark. I don't think I can go home _____.

   B Don't worry. I will give you a ride.

[5~8] 보기 teach oneself   make oneself at home   between oneself   enjoy oneself

5 A Hello, Nancy. I just stopped by to say hello.

   B Come on in. Please _____.

6 A Don't tell the secret. It's just _____.

   B OK. I won't tell anybody.

7 A Did you _____ at the concert?

   B Yes. The concert was amazing, and we had a really good time.

8 A Wow, you speak French so fluently. Did you study French in school?

   B No, I didn't. I _____.

C 우리말과 같은 뜻이 되도록 주어진 단어를 이용하여 문장을 완성하시오.

1 Grace가 우리 부모님께 자신을 소개했다. (introduce)

→ Grace _____ _____ to my parents.

2 그들이 직접 이 보트를 만들었다. (make, boat)

→ They _____ _____ _____ _____.

3 그 어린 소녀는 집에 혼자 있었다. (stay)

→ The little girl _____ _____ _____ _____.

4 그는 그 어려운 일을 혼자 끝낼 수 있었다. (finish, the hard work)

→ He could _____ _____ _____ _____ _____.

5 우리는 우리 자신을 자랑스럽게 여겨야 한다. (be proud of)

→ We should _____ _____ _____ _____.

6 네가 직접 그녀에게 사과를 해야 한다. (apologize to)

→ You have to _____ _____ _____ _____.

7 너는 그 실수에 대해 너 자신을 비난하지 않아야 한다. (blame)

→ You shouldn't _____ _____ for the mistake.

D 우리말과 같은 뜻이 되도록 주어진 말을 알맞게 배열하시오..

1 소금은 본래 짜다. (is, in, salty, itself, salt)

→ _____

2 너는 혼자서 그것을 할 수 있어. (by, it, do, can, yourself, you)

→ _____

3 내가 직접 그 자동차 사고를 목격했다. (saw, myself, the accident, I)

→ _____

4 내 이웃은 항상 혼잣말을 한다. (all the time, talks to, himself, my neighbor)

→ _____

5 우리 어머니께서는 자신의 모든 옷을 직접 만드신다. (makes, all her clothes, herself, my mother)

→ _____

6 그 배우는 거울을 보는 데 많은 시간은 보낸다. (himself, much time, looking at, in the mirror, spends)

→ The actor _____.

7 그 영화 자체는 별로 재미가 없었지만, 나는 그 음악이 좋았다. (itself, very, wasn't, interesting, the movie)

→ _____,

but I liked the music.

UNIT 01 현재완료

A 보기 에서 알맞은 것을 골라 현재완료형으로 바꿔 문장을 완성하시오.

보기	do	gain	ride	have	forget

1 Erica _____ her homework already.

2 He _____ a lot of weight recently.

3 Brian _____ a horse three times.

4 They _____ this car for fifteen years.

5 I _____ her cell phone number.

B 밑줄 친 부분을 어법에 맞게 고쳐 쓰시오.

1 Tim has <u>leave</u> his bag on the subway.

2 How long <u>do</u> you known Ashley?

3 I <u>have never try</u> to play golf before.

4 Jennie <u>not has spoken</u> to me for a week.

5 <u>Did</u> you ever read any of Hemingway's novels before?

C 두 문장을 현재완료를 이용한 한 문장으로 바꿔 쓰시오.

1 Jessica was sick last Sunday. She is still sick.

   → Jessica _____ since last Sunday.

2 Dylan went to Paris to study. He is still in Paris.

   → Dylan _____ to study.

3 My mother lost her watch. She doesn't have it now.

   → My mother _____.

4 Jean played the cello when she was young. She still plays it.

   → Jean _____ since she was young.

5 I started wearing glasses when I was a little kid. I still wear them.

   → I _____ since I was a little kid.

D 우리말과 같은 뜻이 되도록 주어진 말을 이용하여 문장을 완성하시오.

1 우리는 태국에 가 본 적이 있다. (be, to)

→ We _____ _____ _____ Thailand.

2 내 차가 방금 고장 났다. (just, break down)

→ My car _____ _____ _____ _____.

3 그녀는 아직 직장에서 돌아오지 않았다. (return)

→ She _____ _____ _____ from work yet.

4 그는 얼마나 오랫동안 영어를 공부했니? (study)

→ How long _____ _____ _____ English?

5 너는 그로부터 메시지를 받은 적이 있니? (receive)

→ _____ _____ _____ any messages from him?

6 나는 한 번도 그를 만나 본 적이 없다. (meet, never)

→ I _____ _____ _____ him.

7 나는 이미 그 요가 수업에 등록했다. (sign up for, already)

→ I _____ _____ _____ _____ _____ the yoga class.

E 우리말과 같은 뜻이 되도록 주어진 단어를 배열하시오.

1 그는 미국에 가 본 적 있니? (he, been, to, has, America)

→ _____

2 Ron과 Sue는 10년 동안 함께 살아 왔다. (ten years, lived together, for, have)

→ Ron and Sue _____.

3 너 숙제 벌써 끝냈니? (you, have, your, homework, done)

→ _____ already?

4 나는 전에 뮤지컬 '레미제라블'을 본 적이 있다. (the musical, have, I, seen)

→ _____ Les Miserables before.

5 Vicky는 끔찍한 교통사고를 당해 기억을 상실했다. (lost, she, has, memory, her)

→ Vicky had a terrible car accident, and _____.

6 우리 부모님은 시골에서 살기를 바랐다. (wanted, the countryside, have, live in, to)

→ My parents _____.

7 우리 조부모님은 이메일을 이용해 본 적이 없다. (never, email, used, have)

→ My grandparents _____.

UNIT **02** 과거와 현재완료

A 주어진 단어를 알맞은 형태로 바꿔 문장을 완성하시오.

1 I _____ born and raised in L.A., but I live in Seattle now. (be)

2 They _____ _____ each other since they first _____. (love, meet)

3 Lily _____ her textbook yesterday, but she has just found it now. (lose)

4 I parked my car outside, but I can't find it now. It _____ _____. (disappear)

5 Brian _____ to Boston five years ago, and he _____ _____ there since then.
(move, live)

B 보기 에서 알맞은 단어를 골라 알맞은 형태로 바꿔 대화를 완성하시오.

[1~4] 보기 be   decide   live   rain

1 A _____ you _____ what to eat?

   B Yes, I have. I would like to eat pizza.

2 A I don't like the rainy weather.

   B Neither do I. It _____ _____ for a week.

3 A _____ the repairman _____ here yet?

   B No, he hasn't. He will come tomorrow.

4 A How long _____ you _____ in Canada?

   B For ten years

[5~8] 보기 start   go out   leave   see

5 A Have you seen Jacob lately?

   B Yes. I _____ him five minutes ago.

6 A How long have you studied Japanese?

   B Since I _____ high school.

7 A Where is Brian?

   B He is not here. He _____ _____ _____ to buy some milk.

8 A Can I borrow your notebook?

   B Sorry. I don't have it now. I _____ _____ it in my classroom.

C 우리말과 같은 뜻이 되도록 주어진 단어를 이용하여 문장을 완성하시오.

1 Dylan은 여러 번 중국에 가봤다. (be, to, China)

→ Dylan _____ _____ _____ _____ several times.

2 너 여름휴가에 어디에 다녀왔니? (where, go)

→ _____ _____ _____ _____ for your summer vacation?

3 나는 최근에 그로부터 소식을 듣지 못했다. (hear from, not)

→ I _____ _____ _____ _____ him recently.

4 Helen은 Jason을 5년 동안 알고 지내왔다. (know, Jason, five years)

→ Helen _____ _____ _____ _____ _____ _____ .

5 Sam은 누구에게도 거짓말을 한 적이 없다. (never, tell a lie)

→ Sam _____ _____ _____ _____ _____ to anybody.

6 그들은 어제 계약서에 서명했다. (sign, the contract)

→ They _____ _____ _____ yesterday.

7 Cindy는 작년에 나에게 수영 강습을 받았다. (take, swimming lessons)

→ Cindy _____ _____ _____ from me last year.

D 우리말과 같은 뜻이 되도록 주어진 단어를 배열하시오.

1 나는 아침 식사 이후로 아무것도 먹지 않았다. (haven't, since, anything, eaten, breakfast)

→ I _____ .

2 그녀는 아직 대학을 마치지 않았다. (not, has, college, yet, finished)

→ She _____ .

3 우리는 작년에 터키를 여행했다. (to, last, year, traveled, Turkey)

→ We _____ .

4 나는 그 소식을 한 시간 전에 들었다. (the news, ago, hour, an, heard)

→ I _____ .

5 그 학생들은 벌써 시험을 끝냈다. (already, have, the test, finished)

→ The students _____ .

6 우리 가족은 지난 휴가 때 런던에 다녀왔다. (last, to, went, London, vacation)

→ My family _____ .

7 그들은 10년 동안 가장 친한 친구로 지내고 있다. (have, for, years, best, friends, been, ten)

→ They _____ .

UNIT 03 진행 시제

A 주어진 단어를 진행 시제로 바꿔 문장을 완성하시오.

1 Sean _____ his teacher now. (talk with)

2 They _____ new bridges these days. (build)

3 The boys _____ at 10 pm last night. (sleep)

4 My parents _____ to my house this weekend. (come)

5 She _____ a birthday present for her mother at that time. (wrap)

B 보기 에서 동사를 골라 알맞은 형태로 바꿔 쓰시오.

보기	cry	water	wait for	jump

1 A What is Karen doing in the garden?

  B She _____ the plants.

2 A What were you doing when you saw the car accident?

  B I _____ the bus.

3 A Look at the monkeys! They _____ from tree to tree.

  B Wow! They are amazing.

4 A The baby _____ now. I don't know how to soothe him.

  B Pick him up and hold him.

C 밑줄 친 부분을 어법에 맞게 고쳐 쓰시오.

1 It is tasting like ketchup.

2 What are you wanting for dinner?

3 Are you understanding what I'm saying?

4 I am knowing the answer to the question.

5 I am not having that much money right now.

D 우리말과 같은 뜻이 되도록 주어진 단어를 이용하여 문장을 완성하시오.

1 내가 창밖을 보았을 때 눈이 내리고 있었다. (snow)

→ When I looked out the window, _____ _____ _____ .

2 너 어젯밤 일곱 시에 무엇을 하고 있었니? (what, do)

→ _____ _____ _____ _____ at 7pm last night?

3 네가 전화했을 때 나는 샤워하고 있었어. (take a shower)

→ I _____ _____ _____ _____ when you called.

4 우리는 이번 일요일에 소풍을 갈 것이다. (go on a picnic)

→ We _____ _____ _____ _____ this Sunday.

5 Bill과 Grace는 그때 식당에서 저녁을 먹고 있었다. (have, dinner)

→ Bill and Grace _____ _____ _____ at the restaurant at that time.

6 나는 저녁을 요리하다가 손에 화상을 입었다. (while, cook dinner)

→ _____ _____ _____ _____ _____ , I burned my hand.

7 Mary가 상사와 이야기를 하는 중이어서 당신과 통화를 할 수 없어요. (talk to, her boss)

→ Mary _____ _____ _____ _____ _____ , so she can't speak to you.

E 우리말과 같은 뜻이 되도록 주어진 단어를 배열하시오.

1 나는 요즘 요가를 배우고 있다. (learning, am, these days, yoga)

→ I _____ .

2 그때 나는 여행 가방을 싸고 있었어. (was, my suitcase, packing)

→ I _____ at that time.

3 그가 도착했을 때 나는 집을 청소하고 있었다. (the house, cleaning, was)

→ I _____ when he arrived.

4 나의 아들이 오늘 밤에 뉴저지에서 집에 올 것이다. (home, coming, my, is, son)

→ _____ from New Jersey tonight.

5 그는 테니스를 치다가 발목을 삐었다. (he, playing, tennis, was)

→ When _____ , he sprained his ankle.

6 그는 지금 자신의 두통에 대해 불평하고 있다. (is, about, he, complaining)

→ _____ his headache.

7 Lucy는 지금 친구와 온라인으로 채팅을 하고 있다. (her friend, with, chatting online, is)

→ Lucy _____ now.

33

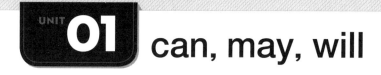

01 can, may, will

A 밑줄 친 부분을 어법에 맞게 고쳐 쓰시오.

1 <u>Will</u> I leave a message?

2 She will <u>can</u> buy a new house.

3 They will <u>visiting</u> the science museum.

4 Look at the sky. It may <u>to snow</u> soon.

5 Tim can <u>drives</u> a car but can't ride a bicycle.

6 <u>May</u> you tell me how to cook seafood spaghetti?

7 Carol is able <u>playing</u> both the drums and the guitar.

B 두 문장의 의미가 통하도록 조동사를 이용하여 문장을 완성하시오.

1 Is it all right if I open the window?

→ _____ the window?

2 Is it OK if I turn off the radio?

→ _____ the radio?

3 Are you able to use chopsticks?

→ _____ chopsticks?

4 Is it possible for you to lend me your notebook?

→ _____ your notebook?

5 Is it possible for you to help me move these boxes?

→ _____ move these boxes?

6 If you are tired, it is OK for you to go to sleep now.

→ If you are tired, you _____ now.

7 Is it all right if I ask you some personal questions?

→ _____ you some personal questions?

C 우리말과 같은 뜻이 되도록 조동사와 주어진 단어를 이용하여 문장을 완성하시오.

1 8시 이후에 다시 나에게 전화해 줄래? (call, back)

→ _____ _____ _____ _____ _____ after eight o'clock?

2 원한다면 내 컴퓨터를 써도 좋다. (use, computer)

→ You _____ _____ _____ _____ if you like.

3 그녀는 여기에 오지 않을지도 모른다. (not, come, here)

→ She _____ _____ _____ _____ .

4 저를 공항까지 태워다 주시겠어요? (give me a ride)

→ _____ _____ _____ _____ _____ to the airport?

5 제가 당신의 신분증을 볼 수 있을까요? (see, ID card)

→ _____ _____ _____ _____ _____ , please?

6 Michael은 100미터를 52초에 수영할 수 있다. (swim, 100 meters)

→ Michael _____ _____ _____ _____ _____ in 52 seconds.

7 Ashley는 그 일을 금요일까지 끝내야만 할 것이다. (finish, the work)

→ Ashley _____ _____ _____ _____ _____ _____ by Friday.

D 우리말과 같은 뜻이 되도록 주어진 단어를 알맞게 배열하시오.

1 저랑 춤 추시겠어요? (dance, me, you, will, with)

→ _____

2 주목해 주시겠습니까? (I, attention, may, your, have)

→ _____

3 James는 말을 탈 수 있다. (ride, able, is, to, a horse)

→ James _____ .

4 그 시험은 쉽지 않을 것이다. (be, easy, the test, won't)

→ _____

5 Annie는 젓가락을 이용할 수 없다. (cannot, chopsticks, use)

→ Annie _____ .

6 그것을 어떻게 하는지 보여주시겠어요? (you, show, can, me)

→ _____ how to do it?

7 그는 그 계획에 동의하지 않을지도 모른다. (with, may, agree, not, the plan)

→ He _____ .

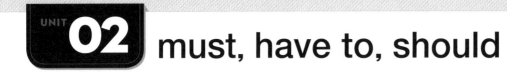

UNIT 02 must, have to, should

A 밑줄 친 부분을 어법에 맞게 고쳐 쓰시오.

1 Do I <u>have</u> wait longer?

2 What should I <u>to do</u> to lose weight?

3 He <u>musted finish</u> the work last night.

4 I will <u>must</u> go to work early tomorrow.

5 You <u>don't must</u> chat with your classmate during class.

6 You <u>have not to</u> bring anything. We will prepare everything.

B 두 문장의 의미가 통하도록 보기 에서 알맞은 말을 골라 문장을 완성하시오. (한 번씩만 쓸 것)

[1~3]

보기	must	must not	have to

1 You must go home and take a rest.

→ You _____ go home and take a rest.

2 It is necessary for us to save more money.

→ We _____ save more money.

3 You are not allowed to take pictures in the museum.

→ You _____ take pictures in the museum.

[4~6]

보기	don't have to	should not	must

4 I'm sure that Jeremy is very angry with me.

→ Jeremy _____ be very angry with me.

5 You don't need to bring your camera. I will bring mine.

→ You _____ bring your camera. I will bring mine.

6 It is not good for you to play computer games too much.

→ You _____ play computer games too much.

C 우리말과 같은 뜻이 되도록 조동사와 주어진 단어를 이용하여 문장을 완성하시오.

1 우리는 교통 규칙을 지켜야 한다. (follow, the traffic rules)

→ We _____ _____ _____ _____ _____.

2 너는 6시까지 집에 들어와야 한다. (come, home, by six)

→ You _____ _____ _____ _____ _____.

3 소방관들은 매우 용감함이 틀림없다. (be, very, brave)

→ Firefighters _____ _____ _____ _____.

4 너는 이런 큰 기회를 놓치면 안 된다. (miss, this big chance)

→ You _____ _____ _____ _____ _____.

5 Linda는 성적을 걱정할 필요가 없었다. (worry about)

→ Linda _____ _____ _____ _____ _____ her grades.

6 성공하고 싶다면 너는 열심히 일해야 할 것이다. (work hard)

→ If you want to succeed, _____ _____ _____ _____ _____.

7 나는 하루에 세 번 이 약을 복용해야 한다. (take, this medicine)

→ I _____ _____ _____ _____ _____ three times a day.

D 우리말과 같은 뜻이 되도록 주어진 단어를 알맞게 배열하시오.

1 우리는 여기서 무단 횡단을 하면 안 된다. (not, here, must, jaywalk)

→ We _____.

2 제가 그녀의 사과를 받아 줘야 할까요? (I, apology, should, accept, her)

→ _____

3 나는 역사 보고서를 다시 써야 했다. (to, report, write, had, history, the)

→ I _____ again.

4 너는 그것에 대해 미안해할 필요가 없다. (it, feel, don't, to, sorry about, have)

→ You _____.

5 나는 내일 남동생을 돌보아야 한다. (my, take care of, will, have to, brother)

→ I _____ tomorrow.

6 그 책은 네가 이해하기에 어려운 것이 틀림없다. (for, must, difficult, understand, to, be, you)

→ The book _____.

7 당신은 영화가 상영되는 동안에는 휴대 전화를 꺼야 한다. (cell phone, turn off, should, your)

→ You _____ during the movie.

had better, used to, would like to

A 밑줄 친 부분을 어법에 맞게 고쳐 쓰시오.

1 I would like <u>have</u> a haircut.

2 They'<u>d be better</u> here soon.

3 I <u>not used to</u> have breakfast.

4 They used <u>to living</u> in a big city.

5 Did you <u>used</u> to take long walks?

6 You'<u>d not better</u> stay here any longer.

7 What would you like <u>doing</u> this weekend?

B 두 문장의 의미가 통하도록 보기 에서 알맞은 말을 골라 문장을 완성하시오. (중복 가능)

> 보기 had better   used to   would like to

1 No one wants to do the work.

→ No one _____ do the work.

2 I think I should not buy those jeans.

→ I _____ not buy those jeans.

3 I want to take you out to lunch.

→ I _____ take you out to lunch.

4 I liked rock music, but not anymore.

→ I _____ like rock music, but not anymore.

5 I think you should finish your homework before dinner.

→ You _____ finish your homework before dinner.

6 Jason worked for a bank before becoming a professor.

→ Jason _____ work for a bank before becoming a professor.

C 우리말과 같은 뜻이 되도록 주어진 단어를 이용하여 문장을 완성하시오.

1 Kevin은 혼자 여행을 하곤 했다. (travel, alone)

→ Kevin _____ _____ _____ _____ .

2 너는 오늘 오후에 쇼핑하고 싶니? (go shopping)

→ _____ _____ _____ _____ _____ this afternoon?

3 너는 새치기를 하지 않는 것이 좋겠다. (not, cut in line)

→ You _____ _____ _____ _____ _____ _____ .

4 너는 그 계단을 조심하는 게 좋겠다. (watch out)

→ You _____ _____ _____ _____ for the stairs.

5 창가 테이블을 하나 예약하고 싶어요. (reserve, a table)

→ I _____ _____ _____ _____ _____ by the window.

6 그들은 그 팝 콘서트에 가기를 원한다. (go to)

→ They _____ _____ _____ _____ the pop conert.

7 그는 어릴 때 부모님 앞에서 노래를 부르곤 했다. (sing, songs)

→ He _____ _____ _____ _____ in front of his parents when he was young.

D 우리말과 같은 뜻이 되도록 주어진 단어를 알맞게 배열하시오.

1 너는 저녁으로 무얼 먹고 싶니? (would, have, like to, what, you)

→ _____ for dinner?

2 너는 그에게 사실을 얘기하는 것이 좋겠다. (him, the truth, had better, tell)

→ You _____ .

3 어릴 때 너는 연 날리기를 즐기곤 했니? (use to, did, flying, you, enjoy, a kite)

→ _____ when you were little?

4 너는 이 강에서 수영하지 않는 것이 좋겠다. (not, swim, had, in this river, better)

→ You _____ .

5 나는 어릴 때 아빠와 캠핑을 가곤 했다. (go, would camping, my dad and I)

→ _____ when I was young.

6 마을에 네 개의 학교가 있었는데, 겨우 하나 남았다. (used, four, in town, there, to, schools, be)

→ _____ , but there is only one left.

7 Dean은 가족과 더 많은 시간을 보내는 것이 좋겠다. (spend, better, more time, had, his family, with)

→ Dean _____ .

UNIT 01 원급 비교, 비교급, 최상급

A 주어진 단어를 알맞은 형태로 고쳐 문장을 완성하시오.

1 Can you swim _____ than him? (fast)

2 Beth is the _____ girl in the class. (pretty)

3 These shoes are as _____ as those ones. (new)

4 Oranges are usually _____ than lemons. (sweet)

5 Carrie is not as _____ as Miranda in school. (popular)

6 My brother has the _____ room in my house. (big)

7 She earns as _____ money as her husband does. (much)

8 This question is a lot _____ than the previous one. (easy)

9 This restaurant serves the _____ chicken soup in town. (delicious)

B 밑줄 친 부분을 어법에 맞게 고쳐 쓰시오.

1 He is the <u>richer</u> guy in town.

2 Today is the <u>hot</u> day of the year.

3 This book is as <u>thickest</u> as that one.

4 I cannot cook as well <u>than</u> Mom does.

5 The game was <u>exciting</u> than I expected.

6 The situation is <u>very</u> worse than I expected.

7 You should listen to me more carefully <u>to</u> usual.

C 문장의 의미가 통하도록 주어진 단어를 이용하여 문장을 완성하시오.

1 Mark is 65 kg. Dean is 70 kg. Jacob is 60 kg.

→ Dean is _____ _____ of the three. (heavy)

2 My math grade is an A. Daniel's math grade is an A.

→ My math grade is _____ _____ _____ Daniel's. (good)

3 Joan has thirty books. Helen has thirty books.

→ Joan has _____ _____ _____ _____ Helen does. (many books)

4 The blue skirt is $30. The black skirt is $20. The red skirt is $15.

→ The blue skirt is _____ _____ _____ of the three. (expensive)

5 I go shopping twice a month. She goes shopping once a month.

→ I go shopping _____ _____ _____ she does. (often)

6 Steve can run 100 meters in 15 seconds. Louise can run it in 13 seconds.

→ Louise can run _____ _____ Steve can. (fast)

D 우리말과 같은 뜻이 되도록 주어진 단어를 이용하여 문장을 완성하시오.

1 나는 엄마만큼 일찍 일어난다. (get up, early)

→ I _____ _____ _____ _____ _____ my mother does.

2 이곳이 우리 동네에서 가장 저렴한 호텔이다. (cheap)

→ This _____ _____ _____ _____ in my neighborhood.

3 이 자동차가 저것보다 훨씬 낫다. (be, much, good)

→ This car _____ _____ _____ _____ that one.

4 나는 내 인생 최악의 실수를 했다. (make, bad, mistake)

→ I _____ _____ _____ _____ of my life.

5 스마트폰은 컴퓨터보다 유용하다. (useful, computers)

→ Smartphones are _____ _____ _____ _____.

6 나는 건강이 돈보다 중요하다고 생각한다. (important)

→ I think health _____ _____ _____ _____ _____.

7 그 어린 소년은 성인 남자만큼 힘이 세다. (strong, an adult man)

→ The little boy is _____ _____ _____ _____ _____ _____.

41

UNIT 02 비교급과 최상급 표현

A 주어진 단어를 알맞은 형태로 고쳐 문장을 완성하시오.

1 Who is _____, your father or your mother? (old)

2 My elder brother is twice as _____ as I am. (heavy)

3 This bridge is three times _____ than that one. (long)

4 No other man in the village is _____ than Richard. (rich)

5 The _____ I try to forget her, the more I miss her. (hard)

6 He is one of the _____ musicians of all time. (talented)

7 Vatican City is _____ than any other country in the world. (small)

8 Winter is coming. The days are getting _____. (short and short)

B 밑줄 친 부분을 어법에 맞게 고쳐 쓰시오.

1 Mike has twice as <u>more CDs</u> as I do.

2 After the sun sets, it becomes <u>dark and dark</u>.

3 <u>The heaviest</u> it rains, <u>the most</u> depressed I feel.

4 Which do you enjoy <u>most</u>, swimming or riding?

5 A human is more intelligent than <u>any other animals</u>.

6 No other worker in the company is <u>diligent than</u> Eddie.

7 Steven Spielberg is one of <u>the most famous director</u> in the world.

C 두 문장이 의미가 통하도록 빈칸에 알맞은 말을 쓰시오.

1 This book is three times thicker than that one.

→ This book is _____ _____ _____ _____ that one.

2 When you walk faster, you will arrive earlier.

→ _____ _____ you walk, _____ _____ you will arrive.

3 When we go up higher, it will become colder.

→ _____ _____ we go up, _____ _____ it will become.

4 My parents' bedroom is four times as large as my bedroom is.

→ My parents' bedroom is _____ _____ _____ _____ my bedroom is.

D 주어진 문장과 의미가 통하도록 문장을 완성하시오.

1 Health is the most important thing.

→ _____ other _____ is _____ _____ _____ health.

→ _____ other _____ is _____ _____ _____ health.

→ Health is _____ _____ _____ any other _____.

→ Health is _____ _____ _____ all the other _____.

2 The cheetah is the fastest animal on land.

→ _____ other _____ is _____ _____ _____ the cheetah.

→ _____ other _____ is _____ _____ the cheetah.

→ The cheetah is _____ _____ _____ _____ _____ on land.

→ The cheetah is _____ _____ all the other _____ on land.

E 우리말과 같은 뜻이 되도록 주어진 단어를 이용하여 문장을 완성하시오.

1 중국은 인도보다 네 배 더 크다. (large)

→ China is _____ _____ _____ _____ India.

2 두통과 치통 중 어떤 것이 더 나쁘니? (bad)

→ _____ _____ _____, headache or toothache?

3 Seth는 학교에서 다른 어떤 소년보다 키가 크다. (tall)

→ Seth is _____ _____ _____ _____ _____ in the school.

4 연설이 계속되자, 그는 점점 더 지루함을 느꼈다. (bored)

→ He felt _____ _____ _____ _____ as the speech went on.

5 우리는 많이 가질수록 더 많이 원한다. (many, have, many, want)

→ _____ _____ _____ _____, _____ _____ _____ _____.

6 프라하는 유럽에서 가장 매력 있는 도시들 중 하나이다. (attractive, city)

→ Prague is _____ _____ _____ _____ _____ in Europe.

7 너는 공부를 열심히 하면 할수록 더 좋은 점수를 얻는다. (much, study, good grade)

→ _____ _____ _____ _____, _____ _____ _____ you get.

UNIT 01 시간, 이유, 결과 접속사

A 보기 에서 알맞은 말을 골라 문장을 완성하시오. (한 번씩만 쓸 것)

[1~4] 보기   until   before   since   so

1 She washes her hands _____ she has a meal.

2 We have known each other _____ we were kids.

3 She kept traveling to Europe _____ all her money ran out.

4 The room smelled bad, _____ she opened the windows wide.

[5~8] 보기   because   after   when   because of

5 Rick felt much better _____ he took a painkiller.

6 _____ Anthony entered the theater, there was no one else there.

7 Everyone is looking at her _____ her unique style.

8 _____ babies are helpless and tiny, we should take care of them.

B 두 문장이 같은 뜻이 되도록 주어진 접속사를 이용하여 문장을 완성하시오.

1 He passed the exam easily because he studied hard.

→ He studied hard, _____. (so)

2 People brush their teeth before they go to sleep.

→ People go to sleep _____. (after)

3 She goes out for a walk after she has dinner.

→ She has dinner _____. (before)

4 Schools were closed because of heavy snow.

→ Schools were closed _____. (because)

5 When I was on my way to school, I met my English teacher.

→ _____, I met my English teacher. (as)

6 We like camping very much, so we go camping as often as possible.

→ We go camping as often as possible _____. (because)

C 우리말과 같은 뜻이 되도록 주어진 단어를 이용하여 문장을 완성하시오.

1 그녀는 나를 보자마자 울음을 터뜨렸다. (see)

→ _____ _____ _____ _____ _____, she burst into tears.

2 우리는 콘서트에 늦어서 택시를 탔다. (take, a taxi)

→ We were late for the concert, _____ _____ _____ _____ _____.

3 그는 축구를 하는 중에 다리가 부러졌다. (play soccer)

→ _____ _____ _____ _____ _____, he broke his leg.

4 그녀는 어렸을 때 수학을 정말 좋아했다. (be, young)

→ _____ _____ _____ _____, she liked math a lot.

5 어두웠기 때문에 우리는 아무것도 볼 수가 없었다. (be, dark)

→ _____ _____ _____ _____, we couldn't see anything.

6 나는 네가 올 때까지 여기 앉아서 커피를 한잔하고 있을게. (come back)

→ I will sit here and have a cup of coffee _____ _____ _____ _____.

7 그 책은 정말 재미있어서 나는 그것을 읽는 것을 멈출 수가 없었다. (interesting, can't, stop)

→ The book was _____ _____ _____ _____ _____
reading it.

D 우리말과 같은 뜻이 되도록 주어진 단어를 알맞게 배열하시오.

1 내가 없는 동안 내 애완견 좀 보살펴 줄래? (I, away, while, am)

→ _____, will you take care of my pet dog?

2 날씨가 점점 추워지면서 곰들이 겨울잠에 들어가기 시작한다. (it, colder, gets, as)

→ Bears start going into their winter sleep _____.

3 우리 어머니가 꽃을 좋아해서 나는 장미를 좀 샀다. (likes, my mother, as, flowers)

→ _____, I bought some roses.

4 너무 더워서 그는 에어컨을 켰다. (hot, turned on, he, that, so, the air conditioner)

→ It was _____.

5 선생님이 나가자마자, 학생들은 말을 하기 시작했다. (as, the teacher, soon, left, as)

→ _____, the students started talking.

6 그녀는 기차가 플랫폼에 도착할 때까지 기다렸다. (the train, the platform, arrived at, until)

→ She waited _____.

7 그는 아기를 깨우고 싶지 않았기 때문에 조용히 걸었다. (he, wake up, want, didn't, to, because, his baby)

→ _____, he walked quietly.

UNIT 02 조건, 양보, 상관 접속사

A 보기 에서 알맞은 접속사를 골라 문장을 완성하시오. (한 번씩만 쓸 것)

[1~5] 보기   unless   although   if   neither   either

1 I like _____ coffee nor soda.

2 _____ you or she has to give him a ride.

3 _____ it rains tomorrow, we can't go on a picnic.

4 _____ you fasten your seat belt, you may get hurt.

5 _____ the weather was terrible, my father went fishing.

[6~10] 보기   as well as   although   if   or   unless

6 _____ you need my help, just ask me.

7 Listen to your parents, _____ you'll get into trouble.

8 We will go swimming _____ the weather is cold.

9 _____ he kept apologizing to her, she didn't forgive him.

10 Balanced meals are important for adults _____ children.

B 두 문장의 의미가 통하도록 주어진 접속사를 이용하여 문장을 완성하시오.

1 My sister lives alone, and I do, too.
   → _____ live alone. (both)

2 Take a note, or you will forget it.
   → _____, you will forget it. (unless)
   → _____, you will forget it. (if~not)

3 The test was not difficult, and it was not easy, either.
   → The test was _____. (neither ~ nor)

4 Go straight, and you will see the post office on your right.
   → _____, you will see the post office on your right. (if)

5 I am satisfied with the result, and my parents are also satisfied.
   → _____ are satisfied with the result. (not only ~ but also)
   → _____ are satisfied with the result. (as well as)

C 우리말과 같은 뜻이 되도록 주어진 단어를 이용하여 문장을 완성하시오.

1 내 남동생뿐만 아니라 나도 피자를 좋아한다. (like)

→ _____ _____ _____ _____ _____ pizza.

2 그와 나는 둘 다 주말에 계획이 없다. (have)

→ _____ _____ _____ _____ _____ any plans for the weekend.

3 우산을 가지고 가라, 그렇지 않으면 젖을 것이다. (get, wet)

→ Take an umbrella with you, _____ _____ _____ _____ _____ .

4 조심하지 않으면 너는 그 칼에 베일 것이다. (be, careful)

→ _____ _____ _____ _____ , you will cut yourself with that knife.

5 우리는 버스를 타거나 아니면 지하철을 탈 수 있다. (take, the bus, take, the subway)

→ We can _____ _____ _____ _____ _____

_____ .

6 음악이 매우 시끄러웠음에도 불구하고 그녀는 깨지 않았다. (the music, be, very, noisy)

→ _____ _____ _____ _____ _____ , she didn't wake up.

7 책을 많이 읽어라, 그러면 너는 많은 지식을 얻게 될 것이다. (get, a lot of, knowledge)

→ Read a lot of books, _____ _____ _____ _____

_____ _____ .

D 우리말과 같은 뜻이 되도록 주어진 단어를 알맞게 배열하시오.

1 만약 네가 피곤하면 집에 가서 쉬어도 좋다. (feel, you, if, tired)

→ _____ , you can go home and rest.

2 내 새 차는 빠르지도 안전하지도 않다. (nor, neither, safe, fast, is)

→ My new car _____ .

3 너는 여기에 머무르거나 아니면 떠날 수 있다. (stay here, leave, or, either, can)

→ You _____ .

4 그는 매우 열심히 공부했음에도 불구하고 시험에 떨어졌다. (very, studied, hard, he, though)

→ _____ , he failed the test.

5 그녀는 음악과 영화에 흥미를 가지고 있다. (both, interested in, movies, music, and, has been)

→ She _____ .

6 Susan은 영국뿐만 아니라 프랑스도 여행했다. (not, England, also, only, France, but, traveled to)

→ Susan _____ .

UNIT 03 that, 간접의문문

A 빈칸에 **that** 또는 **whether**를 넣어 문장을 완성하시오.

1 No one can deny _____ he is guilty.

2 Sam asked me _____ I received her email.

3 I never thought _____ she met someone like you.

4 I wonder _____ he wants to drink something cold.

5 It is certain _____ air pollution is getting worse.

B 주어진 문장을 「It(가주어) ~ that(진주어)」 구문을 이용한 문장으로 바꿔 쓰시오.

1 That she is alive is a miracle.

→ _____

2 That he loves sports is known to everyone.

→ _____

3 That the actress won an Emmy is no surprise.

→ _____

4 That you keep your promise is important.

→ _____

5 That the little girl can understand the book is impossible.

→ _____

C 두 문장을 한 문장의 간접의문문으로 바꿔 쓰시오.

1 I wonder. + Did you meet them?

→ I wonder _____.

2 Please tell me. + When will she come home?

→ Please tell me _____.

3 Do you know? + What did he order for dinner?

→ Do you know _____?

4 They wonder. + Will he come to the party?

→ They wonder _____.

D 우리말과 같은 뜻이 되도록 주어진 단어를 이용하여 문장을 완성하시오.

1 네가 나와 함께 갈 것인지 말해 줘. (go with)

→ Tell me _____ _____ _____ _____ _____ .

2 그가 의사라는 것은 거짓말이다. (be, a doctor)

→ It is a lie _____ _____ _____ _____ _____ .

3 그는 그것이 안전한지 궁금하다. (wonder, be, safe)

→ He _____ _____ _____ _____ _____ .

4 그의 직업이 무엇인지 나에게 말해 줄래? (be, his job)

→ Can you tell me _____ _____ _____ _____ ?

5 나는 네가 더 잘할 수 있다고 믿는다. (believe, do better)

→ I _____ _____ _____ _____ _____ _____ .

6 나는 그녀가 일을 그만뒀다는 소식을 들었다. (hear, the news)

→ I _____ _____ _____ _____ she quit her job.

7 나는 그녀가 항상 최선을 다한다는 것을 알고 있다. (know, do one's best)

→ I _____ _____ _____ _____ _____ _____ .

E 우리말과 같은 뜻이 되도록 주어진 단어를 알맞게 배열하시오.

1 그가 어디에 사는지 아니? (where, lives, know, he, you)

→ Do _____ ?

2 그는 그녀가 아프다는 것을 모른다. (is, that, know, sick, she, doesn't)

→ He _____ .

3 나는 네가 네 일을 사랑한다는 것을 안다. (you, your work, love, that, know)

→ I _____ .

4 그녀가 결혼을 한다는 것이 사실이에요? (is, getting married, it, she, that, true)

→ Is _____ ?

5 내가 너의 휴대 전화를 빌릴 수 있는지 궁금해. (I, cell phone, can, your, borrow, whether, wonder)

→ I _____ .

6 그녀가 노래에 재능이 있다는 것은 행운이다. (she, is, a talent, has, that, lucky, for singing)

→ It _____ .

7 나는 그가 선수권 대회에서 우승할 거라고 믿는다. (win, believe, will, that, the championship, he)

→ I _____ .

UNIT 01 관계대명사 I

A 빈칸에 who(m), which, whose 중 알맞은 것을 써 넣으시오.

1 The book _____ cover is red is Jason's.

2 Lily is the girl _____ is playing the violin.

3 Is there any bookstore _____ is nearby?

4 The friend _____ we trusted betrayed us.

5 The book _____ he wrote became a bestseller.

6 The car _____ he bought last month is very nice.

7 I remember the gentleman _____ helped the elderly woman at the bus station.

B 두 문장을 관계대명사를 이용하여 한 문장으로 만드시오.

1 I didn't get the fax. You sent it.

→ I didn't get the fax _____ .

2 Tom is driving a car. The car is his father's.

→ Tom is driving a car _____ .

3 Helen is the girl. Her brother is a fashion model.

→ Helen is the girl _____ .

4 I have some relatives. I haven't seen them for years.

→ I have some relatives _____ .

5 The gloves look really warm. Amanda is wearing them.

→ The gloves _____ look really warm.

6 Ms. Collins is a new teacher. She starts teaching in March.

→ Ms. Collins is a new teacher _____ .

7 Helen is the woman. She likes planting flowers and trees.

→ Helen is the woman _____ .

C 우리말과 같은 뜻이 되도록 관계대명사와 주어진 단어를 이용하여 문장을 완성하시오.

1 내가 보낸 엽서를 받았니? (the postcard, send)

→ Did you get _____ _____ _____ _____ _____ ?

2 어젯밤에 나에게 전화한 소녀를 아니? (the girl, call)

→ Do you know _____ _____ _____ _____ _____ last night?

3 이것이 내가 너에게 말했던 그 사진이다. (the picture, tell)

→ This is _____ _____ _____ _____ _____ you about.

4 내가 정말 존경하는 사람은 우리 아버지이다. (the one, really, respect)

→ _____ _____ _____ _____ _____ _____ is my father.

5 우리는 계단을 올라가고 있는 노부인을 도와주었다. (an old woman, climb)

→ We helped _____ _____ _____ _____ _____ the stairs.

6 지갑을 도난 당한 남자가 경찰에 전화를 했다. (the man, wallet, be stolen)

→ _____ _____ _____ _____ _____ called the police.

7 Jim이 인도에서 산 접시들은 매우 예쁘다. (the plates, buy)

→ _____ _____ _____ _____ _____ in India are very pretty.

D 우리말과 같은 뜻이 되도록 주어진 단어를 배열하시오.

1 내가 어제 산 옷이 어디에 있지? (I, the clothes, bought, which)

→ Where are _____ yesterday?

2 지금 연주되고 있는 노래를 아니? (the song, is playing, which)

→ Do you know _____ now?

3 위층에 사는 사람들은 일본에서 왔다. (the people, upstairs, live, who)

→ _____ are from Japan.

4 너는 내가 준 선물이 마음에 드니? (you, which, I, the present, gave)

→ Do you like _____ ?

5 내가 함께 일했던 사람들은 매우 친절했다. (I, the people, worked with, whom)

→ _____ were very friendly.

6 7월부터 시작하는 미술 수업이 있나요? (from July, any art classes, start, which)

→ Are there _____ ?

7 Mia는 머릿결이 아주 부드러운 그 여자애를 부러워했다. (very soft, the girl, hair, was, whose)

→ Mia envied _____ .

UNIT **02** 관계대명사 II

A 보기 에서 알맞은 관계대명사를 골라 문장을 완성하시오. (한 번씩만 쓸 것)

| 보기 | who | whom | which | that | what |

1 This is the book for _____ I looked.

2 Do you remember the friend _____ came with me?

3 Please tell me _____ we need to prepare for the trip.

4 I don't know the lady to _____ you talked at the party.

5 Biology is the subject _____ Rachel studied her whole life.

B 밑줄 친 부분을 생략할 수 있으면 O, 생략할 수 없으면 X표 하시오.

1 That is the house in which my sister lives.

2 Titanic is the movie that I like the most.

3 Look at the boy who is dancing on the street.

4 I have good friends that I can tell everything to.

5 Where can I get the bus which goes to the city hall?

C 빈칸에 that과 what 중 알맞은 것을 넣어 문장을 완성하시오.

1 Is that _____ you want to get?

2 They asked _____ I do for a living.

3 Why don't we drink something _____ is hot?

4 I don't know _____ you're talking about.

5 I miss a friend _____ moved to the U.S.A.

6 She has a brother _____ is very good at math.

D 우리말과 같은 뜻이 되도록 주어진 단어를 이용하여 문장을 완성하시오.

1 이것은 내가 주문한 음식이 아니에요. (the food, order)

→ This is not _____ _____ _____ _____ _____.

2 이 카메라는 내가 찾고 있던 것이 아니에요. (look for)

→ This camera isn't _____ I have been _____ _____.

3 나는 침실에서 잃어버린 반지를 찾았다. (the ring, lose)

→ I found _____ _____ _____ _____ in the bedroom.

4 어제 네가 이야기한 예술가가 누구니? (the artist, talk)

→ Who is _____ _____ _____ _____ about yesterday?

5 우리가 간식으로 먹은 쿠키는 정말 맛있었다. (the cookies, eat)

→ _____ _____ _____ _____ for a snack were really good.

6 안경을 쓰고 있는 소년은 우리 오빠야. (the boy, wear, glasses)

→ _____ _____ _____ _____ _____ is my brother.

7 Billy는 자기에게 너무 큰 바지를 입고 있었다. (pants, be, too big)

→ Billy was wearing _____ _____ _____ _____ _____ for him.

E 우리말과 같은 뜻이 되도록 주어진 단어를 알맞게 배열하시오.

1 내가 했으면 하는 걸 말해 봐. (to do, you, want, what, me)

→ Tell me _____.

2 이것들이 우리가 사야 할 품목들이야. (should, that, buy, we, the items)

→ These are _____.

3 현장 학습을 위해 내가 가져와야 할 것을 적어 줄래? (need, I, to bring, what)

→ Can you write down _____ for the school field trip?

4 내가 초대한 모든 사람들이 우리 파티에 왔어. (I, all the people, invited, that)

→ _____ came to our party.

5 네가 Charlie에게서 들은 것은 사실이 아니야. (heard, what, Charlie, from, you)

→ _____ is not true.

6 나는 네가 얻고 싶어 하는 정보를 네게 줄 수 있어. (want, you, the information, that)

→ I can give you _____ to get.

7 이것이 내가 지금까지 본 영화 중 가장 슬픈 영화야. (I, ever, that, the saddest movie, seen, have)

→ This is _____.

53

UNIT 03 관계부사

A 보기 에서 알맞은 관계부사를 골라 문장을 완성하시오. (한 번씩만 쓸 것)

> 보기   when   where   how   why

1 There's no reason _____ you should feel sad.

2 The day _____ I was married was very warm.

3 The town _____ I was born is near the beach.

4 Can you tell me _____ you spend your leisure time?

B 두 문장의 의미가 같아지도록 관계부사를 이용하여 문장을 완성하시오.

1 Friday is the day on which they go to the movies.

→ Friday is the day _____.

2 I'd like to know the way in which you made this pumpkin pie.

→ I'd like to know _____.

3 I can't understand the reason for which some people hate pets.

→ I can't understand the reason _____.

4 This is the restaurant in which I had my birthday party last year.

→ This is the restaurant _____.

C 두 문장을 관계부사를 이용하여 한 문장으로 만드시오.

1 I can't forget the day. I first visited Paris on that day.

→ I can't forget the day _____.

2 Miranda told me the way. She learned Chinese in that way.

→ Miranda told me _____.

3 This is the drawer. My mother keeps her scarves in the drawer.

→ This is the drawer _____.

4 Do you know the reason? The meeting was canceled for that reason.

→ Do you know the reason _____?

D 우리말과 같은 뜻이 되도록 관계부사와 주어진 단어를 이용하여 문장을 완성하시오.

1 나는 Rachel을 처음 만났던 날을 기억한다. (first, meet)

→ I remember _____ _____ _____ _____ _____ _____ Rachel.

2 일요일은 그들이 소풍을 가는 날이다. (go)

→ Sunday is _____ _____ _____ _____ _____ for a picnic.

3 그녀가 그렇게 일찍 떠난 이유를 나에게 말해 줄래? (leave)

→ Can you tell me _____ _____ _____ _____ _____ so early?

4 이곳이 내 친구들이 주로 모이는 장소이다. (the place, usually, gather together)

→ This is _____ _____ _____ _____ _____ _____

_____ .

5 내가 그들이 시험에 통과할 수 없었던 이유를 설명해 줄게. (can't, pass, the exam)

→ I will explain _____ _____ _____ _____ _____ _____

_____ _____ .

6 나에게 네가 어떻게 그 수학 문제를 풀었는지 말해 줘. (solve, the math problem)

→ Tell me _____ _____ _____ _____ _____ _____ .

E 우리말과 같은 뜻이 되도록 주어진 단어를 배열하시오.

1 너는 그가 그렇게 화가 난 이유를 아니? (so, why, is, the reason, angry, he)

→ Do you know _____ ?

2 지난밤에 울었던 이유를 말해 줄 수 있겠니? (last night, why, cried, the reason, you)

→ Can you tell me _____ ?

3 우리는 당신을 다시 만나는 날을 고대하고 있습니다. (again, you, the day, we, when, meet)

→ We're looking forward to _____ .

4 2008년은 Abbie가 대학을 졸업한 해였다. (graduated from, the year, college, Abbie, when)

→ 2008 was _____ .

5 그 할머니가 비법 소스를 만드는 방법을 아무도 모른다. (her secret sauce, the grandmother, makes, how)

→ Nobody knows _____ .

6 제가 훌륭한 샌드위치를 파는 곳을 알려드리겠습니다. (the place, can get, you, where, great sandwiches)

→ I'll show you _____ .

7 Harry는 자신이 10년 동안 살았던 아파트를 돌아보았다. (where, the apartment, he, for ten years, had lived)

→ Harry looked around _____ .

UNIT 01 현재분사, 과거분사

A 주어진 단어를 과거분사나 현재분사로 바꿔 문장을 완성하시오.

1 This is a picture _____ by my daughter. (draw)

2 Park Hotel is an old hotel _____ in the 1950s. (build)

3 I saw a man _____ the violin on the street. (play)

4 The man _____ over there is my husband. (stand)

5 I enjoy listening to the sound of the _____ rain. (fall)

6 My grandfather often tells us _____ stories. (interest)

7 Whose is the car _____ in front of my house? (park)

8 When she heard the _____ news, her face hardened. (disappoint)

B 보기 와 같이 문장을 완성하시오.

> 보기　Two kids are carrying a box. It is filled with toys.
> → Two kids are carrying a box filled with toys.

1 Look at the kite. It is flying in the sky.

　→ Look at the kite _____.

2 The boy is reading a book. It is written in English.

　→ The boy is reading a book _____.

3 The lady is wearing a red skirt. She is my aunt, Annie.

　→ The lady _____ is my aunt, Annie.

4 The house is my grandparents' house. It is painted blue.

　→ The house _____ is my grandparents' house.

5 There are many children. They are swimming in the sea.

　→ There are many children _____.

6 Mary showed me some pictures. They were taken in Europe.

　→ Mary showed me some pictures _____.

C 우리말과 같은 뜻이 되도록 분사와 주어진 단어를 이용하여 문장을 완성하시오.

1 그녀는 깨진 유리 조각에 베었다. (break, glass)

→ She cut herself on a piece of _____ _____.

2 Julia는 자신의 잃어버린 가방을 찾고 있다. (lose)

→ Julia is looking for _____ _____ _____.

3 그 영화가 너무 지루해서 나는 잠이 들었다. (so, bore)

→ _____ _____ _____ _____ that I fell asleep.

4 그들은 나무로 만들어진 상자를 하나 샀다. (make, of, wood)

→ They bought _____ _____ _____ _____ _____.

5 내 침대에서 자고 있는 그 소년이 누구니? (the boy, sleep, on, bed)

→ Who is _____ _____ _____ _____ _____ _____ ?

6 그의 승리는 우리에게 너무나도 놀라웠다. (victory, be, really, amaze)

→ _____ _____ _____ _____ _____ to us.

7 그녀는 무언가가 자신의 가슴을 압박하는 것을 느꼈다. (something, press on, chest)

→ She felt _____ _____ _____ _____ _____.

D 우리말과 같은 뜻이 되도록 주어진 말을 알맞게 배열하시오.

1 스토브 위에 있는 물을 조심해라. (the, water, boiling)

→ Be careful of _____ on the stove.

2 나는 정원에서 낙엽을 조금 주웠다. (leaves, picked up, fallen, some)

→ I _____ in the garden.

3 Jake는 빈집을 응시하며 서 있었다. (the empty house, staring at, was standing)

→ Jake _____.

4 개를 산책시키던 여성이 그 남자에게 말을 건넸다. (her dog, walking, the woman)

→ _____ talked to the man.

5 Peter는 모든 마을 사람들에게 알려진 화가이다. (everyone, known, an artist, to)

→ Peter is _____ in town.

6 우리 부모님은 그 소식에 많이 놀라신 것 같다. (very, at, seem, the news, surprised)

→ My parents _____.

7 나는 우리 할머니가 만드신 음식을 가장 좋아한다. (by, cooked, the food, my grandmother)

→ I like _____ most.

02 분사구문

A 두 문장이 같은 의미가 되도록 분사구문을 이용하여 문장을 완성하시오.

1 As he listened to the music, he lay on the bed.

→ _____, he lay on the bed.

2 Even though she lives alone, she still has many visitors.

→ _____, she still has many visitors.

3 If you turn to the left, you will find the post office.

→ _____, you will find the post office.

4 Because he was busy, he couldn't go to the party.

→ _____, he couldn't go to the party.

5 Because he had a bad cold, he went to see a doctor.

→ _____, he went to see a doctor.

6 As he smiled brightly, the boy ran toward his mother.

→ _____, the boy ran toward his mother.

7 When I cleaned the attic, I found an old baby picture of me.

→ _____, I found an old baby picture of me.

B 주어진 접속사를 이용하여 두 문장의 의미가 통하도록 부사절을 완성하시오.

1 Stella stood up, shouting loudly. (as)

→ Stella stood up _____.

2 Hearing the sad news, she began to cry. (when)

→ _____, she began to cry.

3 Taking the subway, you will get there on time. (if)

→ _____, you will get there on time.

4 Winning the game, they screamed with excitement. (after)

→ _____, they screamed with excitement.

5 Waiting for the bus, he talked on the phone. (while)

→ _____, he talked on the phone.

6 Not having enough money, Sam decided to not to buy the house. (because)

→ _____, Sam decided to not to buy the house.

C 우리말과 같은 뜻이 되도록 주어진 단어와 분사구문을 이용하여 문장을 완성하시오.

1 그는 커피를 마시면서 신문을 읽었다. (drink)

→ ＿＿＿＿＿＿＿ ＿＿＿＿＿＿, he read a newspaper.

2 그 선수는 부상을 당했음에도 불구하고 경기를 끝마쳤다. (be, injured)

→ ＿＿＿＿＿＿＿＿＿ ＿＿＿＿＿＿, the player completed the match.

3 작별 인사를 한 후에 그는 버스를 탔다. (say, goodbye)

→ ＿＿＿＿＿＿＿＿＿＿, he got on the bus.

4 창밖을 보면 눈이 내리는 것을 볼 수 있을 것이다. (look out, the window)

→ ＿＿＿＿＿ ＿＿＿＿＿ ＿＿＿＿＿ ＿＿＿＿, you can see snow falling.

5 클래식 음악을 들으면 그녀는 차분해진다. (listen to, classical music)

→ ＿＿＿＿＿ ＿＿＿＿＿ ＿＿＿＿＿ ＿＿＿＿, she feels relaxed.

6 Steve는 친절하기 때문에 모든 사람들에게서 사랑을 받는다. (be, kind)

→ ＿＿＿＿＿＿ ＿＿＿＿＿, Steve is loved by everyone.

7 충분한 용기가 없었기 때문에 그는 그녀에게 말을 걸지 못했다. (not, have, enough courage)

→ ＿＿＿＿＿＿ ＿＿＿＿＿ ＿＿＿＿＿ ＿＿＿＿, he couldn't talk to her.

D 우리말과 같은 뜻이 되도록 주어진 말을 알맞게 배열하시오.

1 그녀는 너무 놀랐기 때문에 얼굴이 창백해졌다. (so shocked, turned, she, pale, being)

→ ＿＿＿＿＿＿＿＿＿＿＿＿＿＿＿＿＿＿＿＿＿＿＿＿＿＿＿

2 경찰을 보자 그는 도망치기 시작했다. (to run away, he, seeing, the police officer, started)

→ ＿＿＿＿＿＿＿＿＿＿＿＿＿＿＿＿＿＿＿＿＿＿＿＿＿＿＿

3 매일 운동을 한다면 너는 건강해질 것이다. (be, every day, healthy, exercising, will, you)

→ ＿＿＿＿＿＿＿＿＿＿＿＿＿＿＿＿＿＿＿＿＿＿＿＿＿＿＿

4 나는 최선을 다했지만, 경주에서 이길 수 없었다. (the race, I, my best, win, doing, still couldn't)

→ ＿＿＿＿＿＿＿＿＿＿＿＿＿＿＿＿＿＿＿＿＿＿＿＿＿＿＿

5 나는 목욕을 하는 중에 문 두드리는 소리를 들었다. (at the door, a bath, heard, taking, I, a knock)

→ ＿＿＿＿＿＿＿＿＿＿＿＿＿＿＿＿＿＿＿＿＿＿＿＿＿＿＿

6 그 소식을 들었을 때 학생들은 기뻐서 펄쩍 뛰었다. (the news, jumped, the students, for joy, hearing)

→ ＿＿＿＿＿＿＿＿＿＿＿＿＿＿＿＿＿＿＿＿＿＿＿＿＿＿＿

7 뭐라고 말해야 할지 몰랐기 때문에, 그녀는 침묵을 지켰다. (silent, not, she, knowing, what to say, remained)

→ ＿＿＿＿＿＿＿＿＿＿＿＿＿＿＿＿＿＿＿＿＿＿＿＿＿＿＿

UNIT 01 능동태와 수동태

A 보기 에서 알맞은 말을 골라 문장을 완성하시오.

> 보기   are caused   being built   was broken   will be done   was taken

1 A new hospital is _____.

2 The dishes _____ by my sister.

3 Many car accidents _____ by sleepy drivers.

4 Suddenly, the window _____ by a snowball.

5 The first step on the moon _____ by Neil Armstrong.

B 밑줄 친 부분을 바르게 고쳐 쓰시오.

1 A car is be repaired by a repairman.

2 *Romeo and Juliet* wrote by Shakespeare.

3 The travel schedule will change by them.

4 A lot of clothes are donate by the students.

5 The chairs will moved to the living room by Kevin.

6 The National Anthem is playing now by the marching band.

C 능동태 문장을 수동태 문장으로 바꿔 쓰시오.

1 His mother is feeding the boy.

→ The boy _____.

2 Patrick will find the solution.

→ The solution _____.

3 Levi Strauss made denim jeans.

→ Denim jeans _____.

4 A lot of people have admired Mother Teresa.

→ Mother Teresa _____.

5 Helen took these brilliant photographs.

→ These brilliant photographs _____.

D 우리말과 같은 뜻이 되도록 주어진 단어를 이용하여 문장을 완성하시오.

1 저녁식사가 준비되고 있다. (prepare)

→ Dinner _____ _____ _____ .

2 음료는 메뉴에 포함되어 있다. (drinks, include)

→ _____ _____ _____ in the menu.

3 아무도 그 화재로 다치지 않았다. (hurt)

→ No one _____ _____ in the fire.

4 그 질문에 Ryan이 답변을 하였다. (answer)

→ The question _____ _____ _____ Ryan.

5 그 회의는 Jason에 의해 준비될 것이다. (organize)

→ The meeting _____ _____ _____ _____ Jason.

6 시간이 지나면서 모든 것이 잊혀질 것이다. (forget)

→ Everything _____ _____ _____ with time.

7 초콜릿은 아이들에 의해 사랑받는다. (love, children)

→ Chocolate _____ _____ _____ _____ .

E 우리말과 같은 뜻이 되도록 주어진 단어를 배열하시오.

1 우유는 Eric이 사 올 것이다. (be, Eric, bought, will, by)

→ Milk _____ .

2 프랑스어는 세계 많은 곳에서 이용된다. (spoken, is, French)

→ _____ in many parts of the world.

3 모든 비행이 짙은 안개로 취소되었다. (cancelled, all flights, were)

→ _____ because of heavy fog.

4 우리의 대화가 녹음되고 있다. (being, is, our conversation, recorded)

→ _____

5 이 차들은 독일에서 생산된 것이다. (in Germany, produced, are, these cars)

→ _____

6 지금 우리 가족이 야구 경기를 보고 있다. (my family, watched, is, by, being)

→ A baseball game _____ .

7 내 지갑이 지하철에서 발견되었다. (my purse, found, was)

→ _____ in the subway.

UNIT 02 여러 가지 수동태

A 밑줄 친 부분을 어법에 맞게 고쳐 쓰시오.

1 <u>Did</u> the flowers planted by Susan?

2 He was seen <u>run</u> in the park.

3 My dog <u>named</u> Wow by my brother.

4 Chemistry is taught <u>for</u> us by Mr. Connie.

5 These books <u>should return</u> to the library.

6 The apples on the table <u>were eaten not</u> by Watson.

B 능동태 문장을 수동태 문장으로 바꿔 쓰시오.

1 He doesn't clean his room.

→ His room _____ .

2 Did a volcano destroy Pompeii?

→ _____ Pompeii _____ ?

3 The witness didn't tell the truth.

→ The truth _____ .

4 Brian should finish his homework tonight.

→ His homework _____ .

C 능동태 문장을 수동태 문장으로 바꿔 쓰시오.

1 Ann asked me a big favor.

→ A big favor _____ .

2 They made my uncle a captain.

→ My uncle _____ .

3 He wrote Liz a love letter.

→ A love letter _____ .

4 Someone gave me this package.

→ I _____ .

→ This package _____ .

D 우리말과 같은 뜻이 되도록 주어진 단어를 이용하여 문장을 완성하시오.

1 모든 답은 영어로 쓰여져야 한다. (must, write)

→ All the answers _____ _____ _____ _____ _____ .

2 과학관은 주말에 문을 닫는다. (close)

→ The science museum _____ _____ on weekends.

3 그 선물은 나에게 보내진 것이 아니었다. (send)

→ The gift _____ _____ _____ _____ .

4 만리장성은 우주에서도 보이나요? (see)

→ Can the Great Wall _____ _____ from space?

5 Jack으로 하여금 모든 것을 말하게 했다. (make, tell)

→ Jack _____ _____ _____ everything.

6 이 스파게티는 언니가 나를 위해 요리한 것이다. (cook)

→ This spaghetti _____ _____ _____ _____ by my sister.

7 그 가수가 무대 위에서 노래하고 있는 것이 보였다. (see, sing)

→ The singer _____ _____ _____ on the stage.

E 우리말과 같은 뜻이 되도록 주어진 단어를 배열하시오.

1 이 건물은 1996년에 지어졌니? (built, this building, was)

→ _____ in 1996?

2 우승자에게 메달이 수여되었다. (given, the winner, to, was)

→ A medal _____ .

3 Jerry가 줄넘기 하는 것을 보았다. (jumping rope, seen, was)

→ Jerry _____ .

4 이 약은 하루에 두 번 복용해야 한다. (a day, taken, twice, be, should)

→ This medicine _____ .

5 그 계산서는 웨이터가 우리에게 가져온 것이었다. (brought, the waiter, us, was, to, by)

→ The bill _____ .

6 그는 회의에 참석해 달라는 요청을 받았다. (asked, the meeting, was, attend, to)

→ He _____ .

7 그 모형 비행기는 Dylan에 의해 만들어진 것이 아니었다. (made, Dylan, not, by, was)

→ The model airplane _____ .

UNIT 03 주의해야 할 수동태

A 빈칸에 알맞은 말을 보기에서 골라 쓰시오. (한 번씩만 쓸 것)

[1~4]

> 보기   with   about   in   of

1 My house is made _____ wood.

2 I'm worried _____ what will happen.

3 Are you interested _____ science fiction?

4 My parents will be pleased _____ the news.

[5~8]

> 보기   at   with   to   from

5 Wine is made _____ grapes.

6 This movie is not known _____ young people.

7 I was surprised _____ his decision to study abroad.

8 About three fourths of the earth is covered _____ water.

B 능동태 문장을 수동태 문장으로 고쳐 쓰시오.

1 A truck ran over a poor cat.

  → A poor cat _____ .

2 All my classmates laughed at me.

  → I _____ .

3 My grandparents brought me up.

  → I _____ .

4 I took care of my nephews yesterday.

  → My nephews _____ yesterday.

5 People make use of the Internet for many purposes.

  → The Internet _____ for many purposes.

C 우리말과 같은 뜻이 되도록 주어진 단어를 이용하여 문장을 완성하시오.

1 그 어린 소녀는 패션에 관심이 있다. (interest, fashion)

→ The little girl _____ _____ _____ _____.

2 그 아이들은 유모의 돌봄을 받을 것이다. (look after, a nanny)

→ The children _____ _____ _____ _____ _____ _____ _____.

3 그 소문은 학교의 모든 학생들에게 알려졌다. (know, all students)

→ The rumor _____ _____ _____ _____ _____ in school.

4 수학여행이 교장선생님에 의해서 연기되었다. (put off, the principal)

→ The school trip _____ _____ _____ _____ _____.

5 그들은 고객서비스에 만족하지 못했다. (satisfy, the customer service)

→ They _____ _____ _____ _____ _____ _____.

6 아이들의 얼굴은 기쁨과 행복으로 가득 차 있다. (fill, joy and happiness)

→ The children's faces _____ _____ _____ _____ _____.

7 그는 마을 사람들에게 존경을 받는다. (look up to, the villagers)

→ He _____ _____ _____ _____ _____ _____ _____.

D 우리말과 같은 뜻이 되도록 주어진 말을 알맞게 배열하시오.

1 남극은 얼음으로 덮여 있다. (with, is, ice, the South Pole, covered)

→ _____

2 그 선물 상자는 초콜릿으로 가득 차 있다. (chocolate, filled, is, with)

→ The gift box _____.

3 사람들은 선거 결과에 놀랐다. (at, surprised, the election result, were)

→ People _____.

4 동전은 구리와 니켈로 만들어진다. (from, are, copper and nickel, made, coins)

→ _____

5 그 소녀는 조부모님에 의해 길러졌다. (by, was, brought up, her grandparents)

→ The girl _____.

6 그는 아들의 승리에 매우 기뻐했다. (with, pleased, very, was, his son's victory)

→ He _____.

7 우리는 그 식당의 음식에 실망했다. (at the restaurant, were, the food, disappointed, with)

→ We _____.

UNIT 01 가정법 과거, 가정법 과거완료

A 주어진 단어를 이용하여 문장을 완성하시오.

1 If I _____ time, I would help you. (have)

2 If she liked to dance, she would _____ our club. (join)

3 If he weren't sick, he would _____ camping with us. (go)

4 If I _____ harder, I would have passed the test. (try)

5 If he knew her email address, he would _____ her an email. (send)

6 If it _____ in the evening, we would have gone for a walk. (not, rain)

7 If you _____ me, I would have helped you move to a new house. (ask)

B 두 문장이 같은 뜻이 되도록 가정법 문장을 완성하시오.

1 As I am very busy, I can't help you cook.

  → If I _____, I _____.

2 As we didn't hurry, we couldn't catch the train.

  → If we _____, we _____.

3 As he doesn't have courage, he doesn't admit to his mistake.

  → If he _____, he _____.

4 As I didn't do my best, I didn't win the competition.

  → If I _____, I _____.

5 As it wasn't sunny yesterday, we didn't go on a picnic.

  → If it _____, we _____.

6 As I don't have enough money, I can't buy a house for my parents.

  → If I _____, I _____.

7 As Harry didn't behave politely, his mother was angry at him.

  → If Harry _____, his mother _____.

C 우리말과 같은 뜻이 되도록 주어진 단어를 이용하여 문장을 완성하시오.

1 내가 차가 있다면 버스를 타지 않을 텐데. (have, take)

→ If I _____ a car, I _____ _____ a bus.

2 그가 좀 더 조심했다면 다치지 않았을 텐데. (be, hurt)

→ If he _____ _____ more careful, he _____ _____ _____ himself.

3 어제 비가 오지 않았다면, 그들은 밖에서 놀았을 텐데. (rain, play)

→ If it _____ _____ yesterday, they _____ _____ _____ outdoors.

4 내게 돈이 있다면 저 컴퓨터를 살 텐데. (have, buy)

→ If I _____ money, I _____ _____ that computer.

5 그녀가 아프지 않다면 강의에 참석할 텐데. (be, attend)

→ If she _____ sick, she _____ _____ the lecture.

6 우리가 시간이 충분하면, 해외여행을 할 수 있을 텐데. (have, travel)

→ If we _____ enough time, we _____ _____ abroad.

7 그가 조금 더 일찍 도착했다면, 그녀를 만날 수 있었을 텐데. (arrive, meet)

→ If he _____ _____ earlier, he _____ _____ _____ her.

D 우리말과 같은 뜻이 되도록 주어진 단어를 배열하시오.

1 내가 그녀라면 그렇게 말하지 않을 텐데. (talk, were, wouldn't, like that, her, I)

→ If I _____ .

2 내가 도시에 산다면 더 편할 텐데. (more convenient, the city, it, be, lived in, would)

→ If I _____ .

3 네가 그 영화를 봤다면 많이 좋아했을 텐데. (it, seen, would, liked, had, have, the movie, you)

→ If you _____ very much.

4 오늘 밤 내가 시간이 있다면 영화를 보러 갈 텐데. (go, had, would, tonight, to the movies, time, I)

→ If I _____ .

5 그들이 그 음식을 먹었다면, 매일 먹고 싶어 했을 텐데. (would, had, have, the food, wanted, eaten, they)

→ If they _____ to eat it every day.

6 안경을 끼지 않으면 너는 훨씬 더 나아 보일 텐데. (look, wear, didn't, would, much better, glasses, you)

→ If you _____ .

7 내가 약속을 잊어버리지 않았으면 그곳에 갔을 텐데. (gone, forgotten, I, the appointment, have, hadn't, would)

→ If I _____ there.

UNIT 02 I wish, as if

A 주어진 단어를 이용하여 문장을 완성하시오.

1 Jane works until 9 pm. I wish she _____ that late. (not, work)

2 The concert was great! I wish you _____ there with me. (be)

3 It snowed a lot yesterday. I wish it _____. (not, snow)

4 I caught a cold. I wish I _____ last night. (not, go out)

5 They are not close friends, but they act as if they _____ close friends. (be)

6 Lena couldn't sleep at all, but she looks as if she _____ a good sleep. (have)

7 Rachel hasn't been to Mexico, but she talks as if she _____ to Mexico. (be)

B 두 문장의 의미가 통하도록 가정법 문장을 완성하시오.

1 I'm sorry I didn't bring my coat.

   → I wish I _____.

2 I'm sorry I'm not eighteen years old.

   → I wish I _____.

3 I'm sorry Cathy isn't interested in me.

   → I wish Cathy _____.

4 In fact, I haven't met him before.

   → I feel as if I _____.

5 In fact, Ted doesn't know about the issue.

   → He talks as if he _____.

6 In fact, my boss didn't see the document.

   → My boss talks as if she _____.

7 In fact, he has a problem to solve.

   → He acts as if he _____.

C 우리말과 같은 뜻이 되도록 주어진 단어를 이용하여 문장을 완성하시오.

1 나는 남자친구가 없어. 있으면 좋을 텐데. (wish, have)

→ I don't have a boyfriend. I _____ _____ _____ one.

2 나는 지금 떠나야 해. 더 머무를 수 있으면 좋을 텐데. (wish, stay)

→ I should leave now. I _____ _____ _____ _____ longer.

3 나는 마치 아무것도 먹지 않은 것처럼 배가 고프지만, 이미 점심을 먹었다. (as if, eat)

→ I'm hungry _____ _____ _____ _____ _____ anything, but I already had lunch.

4 Angela는 마치 20대인 것처럼 보이지만, 20대가 아니다. (as if, be)

→ Angela looks _____ _____ _____ _____ in her 20s, but she isn't.

5 우리는 그 경기에서 졌어. 우리가 이겼다면 좋을 텐데. (wish, win)

→ We lost the match. I _____ _____ _____ _____ the match.

6 James는 마치 이해한 것처럼 고개를 끄덕였지만, 이해하지 못했다. (as if, understand)

→ James nodded his head _____ _____ _____ _____ _____, but he didn't.

D 우리말과 같은 뜻이 되도록 주어진 단어를 배열하시오.

1 그는 마치 요리사처럼 요리를 잘한다. (a chef, as if, were, he)

→ He is good at cooking _____.

2 나는 도시에 산다. 시골에 살면 좋을 텐데. (lived in, wish, the countryside, I)

→ I live in the city. I _____.

3 Bob은 복권에 당첨된 것처럼 돈을 많이 쓴다. (the lottery, won, he, as if, had)

→ Bob spends a lot of money _____.

4 Simon은 아무것도 보지 못한 것처럼 행동한다. (anything, seen, he, as if, hadn't)

→ Simon behaves _____.

5 중국어를 유창하게 할 수 있다면 좋을 텐데. (Chinese, speak, fluently, could, I, wish)

→ I _____.

6 용돈을 지난주에 다 쓰지 않으면 좋을 텐데. (spent, wish, all of my allowance, hadn't, I)

→ I _____ last week.

7 우리 오빠가 쿠키를 다 먹어버렸다. 나를 위해 좀 남겼으면 좋을 텐데. (some cookies, left, he, wish, for me, had)

→ My brother ate up all the cookies. I _____.

UNIT 03 시제 일치

A 주어진 동사를 가장 알맞은 형태로 바꾸어 빈칸을 채우시오.

1 I didn't know you _____ there. (be)

2 I thought you _____ watching TV. (be)

3 We learned that the sun _____ in the east. (rise)

4 I thought she _____ me as well, but she didn't. (like)

5 My teacher said that World War II _____ in 1945. (end)

6 Galileo Galilei said that the earth _____ around the sun. (go)

7 My teacher taught us that where there _____ a will, there is a way. (be)

B 주절의 시제를 과거 시제로 바꾼 문장을 완성하시오.

1 He knows that I will visit him.

→ He knew that I _____.

2 Jeff says that he will come to see me.

→ Jeff said that he _____.

3 We learn that oil and water don't mix.

→ We learned that oil and water _____.

4 He says that he is glad to see me again.

→ He said that he _____.

5 The book says that General Lee made the turtle ship.

→ The book said that General Lee _____.

6 My father says that slow and steady wins the race.

→ My father said that slow and steady _____.

7 She says that she is happy to have a friend like me.

→ She said that she _____.

C 우리말과 같은 뜻이 되도록 주어진 단어를 이용하여 문장을 완성하시오.

1 나는 그가 졸업 후에 일자리를 얻게 될 거라고 믿는다. (believe, will, get)

→ I _____ he _____ _____ a job after graduation.

2 Sara는 많은 연극을 보고 싶다고 말했다. (say, want)

→ Sara _____ that she _____ to watch many plays.

3 Jack이 말하길 그들은 내가 그곳에 도착하기 전에 떠났다고 했다. (say, leave)

→ Jack _____ that they _____ _____ there before I arrived.

4 그 책에는 콜럼버스가 1492년에 아메리카 대륙을 발견했다고 쓰여 있다. (discover)

→ The book says that Columbus _____ America in 1492.

5 나는 Shiu 부인이 책을 빌리러 도서관에 자주 간다고 들었다. (hear, go)

→ I _____ that Mrs. Shiu often _____ to the library to borrow books.

6 우리는 빛이 소리보다 빠르게 이동한다고 배웠다. (learn, travel)

→ We _____ that light _____ faster than sound.

7 우리 부모님께서는 네가 좋은 학생이라고 생각하신다. (think, be)

→ My parents _____ that you _____ a good student.

D 우리말과 같은 뜻이 되도록 주어진 단어를 배열하시오.

1 나는 Sam이 3년 동안 부산에 살았다고 들었다. (Sam, had lived, that, heard)

→ I _____ in Busan for 3 years.

2 Michael은 구내식당에 점심을 먹으러 갔었다고 말했다. (he, that, visited, said, had)

→ Michael _____ the cafeteria to eat lunch.

3 그녀에게 내가 다음 주에 책을 보낼 거라고 말해주세요. (her, send, will, I, that, tell)

→ Please _____ her the book next week.

4 Bob은 나에게 매일 아침 다섯 시에 일어난다고 말했다. (me, gets up, he, that, told)

→ Bob _____ at 5 every morning.

5 Smith 씨는 조수에게 그 우편물을 부치도록 했다고 말했다. (get, he, that, said, would)

→ Mr. Smith _____ his assistant to send the mail.

6 우리 선생님이 달이 조류를 만든다고 가르쳐 주셨다. (the moon, that, us, taught, causes)

→ My teacher _____ the tides.

7 우리는 한국 전쟁이 1953년에 끝났다는 사실을 알고 있다. (ended, the Korean War, that, know)

→ We _____ in 1953.

화법

A 직접화법 문장을 간접화법 문장으로 바꿔 쓰시오.

1 Mark said to me, "What do you want to eat?"

→ Mark asked me _____.

2 Catherine said, "I went downtown."

→ Catherine said _____.

3 Jia said to me, "Did you do your homework?"

→ Jia asked me _____.

4 Kelly said to me, "I am not cleaning my room now."

→ Kelly told me _____.

5 Mac said to me, "Did you see the accident?"

→ Mac asked me _____.

6 Sandra said to me, "Where did you buy the game CD?"

→ Sandra asked me _____.

B 간접화법 문장을 직접화법 문장으로 바꿔 쓰시오.

1 I asked Luke whether he had caught a cold.

→ I said to Luke, "_____?"

2 Mia asked me if I liked pumpkin pies.

→ Mia said to me, "_____?"

3 Ned said that he was learning swimming then.

→ Ned said, "_____."

4 Julia told me that she wanted to come with me.

→ Julia said to me, "_____."

5 Tom told me that everything was going to be fine.

→ Tom said to me, "_____."

6 Tina asked me who I would bring to the party.

→ Tina said to me, "_____?"

7 Sam asked his new neighbors when they moved there.

→ Sam said to his new neighbors, "_____?"

C 우리말과 같은 뜻이 되도록 주어진 단어를 이용하여 간접화법 문장을 완성하시오.

1 Rachel은 나에게 어떻게 지내고 있냐고 물었다. (ask, how, do)

→ Rachel _____ me _____ _____ _____ .

2 Jamie는 Chris에게 Ted를 결혼식에 초대했는지 물었다. (ask, invite)

→ Jamie _____ Chris _____ _____ _____ _____ Ted to the wedding.

3 Barbara는 나에게 우리가 몇 시에 만날 건지 물었다. (ask, what time, will, meet)

→ Barbara _____ me _____ _____ _____ _____ _____ .

4 나는 Jessica에게 전화를 걸어서 수업에 올 건지 물었다. (ask, will, come)

→ I _____ Jessica _____ _____ _____ _____ to the class.

5 나의 비서는 나에게 Evans씨가 사무실에서 나를 기다리고 있다고 말했다. (tell, wait for)

→ My secretary _____ me _____ Mr. Evans _____ _____ _____ me in the office.

6 Joan은 Amy에게 Ben을 소개시켜줄 예정이라고 말했다. (say, be going to, introduce)

→ Joan _____ that she _____ _____ _____ _____ Ben to Amy.

7 Tim과 Phil은 자신들의 유럽 여행이 굉장했다고 말했다. (say, their trip to Europe, be)

→ Tim and Phil _____ that _____ _____ _____ _____ _____ great.

D 우리말과 같은 뜻이 되도록 주어진 단어를 배열하시오.

1 Jackie가 나에게 거기서 무엇을 하고 있냐고 물었다. (me, what, was doing, asked, I)

→ Jackie _____ there.

2 Eric은 나에게 점심시간에 들르겠다고 말했다. (stop by, me, would, he, that, told)

→ Eric _____ during lunchtime.

3 Sandra는 나에게 시험에 통과했냐고 물었다. (me, passed, I, if, asked, had, the test)

→ Sandra _____ .

4 James는 나에게 전에 어디에 살았냐고 물었다. (me, where, I, lived, asked, had)

→ James _____ before.

5 Nick이 나에게 회의에 참석할 거냐고 물었다. (attend, me, would, I, whether, asked)

→ Nick _____ the meeting.

6 Martin은 유럽에서 그 다음 달에 돌아온다고 말했다. (come back, said, would, he, that)

→ Martin _____ from Europe the following month.

Memo

새 교과서 반영
중등 내신 완벽 대비서
GRAMMAR 공감

- 최신 교과서의 학습 내용을 반영한 체계적인 문법 설명
- 2,500여 개의 전국 중학교 기출 문제 완전 분석 후 문법 포인트, 문제 반영
- 공부감각을 업그레이드 시켜주는 다양한 서술형 평가 코너 수록 및 워크북 제공
- 놓치기 쉬운 문법 포인트를 잡아 주는 Plus α, Tips 코너 수록
- 말하기, 쓰기, 읽기의 실용적 쓰임을 생각한 통합형 문법 학습
- 2,000여 개 이상의 충분한 문제풀이를 통한 문법 감각 향상

넥서스 중등 영어
공감시리즈로
공부감각을
키우세요!

NEXUS makes your next day
www.nexusEDU.kr | 책에 대해 궁금한 사항은 넥서스에듀 홈페이지 1:1 고객상담 게시판을 이용하세요.

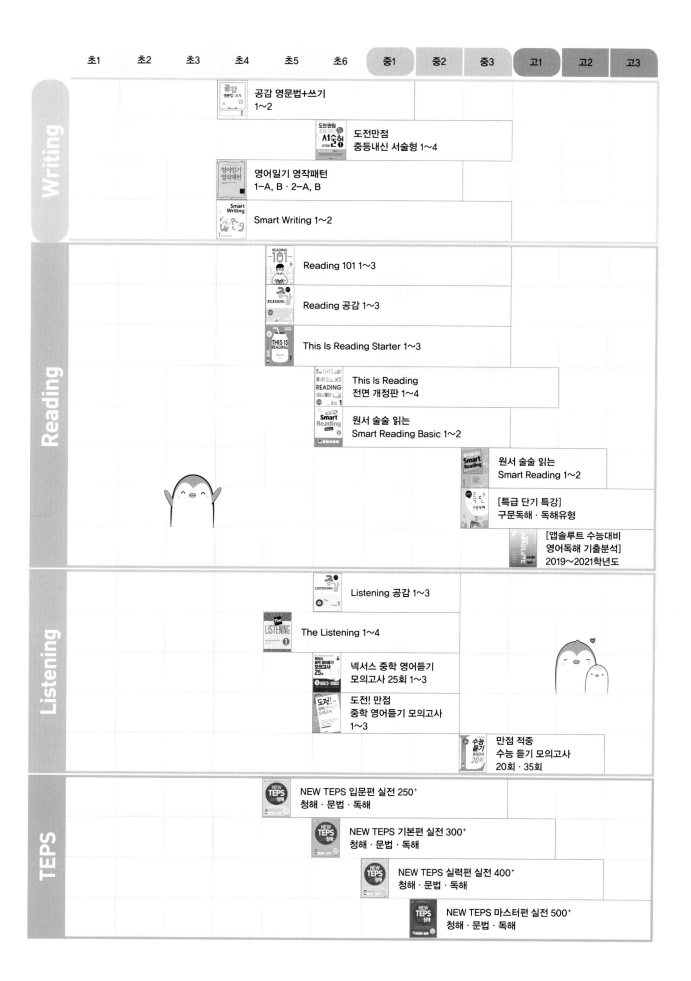

	초1	초2	초3	초4	초5	초6	중1	중2	중3	고1	고2	고3

Writing

공감 영문법+쓰기 1~2

도전만점 중등내신 서술형 1~4

영어일기 영작패턴 1-A, B · 2-A, B

Smart Writing 1~2

Reading

Reading 101 1~3

Reading 공감 1~3

This Is Reading Starter 1~3

This Is Reading 전면 개정판 1~4

원서 술술 읽는 Smart Reading Basic 1~2

원서 술술 읽는 Smart Reading 1~2

[특급 단기 특강] 구문독해 · 독해유형

[앱솔루트 수능대비 영어독해 기출분석] 2019~2021학년도

Listening

Listening 공감 1~3

The Listening 1~4

넥서스 중학 영어듣기 모의고사 25회 1~3

도전! 만점 중학 영어듣기 모의고사 1~3

만점 적중 수능 듣기 모의고사 20회 · 35회

TEPS

NEW TEPS 입문편 실전 250⁺ 청해 · 문법 · 독해

NEW TEPS 기본편 실전 300⁺ 청해 · 문법 · 독해

NEW TEPS 실력편 실전 400⁺ 청해 · 문법 · 독해

NEW TEPS 마스터편 실전 500⁺ 청해 · 문법 · 독해

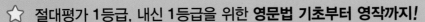